Crimes Against Nature

Crimes Against Nature
Environmental criminology and ecological justice

Rob White

WILLAN
PUBLISHING

Published by

Willan Publishing
Culmcott House
Mill Street, Uffculme
Cullompton, Devon
EX15 3AT, UK
Tel: +44(0)1884 840337
Fax: +44(0)1884 840251
e-mail: info@willanpublishing.co.uk
website: www.willanpublishing.co.uk

Published simultaneously in the USA and Canada by

Willan Publishing
c/o ISBS, 920 NE 58th Ave, Suite 300,
Portland, Oregon 97213-3786, USA
Tel: +001(0)503 287 3093
Fax: +001(0)503 280 8832
e-mail: info@isbs.com
website: www.isbs.com

First published 2008

ISBN   978-1-84392-361-9 paperback
       978-1-84392-362-6 hardback

British Library Cataloguing-in-Publication Data

A catalogue record for this book is available from the British Library

Typeset by GCS, Leighton Buzzard, Bedfordshire
Printed and bound by T.J. International, Padstow, Cornwall

Contents

List of boxes, case studies and figures

Boxes

Case studies

Figures

Preface

This is a work in progress. It is a work that has been in progress for at least the last ten years if not more. It is a work that has much more yet to come.

The study of environmental harm is relatively new for most criminologists. For myself, in writing this book I have had to draw upon my own work over the last decade plus that of a relatively small handful of criminologists who are fellow travellers in this area.

On the other hand, there is a wealth of material from other fields and disciplines that is entirely relevant and useful to a study such as this – environmental studies, politics, law, sociology – and the work of activists and NGOs, as well, has been invaluable in trying to pull the pieces together. To my criminology colleagues and to the many others struggling to turn the tide in favour of social and ecological justice, my great thanks.

I am grateful to Brian Willan for supporting this project and others of similar ilk within the Willan Publishing list. The staff at Willan have been most helpful and I wish to thank them all for their contributions to the production of this book, with special thanks to production editor Emma Gubb.

Thanks as well go to Di Heckenberg and Hannah Graham for reading the preliminary draft. Without their comments and reassurance things would have been much more difficult. Della Clark, Lyn Devereaux and Denise Jones, general support staff at the University of Tasmania, have also all contributed to the conditions which allowed this work to happen and for this I am most appreciative. I am also grateful for the helpful comments and suggestions provided by Michael Lynch and Steve Tombs during the final stages of the book.

Finally, I wish to thank and dedicate this book to my four 'girls' – my wife, Sharyn, and Sienna, Hannah and Frances – for whom anyone, and especially I, would want to make the world a better place.

Part I
Green Theoretical Perspectives

Chapter I

Criminology and environmental harm

The link between environmental issues and criminology finds its expression in environmental or green criminology, itself a development that has arisen from advances and concerns from outside the field as such. In this relatively new area of research and scholarship the concern is to stretch the boundaries of mainstream criminology to accommodate issues of global significance, while also utilising the insights of conventional criminology to illuminate ways in which to understand and to respond to environmental harm.

Introduction

Environmental issues dominate media headlines today and are forcing many people to re-evaluate their day-to-day practices as citizens, as workers, as parents and as members of communities. So, too, concern about the environment is now starting to have greater resonance within the criminal justice field, albeit in a still fairly modest fashion. Within this context of social and professional concern about environmental matters we have also seen in recent years the emergence of a distinctly 'green' criminology.

The aim of this book is to consider the key concerns, concepts and conundrums of environmental or green criminology. The intention is to explore and to question, to initiate and to summarise, to provoke and to stimulate. The book as a whole is meant to develop further this particular approach to criminological study.

The book is based on work undertaken specifically on environmental crime over the last fifteen years or so. It incorporates current research and scholarship that spans diverse disciplines and fields. It is also based on an appreciation that there are pressing issues that ought to be of more central concern to criminologists. Hence the book offers something 'old', something 'new', and a guide to that which still requires critical scrutiny and practical action.

The book deals with specific issues that pertain to the nature of and responses to environmental harm. These particular crimes against nature include a wide variety of transgressions against humans, against environments, and against nonhuman animals. The book also deals with broad agendas, in the sense of trying to apply and generate conceptual understandings of harm, victimisation, law enforcement and social regulation that are relevant for a criminological approach to environmental issues. The combination of, and dialectic between, practical example and theoretical conceptualisation is essential to mapping out the terrain occupied by green criminology.

This chapter describes three frameworks that inform how green criminologists conceptualise the nature of the problem – what they see as most important for analysis and action, and which thus shape their conceptions of harm and criminality. It begins by discussing the broad approach taken in green or environmental criminology, followed by a discussion of how, in abstract terms, ecophilosophy shapes and informs how 'harm' itself is conceptualised. The main part of the chapter elaborates on three distinct approaches to the study of environmental harm, one based on notions of *environmental justice*, one on *ecological justice*, and one on *species justice* or *animal rights*. The chapter then briefly outlines some of the key tasks of a green or environmental criminology. It concludes with a discussion of 'where to from here' for environmental criminology, as a lead in to the rest of the book.

For some readers this chapter may seem a bit 'hard going'. This is because it deals with issues of a more abstract theoretical nature than other chapters in the book. However, as demonstrated in this chapter, *philosophy is always the driver of action*: it is intertwined with how we perceive the world around us, our location in this world, and what we feel ought to be done to preserve or make the world a better place. The environmental issues that we think matter most, and the issues which become transformed into environmental problems, are shaped by different understandings of the nature–human nexus. To investigate environmental harm, therefore, we need to first explore core concepts and overarching perspectives relating to the relationship between humans and 'nature'. This provides a foundation for the discussions to follow in later chapters that deal with specific environmental crimes and harms, and societal responses to these.

While philosophy is the driver of action, it is the material reality of environmental harm that is the impetus to action. That is, the scale and scope of many of our environmental problems is now so huge, and the evidence so incontrovertible, that we cannot ignore them. The reality of environmental degradation confronts us daily, in the form of oil spills, air pollution, energy crisis and inadequate drinking water. Furthermore, scientists have provided substantial objective confirmation of our personal anxieties and subjective concerns. Global and local analysis, selective and systematic sampling, and snap-shot and longitudinal studies drawing from many different scientific disciplines have collectively, and conclusively, demonstrated that the well-being of planet Earth is indeed imperilled (United Nations Environment Programme 2007). It is the science of climate change that likewise has formed the basis for extrapolating the economic and social consequences of environmental problems (Stern 2007). What is happening to the biosphere, to species generally, and to humans specifically, is measurable, scientifically. Debate may occur over particular methodologies and over specific claims, but the sheer weight of evidence pertaining to issues such as global warming means that no one can now seriously dispute its existence and pressing nature.

What to do about environmental trends, issues and problems is, however, the source of considerable debate. In political terms, this is apparent in the reluctance of the United States and Australia to ratify the Kyoto Protocol relating to the reduction of greenhouse gases. Everyone agrees that a problem exists; differences arise, however, over how best to tackle it and whose interests are to be preserved or privileged in the process. This is not about science, it is about philosophy and values, power and interests. For example, it was a change in government that led Australia to finally ratify Kyoto, not new scientific evidence. Yet, the impetus to sign was provided by objective evidence of climate change.

More generally, the level of harm that is deemed to be acceptable or unacceptable always involves some combination of scientific knowledge and values-based judgement. Environmental issues are interpreted through the lens of philosophy, even though the material basis for understanding lies in direct experience and scientific experiment. Responding to environmental harm likewise incorporates different perspectives on the nature–human relationship, conflicts over values

5

and interests, and contested notions as to what is considered the 'best of all worlds'. For a criminology that deals with environmental issues this makes the task all that much more complicated and challenging.

Environmental / green criminology

Before beginning our exploration, it is necessary to say a word or two about terminology. While the descriptions 'green criminology' and 'environmental criminology' can be used interchangeably, in other contexts they can also refer to distinct areas of criminological inquiry that are quite separate from each other (see Box 1.1). For the reasons outlined, this book will use them as synonymous or equivalent terms.

Box 1.1 What's in a name?

The term 'green criminology' was first coined by Lynch in 1990 (Lynch 1990) and has now been widely accepted as describing criminological work that focuses specifically on issues pertaining to environmental harm (see Beirne and South 2007; South and Beirne 2006). Another related formulation has been 'conservation criminology' (see Herbig and Joubert 2006). In each instance, the main concern has been to focus criminological attention on issues of environmental importance. To some extent, the choice of words has also been used to distinguish this focus from another strand of criminology that (likewise) is referred to as 'environmental criminology'.

The latter refers to a particular kind of urban study and crime mapping, in essence the linking of urban environments to specific types of crimes (see Brantingham and Brantingham 1981). This type of environmental criminology has been interested in the spatial and temporal dimensions of crime, usually within an urban setting, and frequently related to particular types of crime prevention measures and agendas. The emphasis has been on modifying urban environments, through better lighting for instance or better sightlines on public walkways, in order to decrease fear of crime and improve public safety. This type of criminology likewise has a range of related titles: situational crime prevention, planning for defensible space, crime prevention through environmental design, pattern theory and so on (see Schneider and Kitchen 2002). Moreover, there is some suggestion within these circles

---

that the term 'environmental' should perhaps be deleted in favour of less encompassing yet more precise terminology – such as 'place-based crime prevention'.

There are also several reasons why 'green criminology', likewise, needs to rethink its particular label. For instance, in many jurisdictions there are now green parties. These are formal political entities that contest democratic elections and that in many places have elected representatives to local, State and national governing bodies. A dilemma with using the word 'green', as in green criminology, is that such work may inadvertently be considered politically partisan – that is, aligned with a particular political group or party.

Exponents of green criminology make it clear that, while philosophically aligned to social and ecological justice, this does not reduce down to any particular social and political organisation. Environmental social movements and distinct green political parties may be fellow travellers politically, but the brief of green criminology goes well beyond these particular projects and includes agendas and issues that may not be pursued by any one particular group. To put it differently, environmental or green criminology may have a specific political flavour, but it is non-partisan and 'independent' of direct organisational links to green parties and social movement groups such as Greenpeace. Green criminology, in other words, does not present as the intellectual wing of the green parties, although it may well inform the policies and practices of the Greens, amongst other political formations. It is not tied to any one political organisation.

For these and other reasons, it has been suggested that perhaps the term 'conservation criminology' be adopted (Herbig and Joubert 2006). This refers to study of 'natural resource crime', with a major theme being 'conservation'. However, the classification of crime using this framework is ambiguous and implicitly assumes a particularly narrow understanding of 'resources' as well seeming to ignore the dynamic and changing character of 'nature'. The natural world is somehow seen to stand outside the human world, and the interplay between the two remains largely un-explained. Yet the attempt to produce a new classification pertaining to natural resource crime mirrors the work of other criminologists who share concern about environmental-related harms.

Given that a broad generic use of the word 'environment' can also encapsulate urban environmental analysis as well as wider issues pertaining to environmental harm, the position adopted herein is that it is time to reclaim 'environmental criminology' as a descriptor for the work described in this book. This also reflects a concern to utilise a more politically neutral term than otherwise may be the case. Accordingly, the terms 'green criminology' and 'environmental criminology' will be used interchangeably in the context of the work described in this book, reflecting both the state of existing work in this area and its elaboration into the future.

Green or environmental criminology basically refers to the study of environmental harm, environmental laws and environmental regulation by criminologists. There is a growing network of criminologists across the English-speaking world working in this area, as evidenced in recent book collections (Beirne and South 2007; South and Beirne 2006) and special editions of journals such as *Social Justice*, *Theoretical Criminology* and *Current Issues in Criminal Justice* (Williams 1996; South 1998; White 2005a). Even those who purport to be 'against green criminology' (Halsey 2004) can be considered part of the deliberations surrounding how criminologists approach the study of environmental issues.

The interests of green criminology incorporate specific incidents and events, often within defined geo-political areas, through to issues of global magnitude. Whatever the scale or the type of environmental harm, these are matters of great public importance and criminological concern. A keen motivator for this interest is to try to predict and to prevent disaster and degradation from happening, since these are capable of destroying specific life forms and, indeed, life on the planet generally. The concept of 'ecology' refers to the complex interactions of nonhuman nature, including its abiotic components (air, water, soils) and its biotic components (plants, animals, fungi, bacteria). Humans are implicated in these interactions as the relationship between humans and the environment is crucial to understanding how environments change over time, for better or for worse (Merchant 2005). For criminologists, ecological considerations go to the heart of many conceptualisations of environmental harm.

Case study 1.1 Specific ecological catastrophe

In mid-November 2007 a major storm in the Strait of Kerch, south of Ukraine near the Black Sea, led to the sinking or running aground of some ten ships. At least three sailors died, and a number of others went missing, presumed dead. A tanker broke apart in the heavy seas. More than 30,000 birds were killed by the thousands of tons of oil that leaked from the tanker. No one knows how many fish and other marine creatures died. Concerns were expressed about the environmental impact of oil globs that in winter could drop to the seabed below (The Australian 2007).

As illustrated in Case study 1.1, environmental harm can be specific and localised. Given the particular circumstances surrounding their advent, such events can also be prevented or minimised through the taking of suitable precautions. Environmental harm can also be universal and globalised in nature, as shown in the next case study. The solutions here are less apparent and certain to be far reaching.

Case study 1.2 Global ecological catastrophe

The fourth *Global Environment Outlook*, a report compiled by the United Nations Environment Programme, was released in November 2007. A central finding of the report is that each human being now requires one-third more land to supply their needs than the planet can provide. That is, humanity's ecological footprint is 29.1 hectares per person, while the world's biological capacity is on average only 15.7 hectares per person. The result is net environmental degradation and loss, and things are getting worse rather than better. In essence, environmental problems, across all areas, are now at the stage where they are a threat to humanity's survival (United Nations Environment Programme 2007; see also Powell 2007: 28).

The development of environmental criminology over the last twenty years or so has led to new interests, new conceptualisations and new techniques of analysis. This is because there is increasing *acknowledgement* of the problem of environmental degradation and destruction, and the relevance of this to traditional criminological concerns with social injury and social regulation. There is also greater awareness of the *interconnectedness* of social and environmental issues, such that matters

9

relating to poverty, health, indigenous people's rights, exploitation of nonhuman nature, corporate business misdealings, state corruption and so on are seen in many instances to be inseparable. As well, there is recognition of the need for *multidisciplinary approaches* to the study of environmental harm, involving cooperation between different 'experts', and different areas of academic expertise.

These kinds of observations and interrelationships are forcing many of us to rethink the social and natural universe, to reconceptualise the relationship between humans and nature in ways that accord greater weight to the nonhuman when it comes to assessing issues such as environmental harm. In practical terms, this translates into new and overlapping domains of consideration within green criminology itself. These will be discussed below when we consider the key theoretical frameworks of environmental criminology.

Different writers have different conceptions as to what constitutes the most appropriate way to analyse environment and crime, and indeed what to include as part of such discussions. For some, the important thing is to consider particular *environmental issues* from the point of view of criminological consideration. Issues might include such things as illegal logging, declining biodiversity, transportation of toxic waste, chemical pollution, global climate change, provision of unsafe drinking water, and the list goes on. For others, the approach may be more *conceptual*, in the sense of locating debates over and about the environment within the context of social, political and criminological theory – such as analysis of different ways in which 'nature' is defined and perceived, theorising the relationship between human beings and 'nature' and human beings and nonhuman animals, examining the ways in which globalisation impinges upon environments, and exploring the agency of human beings in relation to their environments and as part of social movements about the environment. The complexity and overlap of issues and approaches surrounding the environment means that there will necessarily be myriad different ways in which to study environmental harm.

Ecophilosophy and environmental harm

Different philosophical perspectives shape varying definitions of crime, and the nature of what are deemed to be appropriate responses to environmental issues. As will be seen shortly, ecophilosophy has a major impact on how criminologists define crime and the varying ways in which they understand the victimisation of humans, specific environments and nonhuman animals.

There exists a considerable disjuncture between what is officially labelled environmentally harmful from the point of view of criminal and civil law, and what can be said to constitute the greatest sources of harm from an ecological perspective. For example, there are profound, long-term adverse environmental effects flowing from such historically *legitimate* practices as using long-lines and drift-nets to catch fish, injecting cyanide and arsenic into the earth to mine precious metals, or destroying nonhuman nature in the course of building freeways. Indeed, many conventional, and legal, forms of human production and interaction do far worse things to the natural environment than those activities deemed illegal.

Although the philosophies employed to explicate the nature of the relation between the 'social' and the 'natural' worlds are numerous (see for example, Lane 1998; Plumwood 2005; Halsey 2004), a useful analytical distinction can be made between anthropocentric (human-centred), biocentric (species-centred) and ecocentric (socio-ecological centred) perspectives (see Halsey and White 1998). The anthropocentric perspective emphasises the biological, mental and moral superiority of *humans* over other living and non-living entities. Biocentrism views humans as simply 'another species' to be attributed the *same* moral worth as such organisms as, for example, whales, wolves and birds. Ecocentrism refuses to place humanity either above or below the rest of nature. However, the unique capacity for humans to develop and deploy methods of production which have global consequences, means that humans also have an explicit responsibility to ensure that such production methods do not exceed the ecospheric limits of the planet (White 2007a). Moreover, this responsibility is a responsibility that extends to human *and* nonhuman life.

Each of these perspectives conceives of the relationship between humans and the environment in a different way, and this in turn has major implications when it comes to defining and responding to instances of environmental harm. Consider, for example, how each philosophy might approach the practice of clearfelling of old-growth forests (see Figure 1.1).

Anthropocentric
An anthropocentric perspective views old-growth forests instrumentally, as a means to satisfy the demands of humans. Economically, the philosophy requires that forests be exploited for their commercial potential and that the production methods used be those which incur the least cost to producers – such as clearfelling. The aim of legislation is to facilitate the extraction and processing of particular resources (e.g. laws relating to the conditions whereby companies are guaranteed long-term access to particular geographical sites for the purposes of commercial activity such as mining, forestry or farming). Legislation is also directed at conserving particular natural resources through prohibiting over-use or over-extraction of particular resources (e.g. imposition of quotas on logging or fishing), or dealing with conflicts between certain industries (e.g. farming and mining), or between certain industries and specific population groups (e.g. mining companies and indigenous people).

Biocentric
Biocentrism views old-growth forests (and the organisms which dwell within them) as having intrinsic worth, whereby such forests have a significance independent of any value placed on them by humans. Biocentrists consider old-growth forests to be significant because they are suitably diverse in structure and age as to provide the only habitat for certain forest dependent species. In terms of conservation, biocentrism demands that there be no human impact on old-growth forests since such ecosystems are considered too fragile to tamper with. Regulatory legislation should be directed first and foremost to preserving the natural environment, particularly those sites identified as being 'wilderness' in order to protect biodiversity and species integrity.

Ecocentric
From an ecocentric perspective, old-growth forests are seen to be crucial to the long-term survival of humans and nonhumans. Ecocentrism attempts to strike a balance between the need to utilise resources for human survival, and the need to develop rules which facilitate the benign use of the ecosphere. From an ecocentric position, ensuring the preservation of biocentric values (such as providing for the widest possible spectrum of species within a forested area), becomes integral to maintaining long-term human needs (such as the continued existence of clean air, unpolluted rivers and fertile soils). Ecocentrism advocates methods of production (such as selective logging techniques) which privilege the long-term requirements of ecosystemic well-being over short-term economic demands. Legislation is ideally framed by the limits of ecology (of which humans are an integral part), instead of instrumental goals relating to economic growth and wealth accumulation.

Figure 1.1 Ecophilosophies and clearfelling of old-growth forests
Source: Drawing from Halsey and White 1998.

As indicated, ecophilosophy as manifested in regulatory practice, leads to very different outcomes. Hence, the importance of acknowledging that how one views the relationship between humans and nature has material consequences in the real world of environmental politics. How ecophilosophy translates into specifically *criminological* understandings of social and ecological issues is discussed in further depth below.

For many of those working on environmental issues, the question of broad philosophy is grounded in specific concerns about eco-human rights or *ecological citizenship* (see for example, Halsey 1997a; Smith 1998). What does this mean in practice? It means that present generations ought to act in ways that do not jeopardise the existence and quality of life of future generations. It also means that we ought to extend the moral community to include nonhuman nature. By doing so, we enter a new politics of obligation:

> In ecological thought, human beings have obligations to animals, trees, mountains, oceans and other members of the biotic community. This means that human beings have to exercise extreme caution before embarking upon any project which is likely to have the possibility of adverse effects upon the ecosystems concerned (Smith 1998: 99).

This particular notion of ecological citizenship thus centres on human obligations to all living things, and the need to carefully assess the impacts of human activity across the human and nonhuman domains.

However, such considerations are not without their problems. Thus, the conceptualisation of 'rights' is itself contentious when extended to the nonhuman (see Christoff 2000). For example, should environmental rights be seen as an extension of human or social rights (e.g. related to the quality of human life, such as provision of clean water), or should human rights be seen as merely one component of complex ecosystems, systems that should be preserved for their own sake (i.e. as in the notion of the rights of the environment)? While increasingly acknowledged in international law, the environmental connection with human rights continues to be somewhat ambiguous and subject to diverse practical interpretations (Thornton and Tromans 1999). Nevertheless, such ambiguities and tensions over 'rights' are essential parts of the criminological debates associated with the shift from ecophilosophy to conceptions of environmental crime.

Within criminology there are significant issues surrounding scale, activities and legalities as these pertain to environmental harm. A strict legalist approach tends to focus on the central place of criminal law in the definition of criminality. Thus, as Situ and Emmons (2000: 3) see it: 'An environmental crime is an unauthorised act or omission that violates the law and is therefore subject to criminal prosecution and criminal sanctions.' However, other writers argue that, as with criminology in general, the concept of 'harm' ought to encapsulate those activities that may be legal and 'legitimate' but which nevertheless negatively impact on people and environments (Lynch and Stretesky 2003). These are issues which we shall return to in later chapters. For the moment, it is essential to anticipate differences in conceptions of crime and approaches to environmental regulation within criminology by considering the main perspectives associated with green criminology as a specific forum of analysis.

Theoretical frameworks of environmental criminology

There is no green criminology *theory* as such. Rather, as observed by South (1998), there is what can loosely be described as a green 'perspective'. Elements of this perspective generally include things such as a concern with specifically environmental issues, social justice, ecological consciousness, the destructive nature of global capitalism, the role of the nation-state (and regional and global regulatory bodies), and inequality and discrimination as these relate to class, gender, race and nonhuman animals. Corporate definitions of a green agenda are sometimes explicitly rejected (Lynch and Stretesky 2003), insofar as corporations are generally seen to be integral to the problems of environmental harm. The green criminology perspective, therefore, tends to begin with a strong sensitivity toward crimes of the powerful, and to be infused with issues pertaining to power, justice, inequality and democracy.

Within the spectrum of ideas and activities associated with green criminology are several different kinds of analytical framework. Some of these pertain to ecophilosophy, that is, to ways in which the relationship between humans and nature can be conceptualised (as seen in the previous section). Less abstractly, however, most environmental criminology can be distinguished on the basis of *who or what precisely is being victimised*. As indicated in Figure 1.2, there are three broad theoretical tendencies that generally frame how specific writers view the nature of environmental issues, including harm and responses to harm.

Environment rights and environmental justice
- Environmental rights as an extension of human or social rights so as to enhance the quality of human life;
- *Intergenerational responsibility*: equity and future generations;
- *Environmental justice*: equity for present generations;
- Environmental harm is constructed in relation to human-centred notions of value and use.

Ecological citizenship and ecological justice
- Ecological citizenship acknowledges that human beings are merely one component of complex ecosystems that should be preserved for their own sake via the notion of the rights of the environment;
- *Global transboundary*: issues of scale and interconnectedness;
- *Ecological justice*: quality of biosphere and rights of nonhuman species;
- Environmental harm is constructed in relation to notions of ecological harm and destructive techniques of human intervention.

Animal rights and species justice
- Nonhuman animals have rights based upon utilitarian notions (maximising pleasure and minimising pain), inherent value (right to respectful treatment) and an ethic of responsible caring;
- *Anti-speciesism*: addressing the discriminatory treatments of animals as Other;
- *Animal rights*: dealing with issues of animal abuse and suffering, and the nurturing of respectful relationships;
- Environmental harm is constructed in relation to the place of nonhuman animals within environments and their intrinsic right to not suffer abuse, whether this be one-on-one harm, institutionalised harm or harm arising from human actions that affect climates and environments on a global scale.

Figure 1.2   Green theoretical frameworks
Source: White 2008a

Environmental justice

Analysis of environmental issues proceeds on the basis that someone or something is indeed being harmed. *Environmental justice* refers to the distribution of environments among peoples in terms of access to and use of specific natural resources in defined geographical areas, and the impacts of particular social practices and environmental hazards on specific populations (e.g. as defined on the basis of class, occupation, gender, age, ethnicity). In other words, the concern is with human beings at the centre of analysis. The focus of analysis therefore is on human health and well-being and how these are affected by particular types of production and consumption.

It is important to distinguish between environmental issues that affect everyone, and those that disproportionately affect specific individuals and groups (see Williams 1996; Low and Gleeson 1998). In some instances, there may be a basic 'equality of victims', in that some environmental problems threaten everyone in the same way, as in the case for example of ozone depletion, global warming, air pollution and acid rain (Beck 1996).

As extensive work on specific incidents and patterns of victimisation demonstrate, however, it is also the case that some people are more likely to be disadvantaged by environmental problems than others. For instance, studies have identified disparities involving many different types of environmental hazards that especially adversely affect people of colour, ethnic minority groups and indigenous people in places such as Canada, Australia and the US (Bullard 1994; Pinderhughes 1996; Langton 1998; Stretesky and Lynch 1999; Brook 2000; Rush 2002). There are thus patterns of 'differential victimisation' that are evident with respect to the siting of toxic waste dumps, extreme air pollution, chemical accidents, access to safe clean drinking water and so on (see Chunn *et al.* 2002; Saha and Mohai 2005; Williams 1996). There are some who challenge the view that this is necessarily a problem (see Box 1.2); however, most would agree that it is the poor and disadvantaged who suffer disproportionately from such environmental inequalities.

Box 1.2 Environmental injustice as a social good?

Critics of environmental justice have pointed to certain 'flaws' in the analysis and in the overall substantive consequences of inequalities in where people live vis-à-vis environments. For example, from an economic instrumentalist perspective, it can be argued that industrial and waste facilities are basically social necessities. They are essential parts of the industrial production process. Moreover, present inequalities simply reflect the fact that a few individuals are forced to bear the external cost of industrial processes from which the public at large receives benefits.

Accordingly, from this utilitarian position (maximum good for the maximum number even if some have to suffer for the greater good), it is argued that the poor ought to be given the opportunity to enhance their economic situation by profiting from hosting polluting and waste facilities. Such 'inconveniences' as odours, increased traffic and unpleasant noise are seen as more or less negligible in the context of negotiations that would bring economic rewards to those communities that suffer the inconveniences. In other words, trading off amenity in this way is construed as a win–win deal for poor people and developer alike (see Boerner and Lambert 1995).

In response to this sort of right-wing apology for environmental injustice, one might reaffirm just why it is important to refuse to cast discussion solely or mainly in monetary terms. As Harvey (1996: 398, emphasis in original) observes: 'seemingly fair market exchange always leads to the least privileged falling under the disciplinary sway of the more privileged and that *costs* are always visited on those who have to bow to money discipline while *benefits* always go to those who enjoy the personal authority conferred by wealth.' Furthermore, empirical study of actual neighbourhoods dealing with issues of waste disposal indicate complex micro-processes that nevertheless serve to disadvantage the poor, regardless of whether the waste disposal is legal or illegal (see Pellow 2004).

Another dimension of differential victimisation relates to the subjective disposition and consciousness of the people involved. The specific groups who experience environmental problems may not always describe or see the issues in strictly environmental terms. This may be related to lack of knowledge of the environmental harm, alternative explanations for the calamity (e.g. an act of God) and socio-economic pressures to 'accept' environmental risk (see Julian 2004). The environmental justice discourse places *inequalities* in the distribution of environmental quality at the top of the environmental agenda (see Julian 2004; Harvey 1996).

Within the environmental justice framework, it is humans that matter, but how specifically? Here we can distinguish between two sorts of approach to human interests that stem from considerations of ecophilosophy. An anthropocentric conception privileges the conventional instrumentalist view of the world and human's domination over nature including nonhuman animals. A big divide exists between corporate environmentalism that is premised on such ideas, and a more radical green criminology perspective (Lynch and Stretesky 2003). An ecocentric approach on the other hand is based upon *enlightened human self interest*, one that is informed by notions of interrelationship between humans, biosphere and nonhuman animals. In this perspective there is also a strong link to environmental justice, since different population groups are affected differently in terms of quality of environments. This means that a key issue is human rights and the environment (see White 2007a).

Action based upon perceived interests, however, generally reflects particular social circumstances. In concrete terms, for example, much of the environmental justice movement begins with an anthropocentric view insofar as the main concern is with the quality of environments for humans. The dreadful living conditions experienced by the poor and minorities are themselves the key source of contention, not necessarily 'the environment' as such. The political agenda is set by the unequal environmental quality that is evident in specific locales and by the local people's responses to this. Struggle is directly related to survival and immediate self interest.

By contrast, those who are better off economically have the opportunity to be concerned with issues of general ecological equity, since their immediate living circumstances are generally not disagreeable or threatening to their health. In this respect, the economically well-off are in a position to use environmental justice issues (i.e. social inequality relating to who lives next to polluting factories) strategically in order to promote ecocentric over anthropocentric concerns (i.e. acknowledging the well-being of environments as well as human interests, demands implementation of anti-pollution measures across the board). Not surprisingly, the better off are also more likely to speak about ecological, rather than environmental, justice.

Ecological justice

Starting from a different general analytical focus, *ecological justice* refers to the relationship of human beings generally to the rest of the natural world, and includes concerns relating to the health of the biosphere, and more specifically plants and creatures that also inhabit the biosphere (Smith 1998; Cullinan 2003). The main concern is with the quality of the planetary environment (that is frequently seen to possess its own intrinsic value) and the rights of other species (particularly animals) to life free from torture, abuse and destruction of habitat.

For example, insofar as poor quality drinking water, and diminished clean water resources, are attributable to social practices such as disposal of agricultural, urban and industrial effluents into water catchments and river systems, then it is not only humans who are affected. It is notable that some of Australia's largest waste disposal companies are owned by French transnational water companies. Moreover, in Sydney, approval has been granted to locate a 'megatip', a large waste management facility, in the city water catchment area (Archer 2001: 34–36). The world's major water corporations are also among the top waste management corporations in the world (Beder 2006: 99). The same companies that promise to supply clean water, therefore, are the same companies most likely to contaminate it. Local natural environments, and nonhuman inhabitants of both wilderness and built environments, are negatively impacted upon by human practices that destroy, re-channel or pollute existing fresh water systems. Who does so, and why, are important questions to answer.

Specific practices, and choices, in how humans interact with particular environments present immediate and potential risks to everything within them. Ecological notions of rights and justice see humans as but one component of complex ecosystems that should be preserved for their own sake, as supported by the notion of the rights of the environment. In this framework, all living things are bound together and environmental matters are intrinsically global and transboundary in nature (as witnessed, for example, by the spread of the bird flu virus worldwide or polluted river waters across national borders). Ecological justice demands that how humans interact with their environment be evaluated in relation to potential harms and risks to specific creatures and specific locales as well as the biosphere generally.

Within this broad approach there may be philosophical differences in terms of the value put on the interests of humans and on the environment. Humans may be placed on the same footing as other species, and cherished and valued as part of the ecological whole. In some cases, however, the fate of specific individuals is less important than the prospects facing the biosphere generally. For some exponents of a deep green or biocentric perspective, for example, AIDS or famine may simply be seen as nature's way of controlling population growth and thus as good for the planet as a whole (see White 1994). From this vantage point, an act or omission is not criminal if it ultimately benefits the biosphere generally. This fundamentally misanthropic (anti-human) perspective frequently sees humans as the problem, and therefore it is humans who need to be controlled or in some cases even eradicated. Related to this attitude, it is notable that members of the environmental justice movements are critical of mainstream environmental groups precisely because of their 'focus on the fate of "nature" rather than humans' (Harvey 1996: 386; see also Sandler and Pezzullo 2007). To put it differently, taking action on environmental issues involves choices and priorities. Many communities who suffer from the 'hard end' of environmental harm feel that their well-being ought to take priority over 'natural environments' or specific plants and animals as such.

The other major strand of ecological thinking provides a progressive contrast to the biocentric view. While an ecocentric or social ecology perspective likewise acknowledges human authorship of environmental degradation, it does so within the context of political economy and the different forms and types of social power. Criminality is related to exploitation of both environments and humans by those who control the means of production (Field 1998). Environmental deviance is linked to particular social power contexts, which in the contemporary world are dominated by large corporations and upper-class stakeholders (Simon 2000). The interplay between nature and humans is such that social justice is equally important and inextricably bound to issues of ecology. An ecocentric approach therefore recognises the central role of humans in acting upon the natural world, while simultaneously calling for accountability in how production and consumption processes relate to the ecospheric limits of the planet.

Within the ecological justice framework, it is environments that matter, but how, specifically? As indicated, a biocentric approach privileges the biosphere over and above specifically human interests and considerations. An ecocentric point of view, however, grounds its understanding of humans in terms of social relationships, including relations of power, and links these to wider ecological concerns. Humans and environments are both liable to exploitation, and frequently the two are inseparable institutionally (it is the same social forces, usually related to global capitalism, that drive the exploitation). An ecocentric perspective therefore is premised on the idea that 'the environment' has its own intrinsic qualities that must be incorporated into human understandings and forms of production and consumption.

Species justice

The third strand of green criminology is that represented by those who wish to include consideration of *animal rights* within the broad perspective (Benton 1998, Beirne 2007). In specific terms, concepts such as speciesism may be invoked. This refers to the practice of discriminating against nonhuman animals because they are perceived as inferior to the human species in much the same way that sexism and racism involve prejudice and discrimination against women and people of different colour (Munro 2004). Animal rights supporters argue that there are two kinds of animals – human and nonhuman – and that both have rights and interests as sentient beings; they believe, however, that the dominant ideology of speciesism enables humans to exploit nonhuman animals as commodities to be eaten, displayed, hunted and dissected for their benefit.

***

Case study 1.3 Humans and nonhuman animals

A perennial question in consideration of the relationship between humans and nonhuman animals is where actually does the specific boundary lie? In other words, what is so special about being human compared to the nonhuman animal? Consider, for example, the following qualities in relation to nonhuman animals: 'only humans have rationality or sentience'; 'only humans have true language'; 'only humans use tools'; 'only humans have consciousness'; 'only humans have continuing life plans' and 'only humans are self-aware'. The idea that only humans exhibit these qualities is, of course, incorrect. As Page (1991) wryly observes, typically and with increasing success, biologists have delighted in showing that these defining characteristics are not sharply defined conceptually and not limited to humans empirically.

***

The animal-centred discourse of animal rights shares much in common with the environment-centred discourse of green criminology, but certain differences, as well as the commonalities, are also apparent (Beirne 2007). For example, nonhuman animals are frequently considered in primarily instrumental terms (as pets, as food, as resources) in environmental criminology, or categorised in mainly anthropomorphic terms (such as 'wildlife', 'fisheries') that belie the ways in which humans create and classify animals as Other. From an animal rights theoretical framework, one key issue revolves around how rights are constructed: via utilitarian theory that emphasises the consequential goal of minimising suffering and pain; via rights theory that emphasises the right to respectful treatment;

and via feminist theory that emphasises the ethic of responsible caring (Beirne 2007).

The other key issue is with practical and conceptual action that is needed to better define animal abuse, and how best to respond to this. Investigation of harm involving nonhuman animals generally starts from the premise that the central issue is harm to animals, and that humans are implicated in this process in varying ways and to varying degrees. Within mainstream criminology, the so called progression thesis, for example, inquires into how young people who abuse animals progress to other types of criminal acts, including harm against humans (Dadds *et al.* 2002; Ascione 2001). Other research has argued that systematic abuse of animals via factory farms ought to be considered at the same time as specific instances of harm to particular animals (Beirne 2004).

Traditional theorising about animals, within an animal concern paradigm, can largely be characterised as lying on a scale ranging from a welfarist approach to, at the other end of the scale, a rights-based approach. The focus of the welfarist approach is the humane treatment of animals (Ibrahim 2006). This model advocates for the protection of animals through increased welfare-based interventions but not the prohibition of animal exploitation. The model is focused on improvements to the treatment of animals but does not challenge the embedded exploitation of animals that is a consequence of their social and legal status (Ibrahim 2006). Implicit in this is that animals may still be exploited for their flesh, fur and skin provided that their suffering is not 'unnecessary', or as often put, the animals are treated humanely.

At the other end of the spectrum is the rights-based approach. At the extreme end this approach contends that animals have rights to live free from human interference. This approach argues for the abolition of animal exploitation through both legal and non-legal change and for the legal recognition of rights for animals. Central to this approach is changing the legal character of animals from property to legal, rights-bearing entities (see Wise 2001, 2004).

Within the nonhuman animal concerns framework, it is animals that matter, but how, specifically? Here we can distinguish between two sorts of approach to animal interests. A (radical) animal rights perspective privileges the intrinsic rights of animals to live regardless of conditions of the biosphere and human interests. However, an animal welfare perspective is one that views nonhuman animals as being part of a web of relationships involving humans and the biosphere. There is a link to species justice, since each animal has 'value' – but this, in turn, is contingent upon specific times, places and activities. Nonhuman animals are part of the symbolic, instrumental and value universes of human beings.

Tensions can exist between both animal rights and environmental justice views, and animal rights and ecological justice approaches. Where do we draw the line when it comes to the rights of (which) animals and the rights of humans (does the mosquito biting into my arm have a right to live)? Trees and rocks and streams are not sentient beings capable of suffering, so where do they fit into the ethical universe? Yet, very often conceptualisation of environmental harm encapsulates the concerns of all three strands – protection of biodiversity within our forests is not incompatible with sustaining localised environments, protecting endangered species and ensuring human happiness. Clearfelling of old-growth forests, for example, can be highly problematic from the point of view of human enjoyment, nurturing of nonhuman animals, and conservation of complex eco-systems.

It will be interesting to see how the dialogue between these three theoretical frameworks will unfold in the coming years. For example, recent work examining the relationship between the environmental justice movement and the environmental movement is premised upon the idea of going beyond either/or political choices. Rather, it is asserted that: 'What is ultimately at issue is *not* whether one movement has more worthwhile goals or moral authority over the other, but, rather, *how the goals of both movements might be achieved together effectively*' (Pezzullo and Sandler 2007: 2, emphasis in original). The overarching frameworks, of course, do have major consequences with regard to where individual scholars and researchers put their time and energy. The study of environmental crime, including animal cruelty, is greatly influenced by the perspective one has about the natural world generally, and thereby which issues ought to receive specific priority. But this does not preclude collaboration and interaction with fellow travellers across the movement and theoretical divides (see also Beirne 2007).

Weighing up the nature of harm

There are many concrete links between the health of natural environments, diverse human activity and the exploitation of animals.

And, increasingly, the language of rights is being used to frame responses to harm and abuse that are evident across the three areas of concern (see Beirne and South 2007). This can sometimes lead to conflicts over which rights ought to take precedence in any given situation – human rights, rights of the environment or animal rights (White 2007a). Accordingly, this is now leading writers to go beyond initial considerations of how to *define* harm to consider how we might best *debate* harm. Defining harm is ultimately about philosophical frameworks as informed by scientific evidence and traditional knowledges; debating harm is about processes of deliberation in the 'real world' and of conflicts over rights and the making of difficult decisions.

Figure 1.3 provides a model of decision-making in which information in each of the three areas is weighed up in regards to any specific issue. Thus, the various conceptualisations of harm within a green criminology framework that typically involve reference to different kinds of justice – pertaining to humans, nonhuman animals and the environment itself – can be put into an abstract analytical model that can be used to weigh up harm in relation to humancentric, animalcentric and ecocentric considerations. Of central importance to the model is contextual understanding of the relationship between the interests of humans, animals and the environment in specific given circumstances.

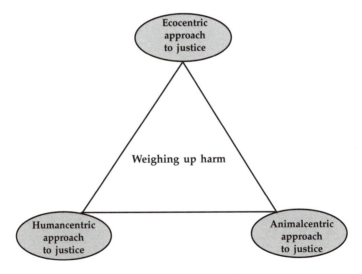

Figure 1.3 Contextual model for weighing up harm
Source: White and Watson 2007.

Analysis that is pitched at too high a level of abstraction, and that correspondingly reinforces rigid definitions and absolutist positions (e.g. humans come first; the earth is most important; any harm to animals is bad) precludes closely considered analysis of specific situations. For example, an absolutist approach may contend that humans should not, in any way, interfere with animals. This approach may be appropriate when dealing with a situation involving dingos and kangaroos in the wilds of the Northern Territory, but may not be appropriate when considering issues of wandering bears in an urban area of Alberta. In applying the model to analyse the harm in a particular activity, consideration is given to three key aspects of the world: humans, the biosphere and animals. This analysis may then be used to inform principles for controlling the harm in the context of the situation. This model does not lead to absolute positions, but rather, provides a method for weighing up and balancing the justice of a particular situation.

In part the model stems from work that has explored the practical realities of decisions that impact on the relationship between particular species (in this case, fish) and humans. In answer to the question, 'what harm is there in fishing?', the dialectical or reciprocal relationship between species was exposed. This is summarised as follows (White 2007b):

> What HUMANS do to fish (over-fishing; contaminated fish feed) and to fish environments (pollution; over-crowding; denuding of environments via technologies related to industrial open seas fishing and aquaculture) affects the basic nature of fish (stocks; genetics; health).

> These activities, in turn, affect what FISH do to humans (dioxins; carcinogens; scarcity) and to human environments (amenity; tourism; reputation; traditions; international relations), thus impacting upon the basic nature of humans (source of food stocks; work opportunities; genetics; health).

The sense of overlapping interests, in the context of 'real world' decision-making, alerts us to the need for a model of action that will enhance deliberations in cases where interests seem at cross-purposes. To put it differently, and as represented in Figure 1.3, there is a need for a model that is 'open-ended', one that does not assume that we know the right or correct answers in advance. In part, this simply recognises that in any discussion of harm (particularly within a

25

green criminology framework), there is always going to be conflicting interests and conflicting rights.

From a green criminology perspective, the key questions are: how do we engender a system of regulation and human intervention that will provide the best outcome for human and nonhuman, and what criteria do we use to conceptualise the nature of harm arising from human actions? To answer these, we need to appreciate why it is that human societies simultaneously respect and protect certain creatures (especially animal companions such as dogs and cats) while allowing and even condoning the utterly dreadful treatment of others (as in the case of factory farming of battery hens to produce eggs) (see Beirne 2004). We need to know why it is that we strive to preserve some environments (via creation of national parks), while at the same time ensuring the devastation of particular ecosystems (such as clearfelling of old-growth forests). To answer these questions demands some type of measure whereby we can weigh up the interests, options and consequences of particular courses of action: hence, the three-part model.

The contextual model of analysis provides a framework in which issues concerning environmental harm can be assessed and principles established for considering regulation or control of that harm. In the context of issues involving animals the model enables analysis of the issue considering not only animal rights but also environmental rights and human rights. By transcending traditional concepts of legal and illegal it is possible to view harm to animals in a new light. It is essential that we move beyond legalistic analysis of harm as this conception, particularly in respect of farmed animals, is already based upon an anthropocentric notion of animals as property of humans. Similarly, the model enables a discussion of animals in the wild beyond the anthropocentric categorisation of 'wildlife', 'endangered species' and the biocentric approaches such as 'biodiversity' and 'sustainability' (see Beirne 2007).

In applying the model to analyse the harm in a particular activity, consideration is given to three key aspects of the world: humans, the biosphere and animals. This analysis may then be used to inform principles for controlling the harm in context of the situation. This model does not lead to absolute positions, but rather, provides a method for weighing up and balancing the justice of a particular situation. For the model to work, it is essential that objective data be collected, that scientific studies be drawn upon, that various types of experiential and traditional knowledge are tapped into, and that baseline information is provided. Informed decision-making demands rigorous methods of data collection and systematic analysis of that data, as well as open dialogue regarding values, perspectives and priorities.

Tasks of environmental criminology

As will be demonstrated throughout the course of this book, environmental criminology has many dimensions and incorporates ideas and materials from a vast array of sources, disciplines and perspectives. Specific questions, specific studies and specific conceptual contributions all bring their own particular aspect to the general melange of what is green criminology. Nevertheless, there are several overarching considerations that tend to bind the disparate writings and investigations together.

Some of these tasks are, and continue, to be addressed by contemporary green criminologists. Others, however, await further devotion of time, energy and skill. Either way, the questions mapped out below (see Box 1.3) provide an illustration of the current activities and potential directions for environmental criminology.

Box 1.3 Tasks of environmental criminology

A central aim of green criminology is to investigate *the nature of environmental harm*. This can incorporate several distinct objectives. These include:

- To identify the varying definitions and types of environment, and to interpret how these can be analysed in a socio-legal conceptual framework. Consideration can be given to ecological factors, human work and settlement patterns, biological diversity, and the determination of 'value' in relation to certain environments (and their inhabitants);
- To identify different types of crime via specific case examples, and to develop a working typology of environmental crime which indicates varying emphasis on issues such as flora and fauna protection, pollution, toxic waste storage and disposal, inappropriate land use and so on;
- To question what constitutes environmental crime from the point of view of legal, social harm, ecological, rights and public interest perspectives. This would involve distinguishing between definitions

---

of harm linked to anthropocentric (human-centred), biocentric (all species are equal) and ecocentric (social ecology) perspectives.

Another aim of environmental criminology is to investigate the *nature of regulatory mechanisms and the social control of environmental harm.* This might be achieved by undertaking work that seeks:

- To identify the regulatory process in relation to environmental crime, as well as to develop a working register of existing control mechanisms and laws. Consideration could also be given to alternative dispute resolution;
- To investigate the pro-active measures available to maintain or protect environments, such as monitoring, preventive intervention and educational programmes;
- To explicate the reactive measures available, such as investigation, prosecution and use of sanctions. This would include consideration of issues pertaining to private property, community control and indigenous rights, as well as the use of statutory law, common law and administrative mechanisms (on a State, national and international level).

A third aim of green criminology might be to investigate the *nature of the relationship between changes in or to specific environments and the criminalisation process.* Here the main concerns might be:

- To investigate the causes or conditions of environmental crime in terms of motivation, propensity, structural capacity to do so, and State involvement (e.g. via subsidy, financial incentive, lack of regulation);
- To examine the nature of environmental harm in the light of factors such as urban planning, industry development, transportation routes, housing markets and so on;
- To explore that harm which may be caused by environmental hazards such as lead poisoning, toxic waste, pollution, inadequate sewerage systems, which may impact upon biological development and social opportunities;
- To consider that criminalisation associated with conflicts over environmental issues, including the actions of protestors and those who are opposed to protest actions.

In undertaking environmental criminology, it is also useful to indicate at the outset what an ideal green criminology programme of research and action would look like. For example, such a programme would acknowledge the importance of such work in the light of the pressing and global nature of environmental issues. The *international nature* of the problems is demonstrated in the transborder nature and effects of environmental degradation and pollution; the development of treaties and protocols in relation to industry development and environmental issues; and the trend toward a more highly integrated world economic and political structure.

Environmental criminology would ideally be based upon development of a socio-legal framework which builds directly upon expertise across a number of disciplines. Given its concerns with a wide range of environments (e.g. land, air, water) and issues (e.g. fishing, pollution), it would necessarily have to develop strong links between disciplines such as botany, zoology, geography, geology, and Antarctic studies, as well as sociology, political science and philosophy.

Environmental criminology ought to involve conceptual analysis, as well as practical intervention on specific environmental issues. Collectively, we can cooperate to build a general repository of knowledge, as well as take on commissioned work requiring expert opinion and professional expertise on specific socio-legal questions relating to the environment. This can also involve multidisciplinary strategic assessment procedures and analysis (e.g. involving economic, legal, social and ecological surveys).

Environmental criminologists also need to liaise and consult with a wide range of private and government bodies. These would include for example government departments charged with environmental regulation (e.g. environmental protection authorities); environmental biosecurity (e.g. customs, quarantine); specialist units within departments (e.g. endangered species – plant and animal); management of parks and reserves, including marine parks (e.g. park rangers); and so on. This could include undertaking organisational analysis and advising on 'best practice' methods of monitoring, assessment, enforcement and education with regards to environmental protection and regulation.

There are, then, many different theoretical and practical tasks with which environmental criminology can be engaged. However, the realities of work, and the politics of environmental study, inevitably mean that what we do will involve tensions and contradictions. For example, exposing environmental harm may make some governments and companies very uncomfortable and, in some cases, positively hostile. On the other hand, working too closely with environmental law enforcement agencies may compromise our ability to speak out on crucial issues of concern. The actual doing of environmental criminology bears with it certain personal and professional challenges. We shall consider these questions again in the concluding chapter.

Conclusion: where to from here?

This book can be read in several different ways. As a whole, it constructs a picture of harm that has many different dimensions. Each chapter also can be read as a self-contained discussion of specific issues. Importantly, the whole and the parts should be read as explorations, rather than authoritative pronouncement. The tension between notions of 'crime' and concepts of 'harm' is intrinsic to the exercise (in its whole and in its parts), and this emerges time and again. There is no 'solution' to this tension as such. The book in its entirety demonstrates that it will be an ongoing issue – which is explicitly recognised in many places throughout the work. In fact, differing conceptions of 'crime' and 'harm' represent the fulcrum upon which environmental politics pivots, and this will continuously shape how green criminology develops in applied and theoretical terms.

The starting point for investigation and action on matters relating to environmental criminology is philosophy. In other words, it is values, assumptions and theories – of life, of nature, of human interests, of ecology, of harm – that inform how individuals, groups and institutions perceive issues and intervene in the real world. Green criminology has generally been associated with philosophies that are liberating and emancipatory, radical and progressive. Its mandate has been not only about understanding the world, but changing it.

The pursuit of social and ecological justice, however, is never straightforward. It is also a never-ending project. By acknowledging shared goals and, equally, differences of opinion, environmental criminology is strengthened in the midst of its great diversity of views, activities and priorities. Having said this, it would be foolish to underestimate the tensions and conflicts that inevitably will accompany the development of green criminology now and into the future.

Posing issues relating to environmental harm in terms of 'rights', for example, is bound to ensure that there will be ongoing debate over the precise nature and terms of these presumed rights. For instance, different constructions of environmental rights lead to quite different emphases in practice. A human-centred concept will see them as an extension of human or social rights. The agenda then becomes one of guaranteeing that each person has adequate access to things such as clean air and clean water. The concept of environmental rights as applied to specific local environments would lead to efforts to conserve and protect these environments from particular kinds of damaging human encroachment. The rights that pertain to specific environments also incorporate, but are not reducible to, maintaining the rights of nonhuman animals to live free from cruelty and from particular kinds of human intrusion.

How different rights are weighed up in practice is, then, an inseparable element of understanding and dealing with environmental harm generally. This is both the challenge and the promise of green criminology. So too, it is important to recognise that if 'rights' or 'ecological citizenship' are the driving force behind social change, then this necessarily also entails consideration of the means to enforce 'justice'. In other words, if harms are viewed as transgressions of certain rights (relating to environments, humans and nonhuman animals), and these are to operate in a political (as distinct from purely moral) context, then such concepts ultimately warrant the use of coercion for their enforcement (see Hayward 2006: 446). It is for this reason that consideration of environmental law enforcement and global regulation must also be a constituent element of green criminology. Conceptualising and identifying the problem(s) is thus only one part of a complex process that is ultimately directed at resolving it.

Chapter 2

Social constructions of environmental problems

Environmental issues do not simply exist 'out there' as if they have an existence separate from human society. Rather, specific environmental problems and harms are always constructed as such through complex social processes of selection and affirmation. Objective harms do exist, but which harms come to public attention depends upon the successful mobilisation of information, opinion and consciousness. It takes issues entrepreneurs to make people sit up and take notice.

Introduction

Determining what is environmentally harmful not only depends upon ecophilosophy and particular conceptions of the nature–human interface. It is also shaped by what gets publicly acknowledged to be an issue or problem warranting social attention.

The aim of this chapter is to explore how environmental problems are socially constructed. From the outset it needs to be asserted that this process always incorporates subjective and objective elements. To put it differently, while there are tensions between a 'realist' position and a 'hard constructionist' position, most commentators now agree that social problems are constructed through a combination of material and cultural factors (Hannigan 2006; Macnaghten and Urry 1998; Higgins and Natalier 2004).

- *Realism* refers to an analytical stance that sees 'nature' as objectively existing in its own right. Environmental problems are seen to originate in what is actually happening in the natural world;

- *Constructionism* refers to an analytical stance that sees 'nature' as a social construct, as something that is always constructed through the lens of a human culture that sifts and selects, names and categorises, the natural world. Environmental problems are seen to be bounded by what humans determine to be important or significant.

In part these positions represent differences in analytical emphasis rather than absolutes. Beck (1992) for example has a tendency to see environmental problems as objectively given phenomena. Others argue that the relationship between 'nature' and 'culture' is such that there is no reality whatsoever outside the symbolic world-building activities of humans (see Lockie 2004).

Today, there appears to be a general consensus that, yes, there is an objective 'nature', and, yes, humans interpret this nature through cultural filters (Lockie 2004; Hannigan 2006). The study of environmental problems is the study of real, existing problems; but these *become* social problems as the products of a 'dynamic social process of definition, negotiation and legitimation' (Hannigan 2006: 31). The problems may be 'real', but the definition, magnitude, impact, risk and origins of phenomena such as pollution, climate change and toxic waste are open to interpretation and dispute.

Box 2.1 The science of environmental harm

It has been noted that 'scientists are integral players in the translation of scientific knowledge into pubic policy' (Silva and Jenkins-Smith 2007: 640). Study of the processes by which this occurs, however, indicates that 'science' and scientific information are not received as 'givens' by policy makers and governing authorities. In addition, research shows that the 'doing' of science is itself a social, rather than simply technical, activity, and that social context influences scientific interpretation of what the 'facts' convey.

From the publication of Rachel Carson's pathbreaking book *Silent Spring* in 1962, contemporary scientists have had a profound impact on public consciousness on issues such as how chemicals and pesticides

---

damage the environment through to the climate implications of the shrinking of the Arctic and Antarctic ice fields. The pleas of scientists to curb the worst excesses of industrial production have particularly resonated with the affluent classes of the advanced industrialised world. A general public that is well off and well educated – itself a reflection of high levels of economic development – has been able to agitate against air and water pollution and inappropriate land use. Social power and scientific knowledge have in combination been able to produce environmental regulation and reform, and scientists have been further called upon to help set the benchmarks and limits of what is or is not acceptable vis-à-vis environmental protection.

The vital role of science in bringing problems to public attention, and in devising methods to monitor or curb environmental hazards, is contingent upon how scientists are integrated into the policy making process. On the one hand, even where there is consensus among scientists about what is scientifically correct, comparison between how scientists deal with scientific certainty and uncertainty in specific cases (e.g. greenhouse gas and global temperatures, radiation doses and cancer) indicate that scientists' application of precaution as a policy recommendation is dependent on context – it is directly linked to the nature of the specific issue at hand (Silva and Jenkins-Smith 2007). Popular understandings and existing policy initiatives shape how scientific knowledge is translated into judgements about appropriate policy.

On the other hand, it is also recognised that the relationship between scientific advice and institutional decisions means considerable variation in how different governments deal with the same issue (even if scientists largely agree on the basic nature of the phenomenon). For example, the United States and the European Union have major policy differences in regards to use of genetically modified organisms (GMOs). This is not simply a dispute over the science involved in study of GMOs; it reflects differences in the vested interests associated with GMO production and distribution (see Chapter 5). Policy differences are apparent in other areas as well, as with the assessment of pesticide hazards in the United States, Britain and the European Union (see Irwin 2001). Whatever the specific science involved, it has been observed that 'institutions do not simply follow broad and established principles, but must instead tread a sensitive path between scientific evidence, social pressures and commercial anxieties' (Irwin 2001: 116). It is rare that scientific evidence is uncontested and that proof of environmental harm is simply a matter of 'let the facts decide'. What counts as 'science', what counts as 'evidence', who counts as being a 'scientific expert' and what counts as 'sensible' public policy are all influenced by factors such as economic situation, the scientific tradition within a particular national context, the scientific standards that are used in relation to specific issues, and the style and mode of government.

Science is one of the backbones of discovery, measurement and explanation of environmental harm, but it, too, is embedded in particular social processes and decision-making frameworks. In this respect, science is inherently social.

This chapter examines some of the ways in which environmental harm comes to be defined as problematic in the public eye. The first part of the chapter describes the ways in which this occurs. This is followed by consideration of how the media contributes to this social construction process. The final section raises issues pertaining to conflicts over rights, and how such conflicts might be resolved.

Social construction of environmental issues

To some extent an abstract model or mapping of environmental harm can be useful in exposing areas of further research and consideration, beyond that dealt with formally by law enforcement agencies and the criminal justice system at present (see Chapters 1 and 4). However, it can also be used to assist in explaining why it is that some types of human activity are more likely to be subject to criminalisation than others. The theme of this section is how environmental crime is socially constructed. Specifically, the concern is to identify those elements that together result in activity being deemed harmful, and thereby worthy of investigation and prosecution.

There are some very dramatic problems facing the planet when it comes to environmental issues. The severity of any particular issue, however, does not necessarily translate into the prominence given to that particular issue. The key question, therefore, is not so much severity but why certain issues become 'known' more so than others. State intervention and social movement action around specific issues similarly rest upon the fact that these specific issues have become important enough to generate widespread, concrete social responses.

What becomes prominent as a social issue reflects a social process in which certain claims – about nature, about environmental harm, about social impacts – are brought into the public domain and gain ascendancy. In this regard, Hannigan (2006: 69) observes that 'in researching the origins of environmental claims, it is important for the researcher to ask where a claim comes from, who owns or manages it, what economic and political interests claims-makers represent and what type of resources they bring to the claims-making process.' Hannigan (1995, 2006) provides a useful analytical model that describes just this process.

There are several key tasks in constructing environmental problems (see especially, Hannigan 2006: 68). One is *assembling*. This is basically determining the claim and supporting it with requisite information and evidence. It involves discovering and naming the problem and constructing 'proof' through appeal to scientific evidence. The more systematic and streamlined the knowledge claims, the more likely they can overcome pitfalls associated with lack of clarity, ambiguity and conflicting scientific evidence. A typical proposition might be, for example, that 'fish farming is bad for the environment'. Protagonists on both sides of this proposition would then engage in assembling their case, using whatever scientific and other evidence they could marshal in support of their position.

The task of *presenting* refers to the process of commanding attention and legitimating the claim. The central forum for this is the mass media, and the message is usually portrayed as a moral claim: fish farming is 'bad', and we should stop it now (or conversely, it is 'good' and should be encouraged). This task requires a communicator, someone who can gain public attention. This can be achieved by use of dramatic verbal and visual imagery, such as pictures of diseased fish or human victims of contaminated salmon. The key is visibility and keeping things in the public sphere.

The third task is that of *contesting*. This means being able to invoke action and mobilising support for the claims being made. This takes the issue into the political realm, and brings with it consideration of legal matters such as burden of proof and potential legislative change. Getting scientists on board, networking with likeminded people and organisations, and initiating public rallies (for example, of fishers, of consumers, of commercial operators) is all part of this process. It can be undermined by cooptation (for instance, allowing fish farms, but only under these rules), issue fatigue (people do not want to hear about it anymore) or countervailing claims (fish farms are vital to the food supply of people in China, Vietnam and other places).

The success or otherwise of claims-making in regard to environmental problems involves several interlocked factors. These are presented in Figure 2.1, which summarises what are in practice quite complicated and fluid social processes.

- Scientific authority for and validation of claims;
- Existence of 'popularisers' who can bridge environmentalism and science;
- Media attention in which the problem is 'framed' as novel and important;
- Dramatisation of the problem in symbolic and visual terms;
- Economic incentives for taking positive action;
- Recruitment of an institutional sponsor who can ensure both legitimacy and continuity.

Figure 2.1 Necessary factors for the successful construction of an environmental problem
Source: Hannigan 2006: 78.

What can further complicate the social construction of environmental problems is what can be called the ambiguities of definition. This refers to the idea that what is environmental harm to one person may not be seen as environmental harm at all by another. For example, some people would say that resource depletion itself is a bad thing; others would argue that the issue is really about how to manage it, not the activity in and of itself that is bad.

The ambiguities of definition also refers to the transposition of issues: an explosion at a gas factory may be a 'workers' issue and/or an 'environmental' issue; contamination of drinking water may be an 'environmental' issue and/or a matter of 'corporate wrongdoing'; lead poisoning from a children's toy may be an 'environmental' issue and/or a 'consumer' issue. How specific issues are defined, and whether they are defined in narrow or broad terms, is part of the social construction process.

Another factor that influences how environmental problems are socially constructed relates to changes in the type and extent of media coverage, and popular participation, over time. For instance, social research has pointed to the phenomenon of the *routinisation* of environmental concerns (Pakulski *et al.* 1998). It is argued that a decline in membership and participation in environmental groups over a ten year period was due in large part to the increasing familiarity of the public with environmental issues (because of persistent media coverage).

A change in the level of public concern about environmental issues was also attributed to a greater reliance upon experts rather than environmental activists to define and shape conceptions of environmental problems. The notion of 'having heard it all before' is also matched by more issues being identified, greater diffusion of concerns, and the clustering of issues into distinct categories (such as urban pollution or forest conservation). For claims-makers, their very success in getting the environment into the public agenda may well undermine later attempts to resuscitate interest in the issues that they specifically wish to mobilise sentiment around.

For scientists, the social processes associated with legitimating or de-legitimating a problem can put them into an invidious occupational and personal situation. Environmental problems generally are bound to put more demands on science to come up with the diagnostic and remediation answers. Simultaneously, this opens science up to public scrutiny and criticism. Great care has to be taken in putting findings into context, and to communicating clearly the strengths and limitations of specific investigations. There is more than this at stake however. The perceived centrality of science and the scientist in determining environmental harm has been linked to the active suppression of environmental scientists through threats to employment conditions and prospects, and through censorship or blocking of publications and presentations (Kuehn 2004). Generally it is those in positions of power and authority who are likely to challenge the reputation, findings and skill of scientists who produce work not to their liking. Protection against suppression is likely to continue to be an issue of pressing concern well into the future.

What gets defined as a 'problem' – its severity, its nature, its identification – is contingent upon the capacity of sectional interests to secure its definitions. In other words, we ought to factor into the social constructionist equation the importance of class and the differential ability of people to mobilise resources around their claims. In the end, environmental problems are always contingent in nature; in answer to the question is this an environmental issue? – the answer is, 'it depends' (see Box 2.2).

Box 2.2 The contingent nature of environmental problems

What is the problem?
In order to determine this we have to deal with issues of definition and evidence of harm. We have to analyse potentially competing

claims as to whether or not the problem exists, and diverse lay and expert opinion on how the problem is interpreted. Does it pose a risk, and if so, to whom, and in what ways? Is the initial problem serious enough in the public's eye to warrant a social response in the form of community action or State intervention?

Why does the problem occur?
To answer this we need to examine the social context, and to investigate the actions of key actors involved with the phenomenon.

What are the social dynamics that allow the problem to persist or ensure that State action is taken to overcome it?
To answer this we need to tackle issues pertaining to the shaping of perceptions, interpretation of events, and intervention processes. Is the problem socially constructed as a *social problem* warranting social action, rather than a personal issue for which the individual has to take responsibility? In what ways is the problem construed from the point of view of *social regulation* and what forms of State and private intervention are mobilised to contain or manage the problem? Is the problem itself to be addressed, or is the focus on how best to avoid, cover-up or manage any *risk* associated with the problem?

Source: adapted from White 2004.

The emergence of global warming or climate change can be used to illustrate how an environmental issue becomes transformed into a social problem.

Case study 2.1 The politics of global warming

Concern about global warming had been expressed for many years, by many scientists in many disciplines. It had been systematically denied and downplayed by governments such as the Bush administration in the United States and the Howard regime in Australia. No evidence, it seemed, was convincing enough to change the mind of these political leaders. The award of the Nobel Peace Prize in 2007 to former Vice-President Al Gore for his film *An Inconvenient Truth* (along with the Intergovernmental Panel on Climate Change), not to mention an

Academy Award for best documentary, went some way to changing this situation. So did the release in 2006 of *The Economics of Climate Change*, a major report by Nicolas Stern in the United Kingdom (Stern 2007). To have a former Chief Economist of the World Bank state categorically that climate change is a serious and urgent issue, and that failure to act will create even more economic damage than the costs of needed expenditure today, was, for many, the final proof that global warming could not be ignored. Nevertheless, the language of 'climate change' seems somewhat muted compared to the previously used popular term 'global warming'. Meanwhile, the scientific evidence keeps mounting up (United Nations Environment Programme 2007).

Part of the reason why climate change and global warming has become increasingly prominent as a social issue is that it seems, in its varied and multiple ways, to now touch or affect every person living on the planet. It does this directly and indirectly, in ways that are understandable and threatening to ordinary people. Unseasonal weather (such as droughts), extreme weather events (such as cyclones/hurricanes) and natural disasters (such as the Indian Ocean tsunami of 2005) bring home the immediate effects of global warming to many millions of people. The longer-term effects, such as rising ocean levels, are also not so long-term for many peoples living in low lying countries of the Pacific and Indian oceans.

The phenomenon of thermal-related deaths in France in August 2003 (Curson and Clark 2004) and the devastation wrought by Hurricane Katrina in New Orleans in 2005 (Hartman and Squires 2006) has also highlighted the lack of adequate preparation for such events and trends. As well, it has demonstrated that environmental injustice not only pertains to the siting of toxic facilities and the dumping of waste, but is entrenched in the priorities assigned to those whose safety, health and well-being matters the most. For the elderly, the poor and people of colour, such differences are, literally, a matter of life and death.

The global media, including the Internet, have been central to bringing climate change into more and more homes, at least in the more affluent nations where computers open many different portals to the world at large. For others, direct experience and changes in traditional social patterns are unmistakeable indicators of profound shifts in global climate (e.g. as with Inuit in northern Canada who find the ice and snow arriving later and melting sooner, which affects their hunting and food gathering activities). The world is smaller, and the issues more transparent. But the causes and solutions still generate considerable disagreement and, it seems, even less substantive action.

Media reporting on the environment

The media obviously play a major role in constructing certain environmental issues as issues of public concern. It is important, therefore, to examine some of the ways in which media reporting of environmental issues takes place. Space precludes extensive and detailed assessment of the media, but even a cursory examination reveals significant trends and features that shape public views, attitudes and perceptions.

The message and the medium

The media consists of a range of specific forms, such as the press (newspapers and magazines), visual electronic (which includes not only free to air television, but pay-TV, videos and Internet sites) and radio (which also can include activity involving downloads off the Internet). The specific medium utilised to convey information also influences the content of the message being delivered. In other words, the content must always fit the format, and is therefore always secondary to the format (Ericson *et al.* 1991). For example, TV news relies upon short, sharp sound-bites with strong emphasis on the visual dimension. If there is no film footage, then there may be no story. So the medium itself determines what gets on, how long it gets on and how it is presented. A radio broadcast is built upon audio communication, which again lends itself to different kinds of formatting and content.

Regardless of medium, there seems to be a longer term trend in media production that has seen entrenched the media practice of replacing complex information with symbols, images and catchwords. Arguably, contemporary audiences have been trained to want nothing else. The emphasis is on theatre and spectacle, images and style, rather than meaning and content. Entertainment and 'infotainment' seem to be the rule of mass media. One consequence of this is a persistent lack of 'historical' sensibility: each day brings an apparently 'new' event.

The gaining of a collective definition of social problems via the media involves issue selection. This is partly determined by the nature of the medium itself. It is also related to notions of what is newsworthy. Disasters, for example, are eminently newsworthy. They command attention and offer much in the way of televisuality. They tend not to be politically threatening. More complex and diffuse issues, such as global warming, are harder to present in simplistic form and in interesting formats (although Al Gore would no doubt argue that this in fact is not the case). The content of the media coverage tends to be event-centred, to focus on milestones, catastrophes and court actions, rather than to be exploratory and explanatory of trends. The activist who risks life and limb against the Japanese whaler makes a good and sensational story. After all, the media are big business and the bottom line is sales and profit. For environmental claims-makers, this puts pressure to be dramatic rather than prosaic in approach to conveying information about issues.

Ownership and control

The nature of media coverage of environmental issues is contingent to a great extent upon who owns and controls the media. Commentators have pointed out, for example, the close ties between media ownership and environmental coverage. NBC television in the US, for example, is owned by General Electric. The latter has major economic interests in nuclear energy. Not surprisingly, this is promoted through the means of NBC TV. Moreover, General Electric funds conservative think tanks which are then used as a source of 'independent' experts for NBC, on issues such as nuclear power (Beder 1997).

Direct ownership is only one way in which economics impinges upon environmental reporting. Another is the influence of advertisers on the content presented by private media providers. Revenue for the mass media is driven by advertisers. Advertisers are basically those companies that want to sell something to the public, and which therefore have a vested interest in promoting consumption and economic growth. Stories that threaten specific corporate interests and images, and those that de-legitimise the economic imperative over the ecological, are more apt to not see the light of day.

On the other hand, there are market opportunities to develop environmentally oriented television that is not about information as such. Nature programmes and programmes about exotic animals and plants might well fall into this category. They bring the rest of the world into the living rooms of the relatively affluent, but in ways that do not compel the audience to engage in anything more than non-demanding action (e.g. provide a donation to a wildlife protection fund). It is the unusual and the spectacular that is emphasised, not the mundane and the ordinary.

Another aspect of environmentalism and the mass media is that for 'hard news', sources of information often include what is provided by company public relations people via media releases, news conferences and staged events. The news thus reflects the power of the news makers. In a similar vein, it has been observed that large corporations that tend to sponsor newscasts and run green advertising campaigns are almost never examined for their environmental record (Beder 1997). Being green, it seems, is in the eye of the beholder, as determined by the beholder.

Case study 2.2 Public profiles and environmental awards

Major Australian forest company Gunns Limited has strived to present itself as a 'clean, green' company, and to use the media to publicise this. In March 2004, Gunns submitted an entry in the Banksia Award and its competition for an award for a business or government enterprise that has demonstrated leadership, commitment and excellence in protecting Australia's environment and contributing to a sustainable future. As a consequence of actions by environmental activists the Banksia Environmental Foundation determined and announced that Gunns was no longer a finalist for the Banksia Award. What is most interesting about this particular event is the way in which Gunns attempted to 'earn' its green credentials by, in effect, buying its way into the awards process and thereby expecting something in return. It was 'understood' by the company that only what the company says about itself was relevant to the award process, and that what outside interests had to say was irrelevant. By exposing Gunns' record to external scrutiny, environmental activists not only provided a critique of a specific company but, in effect, called into question the process of environmental award giving itself (White 2005b).

Corporate interests are protected through various means. This can involve concerted 'greenwashing' campaigns (see Beder 1997; Athanasiou 1996) that provide a green tinge to the corporate image. It also refers to more general processes that serve to maintain the status quo. For example, environmental degradation and specific incidents are seen as 'exceptional circumstances', rather than an intrinsic part of the political economic system. This tendency in reporting is not only due to media-corporate self-serving reportage. It also reflects the manner in which the mass media format and deliver the message generally in ahistorical event-centred ways.

Journalists and journalism

The myth of journalism is that journalists in the field are independent and neutral recorders of history. This belies the many ways in which specific stories can be edited or pulled, depending upon content and potential to disrupt the interests of media owners, advertisers or other powerful élites. It also ignores the ways in which mainstream journalists who 'toe the line' win the awards, while dissident journalists are excluded from this mainstream and frequently derided and complained against for their biases.

The hard reality of journalism is that it is intertwined with big business. Where this is not directly the case (as with national public broadcasters such as the Australian Broadcasting Corporation, the BBC, Canadian Broadcasting Corporation, the US Public Broadcasting Service and so on), there is often political pressure to be 'even handed' and uncritical of certain people, policies and principles. Appeals to the 'national interest' are also used to shut out alternative voices and to deny the more critical perspectives on environmental matters (e.g. getting the Olympic bid requires silence about what to do about the toxic waste on the Olympic site).

A key mechanism that affects the ability of environmental activists to stake their claims via the media is the notion of journalistic neutrality. This notion is based upon three interrelated concepts (see Figure 2.2).

Balance – more radical opinions generally left out; both sides get equal coverage, regardless of numbers of people in demonstration or counter-demonstration; scientists with suspect credentials given equal weight to others.

Depersonalisation – in order to downplay personal views, there is encouragement of uncritical reporting of official statements and those of authority figures; 'In this way, the individual biases of individual journalists are avoided but institutional biases are reinforced.'

Sphere of objectivity – story that supports the status quo is generally considered to be neutral (i.e. no perceived need for balance), while

---

one that challenges the status quo tends to be perceived as having a 'point of view' and therefore biased; the former are 'facts', the latter 'opinions'.

Figure 2.2 Questioning journalistic neutrality
Source: Beder 1997: 202–206.

The idea of being unbiased frequently translates into letting environmental sceptics have much more of the media platform than they deserve. But this seems to work in only one direction. That is, the occasional scientist who has stood against the vast tide of scientific opinion to express doubt about climate change, and who thereby finds favour in places such as conservative political circles within the White House, are more than likely to be given a voice in media 'debates' over the state of the environment. Meanwhile, scientists and environmental activists who for years have been trying to get the message across about specific threats (melting of the Arctic polar ice cap) or general trends (global warming) have been received less favourably.

Even the media, however, is forced into acknowledgement of environmental problems when some events, trends or situations become too big to ignore, downplay or dismiss. Then the issue becomes how do we explain these, and what is to be done about them.

Finally, it has to be said that the mass media, including public and private operations and companies, are not a monolith. The radio talkshow does allow for more than one opinion to be expressed. The environmental activist does have allies in the mainstream media. Media workforces are divided politically and share in a wide range of views and commitments in relation to environmental matters. While there are structural parameters on media work (relating to everything from content–format issues through to editorial control), claims-making only makes sense as an active process if there is some opportunity to make the claim stick. If there were not possibilities to exploit the chinks in the walls of journalist professionalism and media market opportunities, then the present discussion would be about totalitarianism rather than social construction. There are, then, pressures and limits that define the process, but what occurs is nonetheless a process.

Human interests and environmental problems

Another aspect of the social construction of environmental problems relates to the place of human rights and human interests in shaping issues. When it comes to environmental harm, what actually gets criminalised by and large reflects the efforts of claims-makers to make an issue of the harm in question. In part this relates to the ways in which 'environmental rights' have been evolving and are framed in law, particularly in relation to broader developments vis-à-vis human rights legislation (see Thornton and Tromans 1999). It also relates to the strategic interests of industries and indeed humanity as a whole to protect and preserve particular environments and/or species for the 'greater good'.

Part of the dilemma for green criminologists is how to sensibly move the debate beyond standard approaches to environmental crime, and how to shift policy and practice in ways that are more effective than conventional forms of environmental regulation. This involves making certain new claims about the nature of harm, and about the nature of human responsibility. The social construction of environmental problems, for green criminology, must incorporate ideas and practices that link together concerns with environmental justice, ecological justice and species justice.

Importantly, there still is a point at which human interests become privileged in determining the nature of the relationship between 'nature' and 'society'. This is so for several reasons. First, humans are responsible for much of the destruction of ecological systems and, as such, are the key agents of environmental change in the contemporary time period. There may well be a tango between humans and their environments, but the dance tends to be heavily weighted in how humans as a whole transform their immediate environments for their own purposes. The net result is to the detriment of both human and nonhuman, but the causal force for environmental degradation is ultimately human. This is not to deny post-human observations on the powerful shaping of human society by 'nature' and natural phenomena (such as river systems, burning forests and so on). But at a gross, historical level it is what humans do *en masse* that reshapes landscapes, that pollutes air, water and soil, that leads to species decline among plants and animals, that changes the contours of the atmosphere and the level of the seas. The moral responsibility for this lies with us humans.

Secondly, the construction of moral egalitarianism across species and systems is both illogical and impractical (see Low and Gleeson

1998). As discussed in Chapter 1, a strictly biocentric perspective can also lead to a misanthropic perspective that belittles the differences between species and which, by considering human activity out of social context, sees the human species as intrinsically and innately destructive to the environment. Such views quickly lead to racism, élitism and anti-human policies. They are morally repugnant and politically suspect.

A social ecology perspective emphasises humanity and the ability of humans to change themselves and the natural world. It looks to the human causes of environmental destruction, but in so doing attempts to specify which particular categories of humans are responsible for this destruction and which social systems lead inexorably to ecological disaster. It is a perspective grounded in recognition of different social interests, different forms and types of social power, and clear distinctions being drawn between exploiter and exploited, oppressor and oppressed.

The notion of 'universal human interests' is useful here in contradistinction to sectoral human interests. Humanity has common interests – *universal human interests* – namely, the survival of the human race in the face of things like nuclear holocaust or ecological degradation. There are thus common human interests that need to take priority over any other kind of interests if we are, as a species, to survive. However, while everybody on the planet has a common interest in the survival of the human race, the specific class interests of business, of transnational corporations, mean that they are not willing to implement or enact strategies and policies that would, in fact, further the common human interest. In other words the reason why we are not fixing up the planet, even though it is to the advantage of all that we work together in our common interest, is that specific class interests intrude upon the process whereby planetary well-being might be prioritised (see Athanasiou 1996).

The relationship between humans and 'nature' can largely be informed by the notion of the enlightened self-interest of humans. This is, in one sense, a human-centred or anthropocentric viewpoint. But what makes it different from the dominant anthropocentric perspective (see Chapter 1) is the sensitivity to the dialectical nature of change, including those constant changes in the relationship between humans and nature over time. A dynamic concept of 'nature' is complemented by a notion of 'totality' and interconnectedness. Thus, the relationship between humans and the so-called natural environment is seen as one that includes consideration of the impact of humans on particular environments beyond the physical boundaries of human settlement (e.g. pollution in cities affecting forests via acid rain). Respect for nature is integral to the well-being of humans.

What constitutes an environmental harm or environmental crime is partly a matter of visibility of the issues, partly a matter of public policy. As discussed throughout this chapter, what can be identified via personal experiences, expert representation or sectional interest group as being worthy of attention, is that which is most likely to gain recognition as a public issue (see Hannigan 2006). Meanwhile, governments have laws across a wide range of issues, relating to air, water, toxic waste, use of public lands, endangered species and the list goes on. The relationship between public policy and government strategic action is also shaped by contingency – specific events, situations and disasters tend to shake things up rapidly and with immediate effect.

The precise nature of an environmental issue is in itself linked to specific group interests and consciousness of harm. The mobilisation of opinion is crucial to determination of what is or is not considered a 'crime' (or 'harm'), and how the State will in the end respond to the phenomenon in question. This is well known to writers examining the nature of state crime, since state crime is typically denied by the perpetrator – the State itself. In these circumstances it is frequently human rights definitions combined with world opinion that make certain harms *into* state crimes (see Green and Ward 2000, 2004).

In a very similar vein, the actions of states on environmental matters sometimes elude consideration as a criminological matter because of the policy and political context within which the harm occurs. This is especially the case in respect to environmental harms associated with the processes and techniques of war (see Box 2.3).

Box 2.3   Depleted uranium and environmental harm

There are major problems with the use of depleted uranium (DU) in weapons and armour in war situations such as Iraq, the Balkans and Kosovo (see White 2008b). Thus, 'the damage caused by uranium weapons cannot be contained to "legal" fields of battle; they continue to act after the conclusion of hostilities; they are inhumane because they place the health of non-combatants, including children and future generations, at risk; and they cannot be used without unduly damaging the natural environment' (Medical Association for Prevention of War 2003).

The question, from an environmental criminology perspective, is how the use of DU affects the well-being of humans, biosphere and animals. To assess this, we can invoke several concepts that go to the core of a green criminological analysis. One starting point is to consider the precautionary principle. This involves assessment and the presumption of risk (see Chapter 3). In the case of DU, the issue is whether or not it is harmful (and to whom and what), and potential future risks. The issue of risk is highly contentious in regards to DU, as there is sustained denial of risk in official government circles (White 2008b).

The uncertainties surrounding DU are compounded by the fact that DU in its gas form is basically undetectable to unaided human senses. Such risks are thereby invisible, and thus 'unknowable' to the ordinary layperson (see Beck 1992). In such circumstances there is greater reliance upon technical expertise and technological capacity for the measurement and recording of DU levels and impacts. Where these are unavailable, or where direct experience is excluded for being speculative (as in the case of hospital reports linking DU with increased levels of cancer), then knowledge of risk is considered uncertain. Moreover, general knowledge of risk has continued to be actively suppressed and the debate thereby diminished (see White 2008b, for an extended discussion of this).

Environmental justice discourse tends to place inequalities in the distribution of environmental quality at the top of the environmental agenda. Those who suffer, do so precisely because of where they live. Those who will suffer in the future likewise will do so because of geography. The half life of DU is measured in the billions of years. Parts of Iraq are now permanently contaminated. This situation offends against the principle of intergenerational equity, a key principle of ecological sustainability. That is, future generations of Iraqi people will not enjoy the quality of environment experienced by those prior to the Gulf Wars. Without remedial action, the contaminants will continue to pose a hazard to human health and well-being now and far into the future. The cumulative impact of DU, and indeed of low-level radiation generally, is surely a matter of great and ongoing concern.

People also suffer because of where they 'work'. Here it is important to acknowledge the ways in which soldiers (on all sides) are generally ignored and/or dehumanised in regards to DU use in the Gulf. They tend to be treated in terms of functionality (the job of war) rather than humanity (the preciousness of being). The value of the solider is found in military action; they are combatants, not people. As such, they suffer disproportionately now and into the future for decisions made about and for them by others. They simply do not count in the larger scheme of things.

The indiscriminate contamination of people is also simultaneously the indiscriminate contamination of places and other living creatures. From the point of view of ecological justice, this means that human actions have violated basic ecological citizenship principles and the rights of nonhuman animals to be free from abuse and suffering. Respect for the biosphere and for animals has obviously not been built into the war effort. It is also rare to find anyone talking about or studying the impact of DU on nonhuman animals or the biosphere. For example, the only reference to animal welfare or otherwise seems to be in regard to animal studies on the effects of acute, intermediate and chronic duration exposure to DU (see Bertell 1999). In the case of the biosphere, select reference is sometimes made to widespread, low-level contamination of the ground surface by DU, or the possible migration of DU into ground water, but systematic environmental audit and analysis of DU harm does not seem to be a high priority (United Nations Environment Programme 2003).

Green criminology also needs to be concerned, therefore, with how weapons of war affect people and environments, if people, environments and animals are to be protected from hazards and harms that are entirely preventable but which have huge effects and that last for long periods of time (White 2008b).

The complex relationship between human and nonhuman 'rights' is played out in practice through the importance of 'place' in the lives of diverse communities. Aside from global phenomena such as climate change, that sometimes present as too big, too abstract and too difficult to address for ordinary folk, people generally view environmental problems as something pertaining to where they live, holiday or work.

This inevitably leads to conflicts over purposes, as each place or site (such as a forest) is subject to competing demands – jobs (via logging), recreation (via tourism), sustenance (via settlement), aesthetics (via photography) and so on. Disputes over value and use can be settled using the full range of political, ideological, legal, coercive and persuasive means available to stakeholder parties. The complexities of conflict over rights is well captured by Christoff (2000: 204):

> Claims relating to environmental rights potentially conflict with social and economic rights. Consider, for instance, the struggle over the fate of Australia's old-growth forests. On the one hand, timber companies want to harvest 'their' logs (property rights), while timber workers want to preserve their jobs and resource managers want to be able to manage the forests for products such as timber and water for immediate human use (social rights to employment, culture and development). On the other hand, environmentalists want to preserve forests for their wilderness values (reflecting social rights to meet 'abstract' aesthetic and spiritual needs) and biodiversity (reflecting environmental rights protecting an unquantifiable asset benefiting present and future humans, and intrinsic values relating to the existence of species and ecosystems). It is the presence of such – at their most fundamental – irreconcilable value conflicts which makes the relationship between social, environmental and ecological rights (and citizens) so problematic in practice.

Environmental problems are constructed in the crucible of claims and counter-claims over risk and harm (see Chapter 3). They are also socially constituted in the context of competing claims about which or whose rights ought to take precedence. Harm, in this sense, may be about the denial of rights as well as about instances of direct environmental degradation.

There is an array of conflicts and confusions regarding environmental and ecological rights (see for examples, Goldman 1998a, 1998b; Low and Gleeson 1998; Cullinan 2003; Munro 2004). How rights are conceived has a bearing on whether or not there is perception of an environmental problem. Some of the key tensions include:

- Jobs versus environment (where a social right to livelihood conflicts with ecological imperatives to sustain species and environments);

- Intrinsic values (constructing 'value' and drawing lines around speciesism, so that we can identify to what and to whom rights apply in specific circumstances – to the mosquito, the moose, the ant, the zebra?);

- Perils of non-intervention (acknowledging the practicalities of human need vis-à-vis food, shelter, clothing, and the potential problems that arise if management of seal numbers, or deer herds, or kangaroo populations does not occur);

- Individual versus collective notions of rights (the ongoing tensions between bourgeois notions of private property and public interest notions of property);

- Prioritising actions on rights (in specific cases, putting an emphasis on homeless humans rather than loss of bird habitat);

- Constructing the global commons (corporate definitions of what is 'best' for local peoples and transnational interference from afar versus grassroots organising and local input into decision-making).

What complicates this further is the reality that 'nature' by definition is complex, uncertain, interconnected and ever-changing. What is apparently a benign policy prescription one day may lead to disaster the next. For example, one alternative to clearfelling of old-growth forests has been greater reliance on pine forest plantations. However, while some of the old-growth forests may have been protected, the planting of one species of tree lends itself to greater susceptibility to disease and diminishment of biodiversity. Only a flexible approach to logging and forestry will allow change in perspective and practices over time, as we better understand the nuances and dangers of solutions that at time seem to make sense. Responding to an environmental problem one day thus begets a different sort of environmental problem the next.

Conclusion: where to from here?

The theme of this chapter has been the variable ways in which environmental problems are socially constructed – through claims-making processes and media formulations, and in the context of competing notions of rights.

Analysis of the processes whereby environmental issues become translated into issues of public concern once again reaffirms the contingent nature of harm. Environmental harm is objective or material, in that certain trends and events can be discerned, and environmental and social impacts documented. But it is also subjective or cultural, in that which types of social phenomenon are selected and categorised as being environmentally harmful is a social process involving diverse actors. Study of the interplay between 'nature' and 'culture', especially around criminological topical concerns, should reveal further insight into the nature of environmental harm generally.

Specific matters that could also be looked at in greater depth include things such as the displacement of issues. For example, how do media and claims-makers construct environmental issues around different geographical orientations? As alluded to above, local and regional environmental issues may be more volatile politically than those pitched at the level of the global. Acknowledgement of global problems such as climate change is, in one sense, easier than dealing with more localised issues, since the scope of the problem also 'excuses' action on the part of authorities. Similarly, dealing with illegal logging or illegal fishing may appear to be more straightforward than trying to grapple with the complexities of bio-genetics. Both geography and complexity can be used to displace attention from some issues in favour of others.

Environmental problems are socially constructed via public campaigns that legitimate claims and build support for reform and change. Rationality is crucial to this process, insofar as science is enlisted to provide evidence for this or that harm. However, it is often the emotions that go with environmental issues that can win the day for specific campaigns. Thus, affective elements (for example, images of a polar bear scrambling to stay afloat on a rapidly shrinking iceberg) are essential components in how issues are socially constructed.

In the context of competing claims to expertise (e.g. my scientific study is better than your scientific study; my scientist is more qualified than your scientist), it may well be that it is propaganda rather than *bona fide* knowledge that ensures that some issues more than others attain the status of a publicly recognised environmental problem. If this is the case, then big questions can be asked about the veracity of any claims being made and how best to gauge and respond to 'moral panics' associated with environmental issues.

Moral positions, ethical principles, traditional understandings and common sense knowledge each has its part to play in the ways in which claims-making occurs and how well it resonates with particular audiences. The relationship between information and emotion, and the manner in which reception of ideas is linked to local distinctiveness, personal relevance and grounded familiarity, are matters that deserve greater attention.

Chapter 3

Environmental risk and the precautionary principle

Intervention on environmental matters depends in part upon how risk is conceived and whether assessment of risk subsequently leads to action. Responding to environmental harm is not only about reacting to specific events or incidents. It also includes evaluation of potential threats or risks into the future. Taking precaution is central to protecting the planet, humans and nonhuman animals from projected harms. This involves weighing up and recognising which risks actually exist, and for whom.

Introduction

This chapter provides an introduction and overview of how 'risk' features in analysis of environmental harm, and in attempts to minimise existing and potential harms. The first part of the chapter discusses various dimensions of risk. There are multiple kinds of risk; and there are many different disciplinary ways in which risk may be analysed (such as through the lens of actuarial science, sociology, law, psychology, medicine and political science). The intention here is not to elaborate on any one tradition or perspective on risk. Rather it is to describe and survey varying ways in which specific constructs of risk have been related to environmental issues.

The second part of the chapter explores how risk is responded to through the mechanism of the precautionary principle. The precautionary principle is a key concept of environmental study, regardless of discipline background, and thus deserves special attention. This is bolstered by the fact that precaution is exactly called for when investigating issues surrounding environmental risk and environmental harm. After discussing several issues relating to the practical implementation of the precautionary principle (such as risk assessment and risk management), the chapter then discusses the role and importance of community participation in deliberations over environmental matters.

Risk is a multidimensional entity generally incorporating several key elements. One notion of risk sees it as a prediction or expectation that involves:

- A hazard (the source of danger);
- Uncertainty of occurrence and outcomes (expressed by the probability or chance of occurrence);
- Adverse consequences (the possible outcome);
- A timeframe for evaluation;
- The perspectives of those affected about what is important to them.

(Leiss and Hrudey 2005: 3)

Our specific interest is with risk as it is applied to environmental concerns. Drawing upon the list provided by Deville and Harding (1997: 27), a number of threats to the environment can be identified. The list is by no means exhaustive, but it does provide some indication of the types of threats that the precautionary principle aims to avoid.

- Global warming (for example, due to excessive discharges of carbon dioxide);
- Biodiversity loss (for example, due to release and establishment of non-native plant and animal species);
- Stratospheric ozone depletion (for example, due to use of CFCs);
- Desertification and land degradation (for example, due to land clearing for unsustainable agricultural practices);
- Marine ecosystem health (for example, due to oil spills);
- Freshwater ecosystem health (for example, discharge of pollutants);
- Atmospheric pollutants (for example, due to acid rain);
- Damage to specific ecosystems (for example, due to overfishing and overlogging);
- Damage to human and nonhuman physical and mental health (for example, due to chemical residues in food).

Close analysis and thoughtful reflection about this list generates a further set of questions that are relevant to issues surrounding environmental harm. For example, who or what is the victim? What are the actual risks? Can precautions be taken in relation to these risks, and if so, what are they? What are the roles of scientific analysis and non-scientific understandings and experiences (e.g. layperson accounts) in assessing risk? What action is required to address risks, and who, specifically, ought to take the requisite action? These and other questions deserve consideration in any discussion of risk and precaution.

Dimensions of risk

Victimisation is central to the notions of 'risk' and 'precaution', since each is interpreted in terms of potential threat to human and environmental well-being.

From the point of view of environmental criminology, analysis of the nature of environmental harm has to take into account objective and subjective dimensions of victimisation. It also has to locate the processes of environmental victimisation within the context of the wider political economy. That is, the dynamics of environmental harm cannot be understood apart from consideration of who has the power to make decisions, the kinds of decisions that are made, in whose interests they are made, and how social practices based on these decisions are materially organised. Issues of power and control have to also be analysed in the light of global economic, social and political developments.

Risk and political economy

The 'choices' ingrained in environmental victimisation (of human beings, of the nonhuman world), stem from systemic imperatives to exploit the planetary environment for production of commodities for human use. This is not a politically neutral process. In other words, how human beings produce, consume and reproduce themselves is socially patterned in ways that are dominated by global corporate interests (see Athanasiou 1996; White 2002).

Threats to the environment come from a range of activities. Deville and Harding (1997: 27) categorise these as:

- Obtaining resources – either extracting non-renewable minerals and energy or harvesting and managing 'renewable' resources such as fish or forest timbers;
- Transforming or using these resources – constructing buildings, bridges and other infrastructure, manufacturing products, or burning fossil fuels;
- Disposing of unusable 'by-products' – managing, reusing, recycling or disposing of waste materials from obtaining and transforming resources.

Each of these specific activity areas produces environmental threats. Each, as well, embodies risks for particular human populations and biotic communities.

Case study 3.1   Indigenous people at risk

In Canada, governments are not reluctant to allow extraction industries to enter into and fully work lands occupied by indigenous peoples, regardless of the wishes of the local people (Rush 2002). Mining and logging operations create major environmental damage, a process that directly affects the health and well-being of indigenous people. It is tragically ironic that, in the US, the history of repression of indigenous people is such that they were forcibly relocated to unwanted lands that contain some of the richest mineral deposits and other natural resources in the US (such as uranium and low-sulphur coal). Thus, 'The quest for natural resources, then, imposes specific environmental risks on peoples such as Native Americans who reside near, and are dependent on, natural resources' (Field 1998: 80).

The dominance of neo-liberal ideology as a guiding rationale for further commodification of nature, and the concentration of decision-making in State bureaucracies and transnational corporate hands, accelerate the rate and extent of environmental victimisation (Hessing 2002). The power of capitalist hegemony manifests itself in the way in which certain forms of production and consumption become part of a taken-for-granted common sense, the experiences and habits of everyday life (see Chapter 6; also White 2002).

Specific practices, and choices, in how humans interact with particular environments present immediate and potential risks to everything within them. For example, the practice of clearfelling old-growth forests directly affects many animal species by destroying their homes (see Halsey 1997b). Similarly, local natural environments, and nonhuman inhabitants of both wilderness and built environments, are negatively impacted upon by human practices that destroy, re-channel or pollute existing fresh water systems.

Bearing the risk

> By one estimate, three out of every five African-American households currently live near a hazardous-material storage area. Fines imposed on polluters by all levels of government in white communities in the 1980s were 46 per cent higher than those imposed for violations in minority communities. Fines levied against site violations under the federal hazardous-waste statutes were 500 per cent higher in white communities than fines in minority communities ... Until the early 1990s, the US Environmental Protection Agency had conducted no major studies on the possible uneven distribution of environmental cost or benefits across racial or income categories (Rhodes 2003: 5).

The core concern of environmental justice is to highlight and challenge the social inequalities in the distribution of environmental quality. In many cases advocates are sceptical of 'rational' arguments from experts and professionals about environmental impacts. They also take issue with those who argue that the economic trade-off for unhealthy conditions is satisfactory (see Box 1.2, Chapter 1). These experts have often been co-opted by those in power to 'either deny, question, or diminish what were known or strongly felt to be serious health effects deriving from unequal exposure' to environmental hazards (Harvey 1996: 386). Key issues for environmental justice are how discrimination is practiced, and against whom it is practiced.

Box 3.1   Direct and indirect discrimination

According to Stretesky and Hogan (1998) environmental justice researchers try to do at least two things: first, analysis of the placement of active waste facilities in minority and poor areas; and secondly, analysis of the social and political processes that shape racial, ethnic and economic demographic patterns around existing hazardous waste sites.

Direct discrimination relates to the 'prejudice leads to discrimination' model, in which there is express intent to deny or harm another individual or group based on some characteristics that the targeted individual or group possesses (e.g. put the hazard where 'certain' people do not find it so offensive).

Indirect discrimination relates to practices that result in negative and differential impact on minorities even though the policies or regulations guiding those actions were established, and carried out with no intent to harm (e.g. economic and social forces may serve to constrain the choices of minorities and the poor when compared to the choices available to Whites and the affluent – that is, what school to attend, where to live, what kind of work is available, etc.).

Researchers assess broad patterns of urban settlement in order to establish whether or not there are social inequalities related to the siting of waste facilities. They also evaluate the social reasons why this may be the case, incorporating into the analysis consideration of both direct and indirect discrimination. Risk is never socially neutral. Environmental justice explores why and how this is the case.

Consciousness of risk

The subjective disposition and consciousness of people is crucial to perceptions of threat, risk and immanent danger. The specific groups who experience environmental problems may not always describe or see the issues in strictly environmental terms.

In our communities, the smell coming from sewage plants was never perceived as an environmental issue but as a survival issue ... In workplaces, when workers are being poisoned or contaminated ... we do not refer to them as environmental issues but as labour issues. Again, the same thing for farmworkers and the issue of pesticides. In the 60s and 70s, there was organising around the lead-based paints used in housing projects. When the paint curled up and chipped off, children in the projects were eating it and getting sick. When we dealt with this issue, we perceived it as an issue of tenant's rights (Moore 1990: 16).

The unequal distribution of exposure to environmental risks, whether it is in relation to the location of toxic waste sites or proximity to clean drinking water, may not always be conceived as an 'environmental' issue, nor indeed as an environmental 'problem'. For instance, Harvey (1996) points out that the intersection of poverty, racism and desperation may occasionally lead to situations where, for the sake of jobs and economic development, community leaders actively solicit the relocation of hazardous industries or waste sites to their neighbourhoods.

Consciousness of risk can also be studied from the point of view of differential risk within at-risk populations. In others words, a particular suburb or city may be placed in circumstances that heighten risks to well-being and health for everyone (e.g. dumping of toxic waste in Abidjan, Ivory Coast; the spraying of chemical pesticides in New York City). However, particularly where heightened risk is deemed to be 'acceptable' in terms of cost-benefit analysis, as in the use of pesticides to prevent the spread of disease borne by mosquitoes, there are 'hidden' costs that may not be factored in. For instance, children and those with chemical sensitivities will suffer disproportionately if chemicals are sprayed, since they are more vulnerable than others to ill effects arising from the treatment. In such circumstances, the crucial questions are not only 'how many will be harmed' but also 'who will be harmed'? (Scott 2005a: 56). To appreciate this, we need to be conscious of differences within affected populations.

On the other hand, it may well be that it is local residents, local workers and laypeople generally who are more conscious of environmental risk than the scientist or the politician. Some indication of this is provided in a study of interaction between scientists and English sheep farmers in the wake of the 1986 Chernobyl nuclear accident in the Ukraine (Wynne 1996). The study highlighted the accurate, detailed and contextual knowledge of the farmers, even though the scientists considered this layperson knowledge to be lacking in precision. Those who are closer to the 'coal face' and who have lived and worked in the same area for years, are frequently those who notice the small changes that are the harbingers of things to come.

Consciousness of risk is also influenced by the visibility of the potential harm. For example, Beck (1992) observes that many risks in contemporary society are largely invisible to human senses. Radioactivity, for example, cannot be smelt, heard, seen, touched or tasted. Often we do not really know what is in our drinking water. Nevertheless, over time many people have come to appreciate the risks associated with radioactivity, and indeed nuclear energy generally, as well as to be suspicious over everyday consumables such as water (hence, the huge and growing market in bottled water). This reflexivity on risk has been made possible by mediated sources of knowledge, whereby people draw upon multiple sources in order to assess potential threats (e.g. TV programmes, government statements, campaigns by environmental groups). They also draw upon their own experiences, as indicated above (see also Macnaghten and Urry 1998). There are more ways in which to 'know' than simply through the direct senses per se.

Case study 3.2   Chemicals in water

The US Centre for Disease Control and Prevention revealed that in 1993 more than a million people in the US became ill and 900 died from drinking contaminated water (Archer 1998). Yet, in 2001, US President George W. Bush cancelled a health regulation that would have reduced allowable levels of arsenic in US drinking water from 50 parts per billion (ppb) to 10 ppb. In 1993, the World Health Organisation set 10 ppb as the recommended limit for arsenic in drinking water. The European Union adopted 10 ppb as a mandatory standard for arsenic in drinking water in 1998. The (US) Environmental Protection Agency estimated that cutting allowable arsenic from 50 to 10 ppb would prevent 1000 bladder cancers and 2000 to 5000 lung cancers during a human lifetime (Massey 2001). Moreover, the Environmental Protection Agency reports that trace amounts of prescription and non-prescription medications are finding their way into streams and drinking water. The agency cites a US Geological Survey study that sampled 139 streams in 30 states and found 80 per cent of them contaminated with trace amounts of chemicals commonly found in prescription drugs (Marigza 2007).

Exposure of risk is an integral part of raising consciousness about risk. In recent years this has occurred in ways that have seen the globalisation of risk (Macnaghten and Urry 1998) through the actions of environmental activist organisations such as Greenpeace and the Wilderness Society of Australia. What is also peculiar to, and interesting about, these processes of exposure is that very often they involve risk-taking on the part of the protestors. Battling whalers at sea or climbing high up in the tree tops to stop logging are dangerous, and exhilarating, activities. 'Risk' in this context could well refer to the conditions that give rise to an adrenaline buzz. Such activities, regardless of political intention or media importance, are simultaneously sensuous, transgressive and risky. Thus, the risks taken to expose environmental harms are themselves part of the overall risk equation.

Risk and time/space considerations

Environmental harm such as dioxins in water is temporal and spatial in nature. That is, the harm itself actually moves through time and over space. In doing so, it covers wide areas and has long lasting effects. The transformation of environments, and the interplay of water and land, provides interesting challenges to interpretation and analysis of environmental risk. For a start, it is essential to conceive of risk in dynamic rather than fixed terms. Environmental harm may originate in specific locations, but due to natural processes of water movement and flow, they may spread to other parts of a city, region, country or continent. A specific problem thus contains the seeds of the universal dilemma. Moreover, toxins accumulate over time. In other words, there is a cumulative impact on waterways and aquatic life, and small amounts of poison may eventually lead to great concentrations of toxicity in fish and other living creatures of the water.

The social construction of risk is also important to study in respect to spatial and temporal dimensions. For example, in the case of the banning of commercial fishing in Sydney Harbour due to dioxins in the water (see Chapter 4), the boundary of the ban was fixed at the Sydney Harbour Bridge. That is, waters flowing into the estuary up until the Bridge were deemed to be polluted and too toxic for the purposes of fishing; those waters after the Bridge were given the tacit nod of approval. These limits to harm seem to bear no relation whatsoever to actual ecological processes. They do, however, appear to protect the greater Sydney Harbour area from the stigma of toxicity. Harm, and risk, is thus constructed via the interrelationship of location, reputation and perception, as well as on the basis of scientific research.

The local effects of the siting and concentration of toxic waste can be interpreted through the prism of environmental justice, with its concern with social inequality and the residualisation of certain population groups vis-à-vis local amenities. But there are also generalised effects of toxic waste that occur due to cumulative (over time) and additive (more than one originating site) processes of concentration, that in turn are dispersed through the main waterways of large cities. The victims of such processes are thus universalised as the harms expand in their scope and breadth.

The transference of risk manifests itself in other ways as well. For example, we can refer to the monetarisation of risk – structural inequalities exploited by risk producers (e.g. pressures placed on communities to accept toxic landfills on their land in return for financial compensation). At issue here is what to do about LULUs (Locally Unwanted Land Uses), and how the poor and disadvantaged are especially vulnerable to waste transfers relating to these. The traffic in risk also occurs at the global level where developing countries play the same role as the poorer communities within the developed nations (e.g. 'business-friendly' countries that accept hazardous industries and toxic wastes). At issue here is how to respond to NIMBY (Not In My Backyard) opposition within developed countries (Julian 2004).

In regards to temporal questions, the concern is not only how risks and harms can accumulate over time. Risk and harm assessment also has to deal with the problem of scale. For example, the appropriate timescale for even understanding resource and population stability is much longer than we are used to, especially if we think of the usual three to seven-year political cycle. If risk analysis is applicable not only to humans but to the nonhuman animal and the biosphere, then how should we calculate the nature of potential threats? Specifically, the matter of timing and timescale become important considerations. This is perhaps most graphically conveyed in relation to extinction and the urgency for remedial action before entire species disappear forever.

Military risk

Environmental destruction has long been recognised as a consequence of war. The environment has been described as both a casualty and a method of warfare: 'Scorched earths in Norway, defoliated jungles in Vietnam, ignited oil fields in Kuwait, emptied marshes in southern Iraq – the environment is often both a victim and a tool of armed conflict' (Weinstein 2005: 698). Yet, for all the various types of environmental destruction associated with war, no State and no individual has ever been held accountable for this kind of harm. This is for a wide variety of legal, political and economic reasons (Weinstein 2005; White 2008b). Nevertheless, the harms associated with military activity continue to demand some type of response. We can illustrate this by reference to the use of depleted uranium (DU) in weapons and armour.

In the context of great uncertainty regarding existing and potential harm associated with DU, one possible starting point is to make reference to and utilise the precautionary principle (see below). To invoke the precautionary principle is to involve assessment of risk. In the case of DU, the issue is whether or not it is harmful (and to whom and what), and what are the potential future risks. Yet, the issue of risk is highly contentious in regards to DU, for there is sustained *denial of risk* in many official government circles (see White 2008b).

There are also objections to the notion of a *military* precautionary principle, especially in relation to DU. Specifically, it has been argued that there is insufficient scientific evidence to accept whether the threat of harm exists; that alternative armaments to DU weapons could bear worse environmental and health harms to humans; that remediation carries with it its own risks (to removal workers, in regards to the impact of current clean-up methods and in relation to overall costs); and that such prohibitions negatively affect wealthy States with the resources to devote to technological arms change relative to States lacking military resources (Wexler 2006). These are important issues, since they bring to our attention the varying ways in which 'risk' is constructed within a specifically military (and political) context. That is, when proposing courses of action to take, it is crucial to consider the choices made by military planners for this or that sort of weaponry (and the tactical and strategic advantages of each type of ordnance), and the social and environmental impacts that flow from these choices.

While risk analysis ought to be sensitive to the ways in which political leaders and military planners make decisions over weapons, it should not allow such decisions to be enfolded within a black box of 'national security' or 'military technical expertise'. Transparency is crucial to assessment of risk, whether this be in relation to military ventures or environmental issues (White 2008b).

From risk to precaution

Of central importance to contemporary thinking about and responding to risk has been the precautionary principle. This refers to the idea that official action be taken to protect people and environments in cases where there is scientific uncertainty as to the nature of the potential damage or the likelihood of risk. Two definitions of the precautionary principle are frequently mentioned in the literature dealing with it. The first is from a United Nations Conference on Environment and Development held in 1992 in Brazil. The second is from a conference dealing specifically with the precautionary principle held in 1998 (see National Toxics Network Inc., no date).

1992 Rio Declaration
In order to protect the environment, the precautionary approach shall be widely applied by States according to their capabilities. Where there are threats of serious or irreversible damage, lack of full scientific certainty shall not be used as a reason for postponing cost-effective measures to prevent environmental degradation.

1998 Wingspread Conference on the Precautionary Principle
When an activity raises threats of harm to human health or the environment, precautionary measures should be taken even if some cause and effect relationships are not fully established scientifically. In this context the proponent of an activity, rather than the public, should bear the burden of proof. The process of applying the precautionary principle must be open, informed and democratic and must include potentially affected parties. It must also involve an examination of the full range of alternatives, including no action.

The precautionary principle has been generally integrated into the regulatory and legal frameworks of the European Union, but has been less popular in the US. Internationally, the concept is being contested and has 'become a chess piece in the struggles over genetically modified foods, for example' (Leiss and Hrudey 2005: 9).

In order to understand the substance and significance of the precautionary principle we can initially discuss the distinctions between 'burden of proof' and 'standards of proof'. The burden of proof is directed at the question, who has to make the case for safety? (i.e. the originator of the potential harm, or someone else such as a non-government organisation). The standard of proof asks the question, are we confident that the case for safety has been made adequately? (i.e. the level of confidence we have in the data available in regards to a particular phenomenon).

Typically, it has been the case that the law has favoured the status quo in determination of who is to bear the burden of proof in cases involving predictions of risk. However, with the spreading interest in and application of the 'precautionary principle' this is changing. Thus, for many commentators today the dominant perspective is that 'The precautionary principle seeks to shift the burden of proof onto those who create the hazard, benefit from the hazard, or advocate for the hazard' (Scott 2005b: 66). This is justified on a range of grounds: putting the onus on those who introduce new risks into the environment; putting the burden of proof on those who have the economic incentive and information; and for equity considerations, so that the risks and costs are internalised by those wishing to engage in particular kinds of activities.

In the case of pesticide regulation, the onus has tended to already be on the producer to show evidence of acceptable risk. Here the change process is the inverse of what has just been presented as, historically, the traditional pattern of burden.

> Mistakes still happen, and, when they do, it is the legal system that causes a switch to occur, not only in the *burden* of proof but in the *type* of proof required. First, when alleging new evidence showing unacceptable risk against a registered product, the burden of proof falls upon the complainant – a worker or farmer or public-interest group. Second, the product registration, which has vested a property right, cannot be taken away again without 'sufficient' proof that the original decision was mistaken – according to legal (not scientific) conceptions of proof (Leiss and Hrudey 2005: 10, emphasis in the original).

Thus, applications of the precautionary principle demand different burdens of proof and different criteria of proof depending upon particular circumstances and social situations.

Given that disputes over the application of the precautionary principle are disputes over claims, the issue of proof looms large. This raises the issue of 'thresholds' and how the law does or ought to respond to matters pertaining to standards of proof. In other words, at what point do we make a decision, based on available evidence, and how should we interpret what is sufficient evidence in order to make a determination. Here it is argued that 'threshold' approaches utilised in legal proceedings tend to be restrictive in their interpretation of the precautionary principle (Peel 2005). That is, conservative 'scientific' boundaries are set in place by which to measure the application of precaution. If there is insufficient proof as dictated by certain measures of scientific validity, then exercise of the principle is not warranted.

In contrast to this approach, is one that stresses the advantages of going behind simple threshold considerations to emphasise process (Peel 2005; see also Scott 2005b). A process approach to the precautionary principle is seen to allow much greater flexibility and accountability. From this viewpoint, 'the success or failure of efforts to implement the principle will depend upon the manner and extent to which scientific uncertainty is considered in the decision-making process, not the measures that are ultimately adopted' (Peel 2005: 220). There is no 'one size fits all' expression of precaution that will fit every case. In a similar vein, making judgements based solely on what science tells us in the here and now (and whether this is sufficient to demonstrate a likelihood of harm), reduces the scope of decision-makers to 'anticipate harms and to weigh their importance in the decision-making process before serious or irreversible environmental damage becomes evident' (Peel 2005: 221). A process approach demands critical examination of science and uncertainty, transparency in disclosure of the factors influencing decision-making, and incorporation of a range of views in decision-making.

The interplay between 'threshold' and 'process' considerations in application of the precautionary principle is significant from the point of view of social action taken on environmental issues. Where the principle has been taken seriously and integrated into multilateral negotiations between countries, it has impacted upon how State and non-government bodies have responded to perceived risks and threats.

The precautionary principle has functioned therefore to redistribute the burden of scientific uncertainty in ways that foster greater cooperation and policy interdependence among international actors (Maguire and Ellis 2005). This is because it has served to lower the threshold of evidence of threats to human health or the environment required to trigger deliberations about taking action. The lower threshold (i.e. in legal terms, the standard of proof), combined with extensive professional and community concern about process elements (e.g. such as participation and transparency), has meant that application of the precautionary principle has opened up greater space for policy making to be carried out at the international level, especially given the underlying ecological interdependence of environmental issues (see Maguire and Ellis 2005).

Acknowledgement of the precautionary principle has inevitably been accompanied by development of precautionary measures. These are designed to forestall potential harms arising from human actions. Among the precautionary measures are legal measures, some of which are direct and some indirect.

Direct precautionary measures
Direct precautionary legal measures either require behaviours that adhere to the principle, or prohibit those that do not adhere, or both.

Enabling legislation – e.g. guiding principle of regulatory bodies.

Direct prohibition – e.g. specific activities or types of activities.

Reverse listing – e.g. reverse list contains only those substances believed to be safe.

Regulatory standards – e.g. legal requirement to adhere to particular standards.

Indirect precautionary measures
Indirect precautionary legal measures are those that create an environment of incentives and disincentives which will tend to generate behavioural adherence to the precautionary principle.

Procedural requirements – e.g. requirements to follow precautionary procedures such as submitting detailed environmental impact statements in development projects.

Policy measures – e.g. provide a basis for increasing 'cradle to grave' responsibilities for manufacturers generating hazardous wastes.

Public involvement – e.g. laws to assist in the determination of appropriate precautionary measures by written submission or by means of a representative panel.

Liability – e.g. strict liability regime (allows defence of an honest or reasonable mistake: this approach requires only proof that an act took place, but not that there was an intention to carry it out); e.g. absolute liability regime (prosecution need only prove that the act itself occurred, regardless of due diligence).

Figure 3.1 Direct and indirect precautionary legal measures
Source: Deville and Harding 1997: 71–73.

The terms of the precautionary principle are likely to be contested across several dimensions when the principle is applied in practice. This is because each part of the principle involves interpretation of some kind. Thus:

> It is clear that beyond the question of *threshold of scientific evidence* of potential harm, the application of the precautionary principle will be influenced by a number of other factors. These include perceptions of what constitutes a *threat* to the environment, what we regard as *serious* and *irreversible* and what type and level of precautionary *measures* are appropriate (Harding and Fisher 1999: 15, emphasis in original).

Disputes over the terms of the precautionary principle are made even more complicated in cases where a human protagonist (i.e. development company or government department) is not the originator of the decision-making dilemma. Indeed, there are persistent problems associated with *risk tradeoffs*.

Consider, for example, the case of an outbreak of West Nile Virus (WNV) in Toronto, Canada. The uncertainty in this case was complicated by the fact that the precautionary principle seemed to point two ways: 'taking precaution with respect to public health would lead to widespread aerial spraying campaign using chemical pesticides; taking precaution with respect to the environment would preclude that action' (Scott 2005a: 28). The conflict here is not between human protagonists as is often the case when it comes to proposed pulp mills, nuclear facilities and residential developments. Rather, the issue reflected a tension between risks to health and risks to environment stemming from the advent of a mosquito-borne virus (WNV). The concrete application of the precautionary principle had to therefore involve the weighing up of different kinds of knowledge, different risks, and ultimately different courses of action.

From the point of view of process, study revealed that a number of key factors were present that led to a reasonable and satisfactory solution to the risk trade-off dilemma. These are presented in Figure 3.2.

The issue: West Nile Virus

The dilemma: taking precaution with respect to public health would lead to a widespread aerial spraying campaign using chemical

---

pesticides; taking precaution with respect to the environment would preclude that action.

The response: a flexible philosophy of action

Document the uncertainties – i.e. awareness of indeterminacy, chaotic unpredictability.

Examine a wide range of alternative course of action – i.e. go beyond 'either/or' to consider wider range of options.

Engage in a broad public deliberation – i.e. allow a plurality of voices and expertise.

Consider risks in the context of benefits – i.e. consideration of relative benefits of risky action, trade-offs.

Institute continuous monitoring and evaluation systems – i.e. evaluate and re-evaluate the options in light of different perspectives and new evidence.

Figure 3.2 Weighing up the risks
Source: drawn from Scott 2005a.

Importantly, analysis of the event and of responses to the precautionary dilemma demonstrated that as more factors were allowed to come into consideration, the more the dilemma, as such, dissolved. This was because 'when the various elements of precaution were elaborated on and parsed out, the precautionary principle was revealed *not* to demand a single action, to point one way or two ways or all ways, but to set out a useful framework for considering the complexity of risks embedded in an intricate social and ecological matrix' (Scott 2005a: 60, emphasis in the original). This is exemplified in the comment of Dr Sheela Basrur, Toronto's Medical Officer of Health that:

> ... there is growing evidence that human health can be put at risk from pesticide use. And when risks to human health are unnecessary or uncertain, the wisest course of action is to substitute safer alternatives and methods, rather than incurring risks that may prove unacceptable in the long run (quoted in Scott 2005a: 62).

The subsequent plan that was adopted to deal with the threats posed by WNV was guided by this philosophy – to the benefit of all concerned (they did not spray, but a broad educational and preventive campaign was enacted).

Risk assessment and risk management

Putting the precautionary principle into practice is not solely about enabling or stopping things from happening. It also includes coming up with a range of measures that can be used to predict impacts as well as diminish possible negative harms arising from human activity. At the ground level of practitioner activity, this is usually conceived in terms of performing various kinds of environmental impact assessment (EIA).

The broad definition of environmental impact assessment is inclusive of many different types of evaluation. For example, Harvey (1998: 2) favours the following definition:

> Environmental impact assessment is a process of identifying and predicting the potential environmental impacts (including bio-geophysical, socio-economic and cultural) of proposed actions, policies, programmes and projects, and communicating this information to decision makers before they make their decisions on the proposed actions.

Aligned with the precautionary principle, the purpose of EIA is to reduce the impact that development is having on the environment. In doing so, many different strands to assessment have developed, as indicated in Figure 3.3. Moreover, the development of suitable 'sustainability assessment criteria' has increasingly referred to models of good practice that incorporate key facets of human and ecological well-being. The interdependency of the social and the ecological are thus being reflected in efforts to sustain overall socio-ecological systems (see for example, Gibson 2006).

Environmental Impact Assessment (EIA) is generally focused on projects.

Strategic Environmental Assessment (SEA) examines policies, programmes and plans, rather than focusing on the project at issue.

Social Impact Assessment (SIA) looks at the social impact of activities.

Intergenerational Impact Assessment (IIA) examines the environmental impacts on future generations.

Cumulative Impact Assessment (CIA) is the assessment of the accumulated impacts of an activity and previous activities.

Risk Assessment (RA) and Environmental Health Assessment (EHA) can separately or together be included in an Environmental Impact Statement (EIS).

Assessment can also take the form of strategic assessment of government departments and companies, rather than simply environmental effects (on the natural world and on communities).

Figure 3.3 Key terms – environmental impact

The rationale, and processes, of risk categorisation with regard to environmental harm are very different than those applied in relation to street crime (where the focus is on individuals and groups). The targets of risk assessment and management in the case of 'environmental harm' tend to be activities and events. The matrix of risk construction relating to activity in this sphere tends to be centred on the facilitation of production-in-general in ways which maximise profit opportunities for those who head up large business enterprises.

Social control in this instance is meant to ensure a balance between economic needs and environmental sustainability. 'Nature' is generally seen as a resource to be managed for human purposes. Regulation is designed to forestall any economically undesirable destruction of this valuable resource, and to prevent or minimise the harm to human beings arising from specific activities (see Harvey 1996). The focus is on rectifying the damage from past events (e.g. factory pollution) or minimising future harms (e.g. disposal of radioactive waste). At the centre of this process is scientific knowledge and expertise. The main ideological rationale is sustainable development.

Risk assessment

The anticipatory role of environmental risk assessment is complicated from the start by the ingrained difficulties of prediction in relation to the environment. Ecological systems are by their very nature complex. Furthermore, given the focus on 'nature', any criteria of prediction will be based upon speculative, indefinite criteria. Importantly, such assessments rarely, if ever, take into account the past record of companies and individuals that wish to undertake activity affecting particular environments.

Increasingly, environmental assessment has become more reliant upon administrative procedures which spell out in detail the methods and specific criteria allowed in such reviews (Harvey 1998; Marsden 1998). In a similar vein, these assessments are reliant upon specific types of 'research' and particular authorised forms of 'expertise' in undertaking such work. While sometimes presented as a scientific process, environmental assessment is frequently riven by debate over the legitimacy of certain data, and people, associated with the process. Furthermore, in many cases, impact and risk assessment is itself able to be effectively bypassed by the imposition of special legislation or ministerial fiat. As a process, therefore, it can be seen to be simultaneously de-politicised (via exclusion of non-scientific evidence and alternative values-based criteria) and political (through the central role of government administrators and politicians in determining validity or applicability).

An important aspect of environmental assessment, as a procedure, is that it usually involves the compartmentalisation of risk (notwithstanding practitioner efforts to widen the scope of assessment – see Gibson 2006). That is, it is limited, by and large, to specific types of activities and projects. It is not concerned with the 'whole picture', in the sense of wider ecological complexities and connections. This is partly due to the fact that it tends to be framed within the terms of 'sustainable development', an ideological stance which precludes serious discussion and action around alternative value positions which often put into question the very basis of present interactions with, and exploitations of, the environment (Pepper 1993).

Political argument over the environment has, however, led to the generation of a new range of legal concepts (Robinson 1995). These include, for example, cases where certain types of environmental action have been stopped on the basis of preservation of intergenerational equity (e.g. leaving something for our children), through to the development of varying interpretations and applications of the precautionary principle (e.g. basing decisions on proof of 'safety' and proof of 'unsafety'). The precise outcome of any environmental assessment process is contingent upon a range of factors: the mobilisation of expertise; popular interest and activism; the view of judges and magistrates regarding the application of, and conflicts between, diverse legal concepts; the role of bureaucratic structures in circulating information and arranging suitable timeframes and forums for decision-making; and so on. In other words, the nature of environmental assessment is intrinsically ideological and political (Hannigan 1995; Low and Gleeson 1998). It is a class-bound process, and as such reflects the balance of class forces at any one time, in relation to specific areas and events.

What compounds, and in some cases confounds, the assessment of environmental risk is the complexity surrounding the task. Who is going to pay for the scientific research and expert testimony? How are we to judge between environmental/ecological principles and baseline economic criteria? Should risk assessment incorporate concerns about the financial risks taken by companies who wish to invest in particular types of productive activity? The increasingly complex nature of risk assessment, coupled with proposals to increase this complexity (due to the overlapping assessments which, ideally, should be carried out – social, economic, environmental, legal) ensure that issues of power and control will remain central to the process.

For example, the privatisation of risk assessment (and environmental monitoring and testing) is being sought by those governments concerned to limit internal State expenditure on such work. At the same time, the phenomenon of 'commercial confidentiality' is such that the public often does not know what has been agreed to by companies which have 'passed' the environmental assessment checklist. Finally, the politics and complications surrounding environmental assessment gives even greater impetus for the streamlining of such procedures, thereby restricting further the input and scrutiny of 'outside' interests.

Then there is the issue of 'uncertainty' and how this is approached in environmental assessment. Action or inaction on environmental threats has been legitimated one way or the other by claims of scientific uncertainty. The uncertainty has been due to both lack of data, and a more general problem of indeterminacy. The latter refers to processes and systems that cannot readily be captured by the methods of science as such. This is illustrated in the following passage:

> When nutrients accumulate in shallow waters, or when toxic chemicals bioaccumulate in tissues, systems approach a phase-change threshold where conditions can suddenly and dramatically change. This chaotic, inherent unpredictability in natural processes, combined with the conditional and erratic influences of social behaviour, creates contingency in all scientific assessment (Scott 2005b: 60).

Moreover, research on scientific decision-making makes it clear that there are inherent political choices being made in risk assessment (see Scott 2005b). The scientific method is complemented by social decisions that cannot be reduced to technical questions. The scientific and the social are thus permeable parts of a system of information and knowledge about the world around us.

Risk management

In Chapter 1, it was pointed out that environmental victimisation can be defined as specific forms of harm which are caused by acts (e.g. dumping of toxic waste) or omissions (e.g. failure to provide safe drinking water) leading to the presence or absence of environmental agents (e.g. poisons, nutrients) which are associated with human injury (see Williams 1996). The management of these forms of victimisation is generally retrospective (after the fact), and involves a variety of legal and social responses.

The response of the State to these kinds of harm are guided by a concern with environmental protection, which is generally framed in terms of ensuring future resource exploitation, and dealing with specific instances of victimisation that have been socially defined as a problem. Risk management in this case is directed at preventing or minimising certain destructive or injurious practices into the future, based upon analysis and responses to harms identified in the present. The ways in which the State reacts to such harms is based upon classifications of harm and wrongdoing as defined in legislation, including criminal law. The target of such legislation is specific acts and events, usually relating to pollution (see Gunningham *et al.* 1995; Heine *et al.* 1997).

The methods of risk management in this instance tend not to rely upon coercion per se. Indeed, strong arguments have been put forward against the use of criminal law, in particular, in dealing with specific incidents and corporate practices. This is because of the limits inherent in the use of criminal sanctions against the more powerful groups in society (see Haines 1997). For example, corporations have considerable financial and legal resources to contest prosecution, making such prosecutions enormously expensive to run. Technical difficulties of prosecution (such as rules of evidence, multiple offenders, etc.), and the financial and human resource constraints of State legal machinery (e.g. regulatory bodies such as the police, environmental protection agencies and corporate watchdogs), preclude the use of criminal prosecution except in the most extreme or 'winnable' cases. There is, therefore, considerable discretion in prosecution and sentencing decisions (see Chapter 7).

One of the key issues of environmental 'risk management' in relation to existing harmful practices is the matter of benchmark information. That is, what criteria are to be used to evaluate whether or not environmental harm has occurred, whether or not a particular body is responsible for this harm, and whether or not this can be remedied using existing technologies or whether it is something we have to 'live with' given certain economic imperatives? This raises the issues of role of 'expert opinion', and public advocacy, in assessing the nature and dynamics of environmental harm and victimisation. It also raises issues of class interests and environmental philosophy (i.e. the values and analyses that should drive the assessment process), and the place of third party public interest groups, in determination of what is harmful and what ought to be done about it. The import of these matters will be more fully explored below.

The ways in which risk is construed and responded to with respect to environmental harm is socially patterned in ways which reflect and protect the interests of business in general. The basic assumption underlying regulation is that the point is to reduce the impact that development is having on specific environments (e.g. via Environmental Impact Assessment procedures), rather than to challenge the nature of development itself (i.e. issues of material class interests).

There are strong pressures to render the issue of 'risk' in the field of environmental law and regulation to a matter of specialist expertise and legal-technical knowledge, although this varies from jurisdiction to jurisdiction (Hannigan 1995). The emphasis is not on the generic causes of environmental harm (since this immediately raises the issue of control and ownership over the means of production/destruction), but on how to regulate specific instances of actual or potential harm. Insofar as this is the case, it assumes that such issues can only be dealt with within the framework of 'sustainable development', and as such, that control ought to be exercised on a rational, scientific basis which calculates cost-benefit in economic, rather than ecological, terms. There are countervailing approaches to this as well, approaches that emphasise the importance of community participation and citizen deliberation. These will be considered in the next section.

Given this, the question of resource allocation to environmental assessment and management, and issues pertaining to public accountability, tend to be skewed in the direction of less intervention and less transparent processes of regulation. The latter are thus conceived as impediments to the exploitation of the environment, although it is conceded that specific instances of harmful activity do warrant curtailment, since they can undermine public confidence as well as limit the availability of resources (for economic purposes) into the future.

Deliberative democracy and social participation

One of the lessons of the Toronto study of the West Nile Virus is that the contested nature of applying the precautionary principle, in turn, demands that there is a high degree of scientific and community participation surrounding its key elements. The social context within which precautionary principle is applied is thus crucial to understanding how and why environmentally-related risks are socially distributed, in local areas through to around the globe. That is, the precautionary principle is more likely to be applied in some circumstances than others, and action taken on the basis of its application in some situations more than others.

Positive circumstances for the application of the precautionary principle have been identified as including:

- Where new technologies are proposed in well regulated regimes and where public opinion is instinctively or knowledgeably risk averse;
- Where the principles of regulation allow for judgement as to what is socially tolerable;
- Where there is a national culture of care for the less fortunate and the defenceless; and
- Where there is openness and accountability in policy formulation and decision-making.

(O'Riordan and Cameron 1994)

Not every nation-state or society or region in the world is going to allow for these favourable circumstances. This is especially so where States are in transition – experiencing coups, civil war and rebellion, or recovering from colonialism or genocide. Compounding the ability of particular political formations to engage in meaningful precautionary practices are lack of infrastructure and technical know-how, inexperience in liberal and participatory forms of democracy, and immediate survival priorities (e.g. dealing with the aftermath of a tsunami) that preclude action taken now in relation to future risks and threats. This means that some places will be more amenable to the application of the precautionary principle than others.

A vital ingredient in 'good practice' precautionary work is active citizen participation. However, the logic of risk, as a technical scientific exercise, and a narrowly conceived threshold approach to legal decision-making, can diminish the inclusion of popular concerns. In either case, there is a tendency to 'leave it to the experts' whether this is scientific or legal. This can have negative consequences, as Scott (2005b: 69) observes:

> The problem with seeking only truth in science, as I have suggested, is that science does not deliver an objective truth. It delivers truth with a healthy dose of justice mixed in. The cost of blindly pretending that the determination of risk is a 'truth-seeking' technocratic exercise is that the public cedes the power to influence critical political and value choices. They relinquish the power to seek justice in risk management.

Yet, there is a demonstrated need to deliberate extensively on environmental issues, due to their complexity and due to the various conflicts that arise in any given situation. The dialogue must be continuous and extensive. For this deliberation to happen, there is a need to expand democratic space, and to broaden the base of expertise and understanding of environments and environmental issues, often against those who wish to restrict discursive spaces.

A starting point for deliberation, from the point of view of ecological citizenship, is the concept that human laws and human rights have to be tempered by the acknowledgement that human interests are intimately bound up with the well-being of the planet as a whole. Human intervention, of any kind, needs to be considered in the light of this. Hence, the importance of the precautionary principle in gauging potential and real impacts arising from human activity cannot be overstated. Moreover, the concern in many cases is not with the protection of specific individuals, or consideration of particular human rights. Rather, when we plan on the basis of intergenerational equity or biosphere integrity we do so with the collectivity in mind, not the individual per se.

Taking precautions is not only about risk assessment. It is about marshalling requisite expertise in order to best understand the specific problem at hand. Science can and must be a major tool in deliberations over human interventions and human impacts. But this is only one sort of knowledge. Expertise is also very much developed from the ground up, not simply on the basis of experiment and scientific method. Farmers on the land, and fishers of the sea, for example, have generations of expertise built up over time and under varying environmental conditions. Indigenous peoples frequently have knowledge and understandings of their environments that go back to time immemorial. The fact that some indigenous people have survived for thousands of years, and thrived, in extremely hostile environments (the frozen lands of the north, the deserts of the dry continents) is testimony to human practices that are connected, positively, to immediate environs (see Robyn 2002). A public participatory process of deliberation needs to incorporate all of these kinds of voices. It also needs to be able to challenge the 'wisdom' and 'truth' of each, without prejudice and without fear.

There is ample scope for community involvement at all stages of the risk assessment process. This is illustrated in Figure 3.4.

Issue identification: Where community involvement can provide information about the site including weather patterns, local environmental information, health concerns and potential value conflicts. Community input can be sought on what risks deserve priority attention and what information may be available in the general community.

Hazard identification: Where the community may provide information about previous studies and/or data gaps, local perceptions of hazards and the applicability of assumptions to that particular community.

Dose-response relationships: Providing information about community attitudes towards the range and type of technical data and selected tests, as well as the assumptions made in the interpretation of the data.

Exposure assessment: Providing information about the community's attitude to biological monitoring and health monitoring; local knowledge of the range and nature of exposures, relevant exposure settings; the community's attitudes to sampling design and environmental monitoring and to the uncertainties and assumptions in the exposure assessment phase.

Risk characterisation: Providing information on the community's concepts of risk and safety.

Evaluating actions taken: Community involvement will affect how environmental monitoring may be undertaken to ensure that the best decisions are made.

Risk management: Providing information of the communities' concepts of acceptable risk and safety.

Figure 3.4 Community risk assessment in relation to chemical hazards
Source: drawn from National Toxics Network Inc, no date (accessed July 2005).

The obvious problem, however, is that in some risk assessment processes it is the community itself which is seen as threatening to the interests of those in power. Too much democracy, it seems, can be a bad thing, particularly if it adversely affects big business interests and especially if these are, in turn, in close alignment with the interests of particular political parties.

Such was the case in 2007, for example, when the government of Tasmania short-circuited the normal development evaluation process. At the centre of this assessment process was the State's largest company and Australia's largest woodchip exporter, Gunns Limited. The proposal was for a large pulp mill to be built on the Tamar River in the north of the island state. Frustrated with the length of the process, claiming that it was too expensive, and faced with a significant number of negative submissions from a wide range of industry and community groups to the Resource Planning and Development Commission (RPDC), Gunns withdrew from the RPDC process. Nine days later, Tasmania's House of Assembly passed the Pulp Mill Assessment Bill 2007, which was subsequently passed in the Legislative Assembly with minor amendment. The net result was a shift from a reasonably transparent and accountable system to something akin to a closed shop where the final outcome was never in doubt. Most important, for present purposes, is that the new methods of assessment undermined any real opportunity for serious public deliberation of the project proposal. Gunns got its way on the assessment process. However, due to widespread public disagreement, the final fate of the mill is still, at the time of writing, up in the air.

The mobilisation of different kinds of expertise, and confrontations over different values, is an essential part of the deliberation. In 1990 the United Nations Commission on Human Rights adopted its first resolution on human rights and the environment, which affirmed the relationship between the preservation of the environment and the protection of human rights. By 1998 there had been developed an Environmental Rights Convention – the Convention on Access to Information, Public Participation and Decision Making and Access to Justice in Environmental Matters. What this convention expresses is that everyone should have access to information about the environment and that we collectively should have rights to participate in decisions about the environment (see Thornton and Tromans 1999). For this to happen there is a need for transparency and the 'right to know' what governments, community groups and corporations are doing in relation to the environment.

Analysis of recent instances of citizen participation in the area of environmental law appears to signal great potential for increased community engagement on these issues. From a positive affirming perspective, legal research has demonstrated that participation is important not only from the point of view of the legitimacy of environmental decision-making. It also can enhance problem-solving and this, too, ought to be emphasised (Steele 2001; see also Scott 2005a and 2005b). If sustainability is the goal, if precaution requires thinking about multiple courses of action, and if community involvement is to be of benefit, then it is clear that citizens ought to be engaged as deliberators and contributors in their own right.

When environmental harm is contested – conceptually and evidentially – and there are major specific social interests at play (governments, companies, workers, consumers, environmentalists, residents), then those with the power tend to shape public debate in ways that often diminish participation and deliberation. This diminishment and distortion may, for example, take the form of out-and-out propaganda wars. For instance, the forest debates in Tasmania are shaped by the fact that political power is so closely tied up with the industry, and that the media is basically looking for sensationalism (in those instances when it is not reliant upon industry advertising and thus already 'compliant' to industry perspectives). As a consequence, the debate is presented as highly polarised, and each side engages in what might be seen as a propaganda, rather than deliberative, process.

The logic of risk assessment itself may serve to undermine community engagement on environmental issues of importance. This is because the framing of such issues mainly or solely in terms of 'risk' implies that the key questions relate to ascertaining the acceptable level of risk and determining what controls can be imposed to keep the problem within defined risk limits. Field (1998: 76) argues that in relying on this kind of approach 'there is the danger that the debate will become mired in a highly technical discourse over the extent of risk and will lose sight of the equally profound issue of democratic control over the economic aspects of community life which is also presented by this (the environmental justice) movement'. In other words, to assume risk is to ignore who produces risk and whether or not the challenge ought be over the nature of production itself. The problem is not one of management and control, but of basic decisions pertaining to the means of life (and threats to this).

More hopefully, the increasing acceptance of the precautionary principle in scientific, legal and layperson circles may well enhance the prospects for increased community involvement in environmental matters.

> The promise of the precautionary principle, I believe, is in throwing open debate about risks and unleashing a spate of questions about what is at stake and for whom, and about what kind of place we want to live in and how much control we want in shaping it. Precaution invites this exploration because it fosters thoughtful, creative exchange between an activated public and a wider, more inclusive, scientific community (Scott 2005b: 70).

Such exchanges are to be welcomed if crimes against nature are to be nipped in the bud.

Conclusion: where to from here?

This chapter has explored issues revolving around risk as a social phenomenon and the implementation of the precautionary principle as one possible response to threats to environmental health and well-being.

Differences in social interests ensure that questions of inequality, abuse of power, community engagement and democratic governance will continue unabated. How, where and when precautionary measures are put into place depends upon particular social, economic, military and political circumstances. Systematic conceptualisation of basic principles, and case studies of actual practices are nevertheless essential to the promotion of processes and procedures that can provide for a modicum of good sense in planning for the future. So, too, critique can play its part in fostering a climate of openness and participatory deliberation.

Those at risk of environmental catastrophe or who already have experienced the failings of inadequate risk assessment are important players in these matters. More work could be undertaken on the nature and dynamics of citizen participation (and exclusion) vis-à-vis precautionary processes and forums. As part of this, one could track the nature of victim responses to environmental calamity. Williams (1996) describes a series of responses characteristic of environmental victims, ranging from passive to confrontational, collaborative to violent. How victim perspectives can be channelled into environmental assessment processes is an important area for further consideration.

Investigation has to continue to be directed at political and economic developments, especially in regard to appropriation of natural resources and specific market opportunities, and how these impact upon environmental protection and preservation. As mentioned earlier, the targets of risk assessment and management in the case of 'environmental harm' have tended to be activities and events. Greater focus needs to be placed on the companies and individuals who perpetrate the harm. In other words, it is time to conceive of 'risk' in terms of key players rather than just as threats to environments. Publicly exposing the track record of environmental vandals can and should be an integral part of a public accountability process.

Part II
Environmental Crime

Chapter 4

Dimensions of environmental crime

Systems of classification are essential to the process of identifying and responding to environmental harm. Crimes against nature can be conceptualised in abstract philosophical terms, but eventually it is important to ground analysis and action in relation to actual concrete events, incidents and trends. This involves defining environmental harm and exploring the various dimensions pertaining to it.

Introduction

The aim of this chapter is to outline the various ways in which environmental harm can be classified and analysed as a social and legal phenomenon. Environmental harm has a number of dimensions. It can be examined from the point of view of who or what the victim is, where it occurs, when and over what period of time it manifests, and which kinds of issues it encapsulates.

The chapter begins by outlining the kinds of work that has been undertaken by environmental criminologists. As will be seen, this includes a huge diversity of research and scholarship, across many domains of human activity. The chapter then embarks upon a mapping exercise, demonstrating the variety of ways in which environmental harm can be classified and analysed. This is followed by consideration of issues relating to the measurement of environmental harm, and the necessity to develop benchmark data to facilitate contemporary and trend analysis. The final section also discusses the politics of how we might know if a crime has or has not occurred, or if is likely to occur in the future.

Defining environmental harm

There are longstanding issues relating to how 'harm' (and indeed 'crime') is to be defined in criminological terms, and of what the responses to harm should consist. The usual divide is between those who adopt a strict legal-procedural approach to defining harm, and those who opt for a broader socio-legal approach. The former is basically dependent upon legal definitions that proscribe certain action in law (see Tappan 1947). The latter allows for investigation of phenomenon such as white-collar crime and denial of human rights through reference to conceptions of harm which are not limited to definitions solely generated by the State (see Sutherland 1949; Green and Ward 2000). The conundrum of definition is made worse in the specific area of environmental harm in that many of the most serious forms of such harm in fact constitute 'normal social practice' and are quite legal even if environmentally disastrous.

The politics of definition are further complicated by the politics of 'denial' – in which particular concrete manifestations of social injury and environmental damage are obfuscated, ignored or redefined in ways which represent them as being of little relevance to either academic criminological study or State criminal justice intervention. In a manner analogous to the denial of human rights violations (see Cohen 1993, 2001), environmental issues call forth a range of techniques of neutralisation on the part of nation-states and corporations that, ultimately, legitimatise and justify certain types of environmentally unfriendly activities. For example, this takes the form of 'greenwashing' media campaigns that misconstrue the nature of corporate business practices in regards to the environment (Beder 1997). It involves attacking and de-legitimating the arguments of critics of particular kinds of biotechnological development (see for example, Hager and Burton 1999; Hannigan 1995; Hindmarsh 1996). For governments, denial of harm is usually associated with economic objectives and the appeal to forms of 'sustainable development' that fundamentally involve further environmental degradation (for example, see Hessing 2002; White 2002).

The development of environmental criminology as a field of sustained research and scholarship will by its very nature incorporate many different perspectives and strategic emphases. After all, it deals with concerns across a wide range of environments (e.g. land, air, water) and issues (e.g. fishing, pollution, toxic waste). It involves conceptual analysis as well as practical intervention on many fronts, and includes multidisciplinary strategic assessment (e.g. economic, legal, social and ecological evaluations). It involves the undertaking of organisational analysis, as well as investigation of 'best practice' methods of monitoring, assessment, enforcement and education regarding environmental protection and regulation. Analysis needs to be conscious of local, regional, national and global domains and how activities in each of these overlap. It likewise requires cognisance of the direct and indirect, and immediate and long-term, impacts and consequences of environmentally sensitive social practices.

There are, then, significant issues surrounding scale, activities and legalities as these pertain to environmental harm. To define what constitutes environmental harm implies a particular philosophical stance on the relationship between human beings and nature. What is 'wrong' or 'right' environmental practice very much depends upon the criteria used to conceptualise the values and interests represented in this relationship, as reflected for instance in anthropocentric, biocentric and ecocentric perspectives (see Chapter 1). Any attempt to address environmental issues from a criminological perspective must be conscious of the complexities and ambiguities of the subject matter. In recent years, defining the nature of the problem has tended to revolve around the concepts of 'crime', 'harm' and 'victimisation'.

As previously noted in Chapter 1, a strict legalist approach tends to focus on the central place of *criminal law* in the definition of criminality (Situ and Emmons 2000). However, other writers argue that, as with criminology in general, the concept of 'harm' ought to encapsulate those activities that may be legal and 'legitimate' but which nevertheless negatively impact on people and environments (Sutherland 1949; Schwendinger and Schwendinger 1975). Advocates for this position take a wide view of the mandate for green criminology.

In general, criminologists have often left the study of environmental harm, environmental laws and environmental regulations to researchers in other disciplines. This has allowed little room for critical examination of individuals or entities who/which kills, injures and assaults other life forms (human, animal or plant) by poisoning the earth. In this light, a green criminology is needed to awaken criminologists to the types of major environmental harm and damage that can result from environmental harms; the conflicts that arise from attempts at defining environmental crime and deviance; and the controversies still raging over possible solutions, given extensive environmental regulations already in place (Lynch and Stretesky 2003: 231).

Indeed, the emergence of environmental criminology in recent years has been marked by efforts to *reconceptualise the nature of harm in a more expansive manner* (see Chunn *et al.* 2002; White 2003). Much of this work has been directed at exposing different instances of substantive environmental injustice and ecological injustice. It has also involved critique of the actions of nation-states and transnational capital for fostering particular types of harm, and for failing to adequately address or regulate harmful activity.

Drawing upon a wide range of ideas and empirical materials, recent work dealing with environmental harm has ventured across many different areas of concern.

- Exploitation of biotechnology and the corporate colonisation of nature, particularly in regards to the development and marketing of genetically modified food (Walters 2005; South 2007);

- The transborder movement and dumping of waste products (Rosoff *et al.* 1998; Block 2002; Pearce and Tombs 1998);

- The problem of illegal, unreported and unregulated fishing and how best to intervene in preventing overexploitation of ocean resources (Lugten 2005; Anderson and McCusker 2005; McMullan and Perrier 2002);

- Under globalised systems of production, the generation of toxic waste in less developed countries by companies based in advanced industrialised nations (Low and Gleeson 1998);

- The diminishment in the quality and quantity of drinking water worldwide and the influence of transnational corporations in controlling water resources (White 2003; Whelan 2005);

- Environmental degradation on indigenous people's lands perpetrated by governments and companies (Rush 2002);

- Inequalities in the distribution of environmental risk, especially as this relates to poor and minority populations (Bullard 1994; Stretesky and Lynch 1999; Zilney *et al.* 2006);
- The one-on-one and the systematic institutionalised abuse of animals, as well as how changing environments affect the lives and well-being of nonhuman animals (Beirne 2004, 2007);

- The environmental and social damage caused by enforced pursuit of structural adjustment policies generated by the World Bank (Friedrichs and Friedrichs 2002).

In the specific area of environmental criminology, these kinds of broader conceptualisations of crime or harm are deemed to be essential in evaluating the systemic, as well as particularistic, nature of environmental harm. For example, the current environmental regulatory apparatus, informed by the ideology of 'sustainable development', is largely directed at bringing ecological sustainability to the present mode of producing and consuming – one based upon the logic of growth, expanded consumption of resources, and the commodification of more and more aspects of nature (see Chapter 6). Harm is built into the system.

To put it differently, it is important to distinguish (and make the connection between) specific instances of harm arising from imperfect operation (such as pollution spills), and systemic harm which is created by normatively sanctioned forms of activity (such as clearfelling of Australian or Brazilian or Indonesian forests). The first is deemed to be 'criminal' or 'harmful', and thus subject to social control. The second is not. The overall consequence of this is for the global environmental problem to get worse, in the very midst of the proliferation of a greater range of regulatory mechanisms, agencies and laws. This is partly an outcome of the way in which environmental risk is compartmentalised: specific events or incidents attract sanction, while wider legislative frameworks may set parameters on, but nevertheless still allow, other ecologically harmful practices to continue.

Halsey (1997a, 1997b), for instance, identifies a number of social practices that are legal, but environmentally disastrous, such as the clearfelling of old-growth forests. A broader conception of the problem is also vital in developing a critique of existing regulatory measures designed to manage (or, as some argue, to facilitate) such harm. For example, Seis (1993) argues that US legislation that is meant to protect air quality is based upon counter-ecological principles. As such, the legislation necessarily fails to protect and enhance air quality. The problem is not with the lack of criminal or civil law or enforcement powers: it is the anthropocentric assumptions built into the legislation.

Environmental issues have generated considerable public interest in recent years, and as this book demonstrates, criminologists and other social scientists are now likewise turning their attention to how best to define and respond to environmental harm (Lynch and Stretesky 2003; White 2003). Insofar as major environmental changes are occurring on the global scale, with significant impacts at the local level, so too greater urgency and critical analysis about environmental matters has grown. Simultaneously, similar kinds of local issues are being repeated across the globe, making us realise that the global and the local are frequently intertwined and in many ways inseparable. This is often encapsulated in the term 'glocalisation' (see Crowley 1998).

The task of trying to understand, interpret and act upon matters that are often systemic, complicated and intrinsically interconnected poses certain dilemmas for the criminologist. For instance, our interest and knowledge in this area may well be growing (albeit from a rudimentary base), but the more we know, the less secure we seem to be in the knowledge that we have. The very complexities of the issues can make it daunting to tackle them. It certainly makes things analytically challenging. One challenge for environmental criminology is to separate out different levels and kinds of analysis, and to 'make sense' of what is a very complicated whole.

Categorising environmental harm

The objective of this section is to identify some important areas for analytical consideration and to discuss these in abstract conceptual terms. To some extent the discussion is about how best to categorise different kinds of human behaviour and criminal activity. For instance, Carrabine et al. (2004) discuss environmental crimes in terms of primary and secondary crimes. Green crimes are broadly defined simply as crimes against the environment. Primary crimes are those crimes that result directly from the destruction and degradation of the earth's resources, through human actions. Secondary or symbiotic green crime is that crime arising out of the flouting of rules that seek to regulate environmental disasters.

Primary green crimes

Crimes of air pollution (e.g. burning of corporate waste)

Crimes of deforestation (e.g. destruction of rainforests)

Crimes of species decline and against animal rights (e.g. traffic in animals and animal parts)

Crimes of water pollution (e.g. lack of drinking water)

Secondary or symbiotic green crimes

State violence against oppositional groups (e.g. French bombing of the Rainbow Warrior)

Hazardous waste and organised crime (e.g. toxic and general waste dumping both legal and illegal)

Figure 4.1 Types of green crimes
Source: Carrabine *et al.* 2004.

The list of crimes associated with this typology is by no means exhaustive. For example, in recent years researchers have studied environmental harms associated with many different kinds of concern, as was presented earlier in the chapter.

The range of substantive topic areas that green criminology is presently investigating is growing. So too, the complexities involved in studying environmental harm are likewise being acknowledged. For example, environmental harm can be analytically studied in regards to four types of perspective: focal considerations, geographical considerations, locational considerations, and temporal considerations. These are described in the accompanying figure (Figure 4.2).

Focal Considerations:
(Identify issues pertaining to victims of harm)

Environmental Justice (humans)	Ecological Justice (biosphere)	Animal Rights (nonhuman animals)

Geographical Considerations:
(Identify issues pertaining to each geographical level)

International	National	Regional/State	Local

Locational Considerations:
(Identify issues pertaining to specific kinds of sites)

'Built' Environments (e.g., urban, rural, suburban)	'Natural' Environments (e.g., ocean, wilderness, desert)

Temporal Considerations:
(Identify issues pertaining to changes over time)

Environmental Effects (short-term/long-term)	Environmental Impact (manifest/latent)	Social Impact (immediate/lasting)

Figure 4.2 Key considerations of environmental harm
Source: drawing on White 2005a.

Exploration of themes and issues within each of these areas can be used to explore the diversity of perspectives, approaches and concepts that are utilised in contemporary environmental criminology (see White 2005a).

Focal Considerations

Focal considerations refer to concerns that centre on the key actors or players who are central to the investigation into environmental harm. In other words, the emphasis is on identifying issues pertaining to the victims of harm, including how to define who or indeed what is an environmental 'victim' (Williams 1996). Most green criminologists believe that the concept of 'harm' ought to encapsulate those activities that may be legal and 'legitimate' but which nevertheless negatively impact on people, environments and nonhuman animals (Lynch and Stretesky 2003; Beirne and South 2007). As explained earlier in the book, how we understand the relationship between human beings and the environment is crucial to defining and responding to environmental issues (see Chapter 1).

However, such considerations are not without their problems. Thus, as discussed in Chapter 1, the conceptualisation of 'rights' is itself contentious when extended to the nonhuman (see also Christoff 2000). On the other hand, defining environmental crime tends to be easier at an official and institutional level when harm to a particular species (for example, fish) is linked to human economic considerations. This is demonstrated in the discussion of abalone poaching as a crime in Box 4.1. What this shows is that, pragmatically speaking, formal definitions of environmental harm tend to be intertwined with specific types of human interests, rather than to be tied to any intrinsic worth assigned to the abalone itself. Instrumental purposes and anthropocentric conceptions do not necessarily always translate into destructive action as such; they are also crucial to certain notions of 'protection', 'husbanding of resources' and 'conservation' within the context of economic activity. Sustainable development is seen to depend on precisely such concepts and measures.

Box 4.1 Abalone theft as a significant environmental crime

In recent years the stealing of abalone has come to prominence and, indeed, is touted as one of the key areas in which environmental crime, as crime, is being addressed in a concerted way in countries such as Australia. Why is this the case, especially given that environmental harm in many other instances draws much less State attention?

In Australia the abalone industry is highly regulated, with strict quotas enforced, limited numbers of licensed divers and extensive documentation of each catch required. Part of the reason for this high level of regulation is that the industry is a major export earner, bringing in over AUS$100 million a year. Australia produces about one-third of the global wild abalone harvest, and it has been pointed out that:

'Australia's stake in global supply has increased following the decline and/or disappearance of abalone populations in other parts of the world – including Japan, Mexico, South Africa and

---

the United States (California) – due to negative environmental conditions, limited stocks, illegal fishing and poor fisheries management' (Tailby and Gant 2002: 1).

Global demand for abalone and high profits from abalone sales, have contributed to the growth in illegal harvesting.

Given the negative impact of illegal harvesting, use and sale of abalone on the legitimate industry, on royalty/tax revenue to the State, and on abalone stocks generally, concerted efforts have been made to counter the illegal industry. Illegal accessing and processing of abalone is criminalised, both in terms of the law and in terms of resources put into the law enforcement process. Thus, 'Each abalone-producing state has legislation carrying high pecuniary penalties and custodial sentences for abalone offending, and has dedicated abalone-crime investigators' (Tailby and Gant 2002: 5).

There are a number of interrelated reasons why abalone theft has been defined and successfully prosecuted as an environmental crime. The social construction of environmental harm, in this instance, is largely due to the economic bottom line. The framing of abalone poaching as a 'crime' by law enforcement officials is basically achieved precisely because of strong institutional (read economic) pressures to do so. By contrast, environmental harms that are ecologically problematic but economically lucrative, such as clearfelling of old-growth forests, seldom attract official sanction. In such circumstances, it is left to green activists and environmental movements to contest the master definition of the situation and to thereby call into question the political processes by which the 'legal' and the 'illegal' are determined.

Analysis of the different dimensions of environmental issues can be used to both explain why some activities are subject to criminalisation, and why some are not. A case study approach can provide useful insights into how and why this is so.

Geographical considerations

Students of environmental harm have to be conscious of the varying issues that pertain to different geographical levels. Some issues are of a planetary scale (e.g. global warming), others regional (e.g. oceans and fisheries), some are national in geographical location (e.g. droughts in particular African countries), while others are local (e.g. specific oil spills). Similarly, laws tend to be formulated in particular geographically defined jurisdictions. With regard to nation-states such as Australia, relevant laws include international law, federal laws, state laws and local government by-laws.

In the UK, the Environment Agency deals with issues such as fly-tipping, that is, dumping at illegal landfill sites; water, air and land pollution incidents; unlicensed fishing; and cruelty to wildlife including illegal snaring, poaching, poisoning and hunting. The priority issues at any point in time will depend in part upon local contexts, and local environmental and criminogenic factors (e.g. rare species living in particular kinds of habitat). At the country level, different kinds of crimes and harms are linked to specific national contexts and particular geographical regions. For example, threats to biodiversity have been associated with illegal logging and deforestation in the Atlantic Forest of Brazil; illegal wildlife hunting and trade in Chiapas, Mexico; the commercial-scale illegal logging and shipment of illegal logs in Papua Province, Indonesia; and illegal fishing with dynamite and cyanide in Palawan, the Philippines (Akella and Cannon 2004).

Intervention on environmental issues requires not only new concepts of justice and rights, they also require acknowledgement of transnational processes and responsibilities. It has been pointed out that:

> … transnational economic processes, transcontinental cultural links and transboundary environmental impacts have generated a new democratic deficit – the remedy of which requires new forms and institutions for democratic participation which extend beyond the borders of the nation-state (Christoff 2000: 200).

The telecommunications revolution has brought the world into the living rooms of the advanced industrialised countries and extended the scope of our knowledge of the fate of previously unheard of places and species. It has also expanded public or common sense knowledge of the interconnected nature of environmental processes (and harms), which finds expression in the catchphrase: 'think globally, act locally.'

For criminologists, the challenge is to incorporate notions of environmental justice into their overall analytical framework by maintaining a sense of global scale. It also requires understanding of the political economy of environmental harm (White 2002). These issues are dealt with in greater depth in the next two chapters (Chapters 5 and 6) and in Chapter 10.

Locational considerations

We can make a distinction between geographical area and 'place'. The latter refers to specific kinds of sites as described in the language of 'natural' and 'built' environment. There is considerable overlap, interconnection and interplay between these types of environments. Nevertheless, the distinction is useful, particularly when assessing which environmental issues appeal to which sections of the population and for what reasons (Tranter 2004).

In simple terms, we can describe the 'built' environment as basically referring to significant sites of human habitation and residency. It includes urban and rural areas, and areas of cross over between the two consisting of major regional concentrations of people, commuter suburbs and zones, and so on. The 'natural' environment consists of wilderness, oceans, rivers and deserts. These are sites in which human beings may be present, or through which they may traverse, but which are often seen as distinctive and 'separate' from human settlement per se (however, this needs to be qualified by acknowledging different ways in which humans interact with their environments, reflecting different cultural and material relationships to the land – see Langton 1998). Perceptions and consciousness of harm are in part linked to proximity of human habitation to the sources of harm themselves. A toxic spill in the middle of a major city, or contamination of its main harbour, is much more likely to capture public attention, and government action, than something that happens in a remote wilderness area or on the high seas.

In terms of public perceptions and public participation, environmental issues have been categorised according to three different types of harm (Crook and Pakulski 1995; Tranter 2004; see also Curson and Clark 2004). *Brown* issues tend to be defined in terms of urban life and pollution (e.g. air quality); *green* issues mainly relate to wilderness areas and conservation matters (e.g. logging practices); and *white* issues refer to science laboratories and the impact of new technologies (e.g. genetically modified organisms). These are set out in Figure 4.3.

'Brown' issues
- Air pollution;
- Pollution of urban stormwater;
- Pollution of beaches;
- Pesticides;
- Oil spills;
- Pollution of water catchments;
- Disposal of toxic/hazardous waste.

'Green' issues
- Acid rain;
- Habitat destruction;
- Loss of wildlife;
- Logging of forests;
- Depletion of the ozone layer;
- Toxic algae;
- Invasive species via human transport;
- Water pollution.

'White' issues
- Genetically modified organisms;
- Food irradiation;
- In vitro processes;
- Cloning of human tissue;
- Genetic discrimination;
- Environmentally-related communicable diseases;
- Pathological indoor environments;
- Animal testing and experimentation.

Figure 4.3 Colouring environmental issues
Source: drawing from White 2005a.

The significance of conceptualising environmental issues in this way is that it demonstrates the link between environmental action (usually involving distinct types of community and environmental groups), and particular sites (such as urban centres, wilderness areas or seacoast regions). Some issues tend to resonate more with members of the public than others; other issues generally only emerge if an accident or disaster brings it to the fore.

The mobilisation of opinion is crucial to determination of what is or is not considered a 'crime' (or 'harm'), and how the State will in the end respond to the phenomenon in question. The complex relationship between human and nonhuman 'rights' is thus played out in practice through the importance of 'place' in the lives of diverse communities.

It is important to appreciate the interrelationship between built and natural environments. On the one hand, it is long recognised that the lungs of the planet are its forests, and therefore wilderness areas need to be protected not only for intrinsic but instrumental reasons. What happens to the global forests affects how humans, among other creatures, live in the built environments of the city. On the other hand, even where 'natural' areas are subject to conservation orders and State protection, as in the case of national parks, problems may flow from the cities to these areas. For example, some national parks in the US are more polluted than cities; they have ozone levels that are higher than some major metropolitan areas. The source of the problem tends to be located elsewhere, and takes the form of power plant emissions, among other causes (Cooper 2002).

Temporal considerations

Another key issue for consideration relates to issues pertaining to changes over time. To some extent, such considerations are ingrained in contemporary environmental impact assessment in the guise of the 'precautionary principle' (Harvey 1998; Deville and Harding 1997). That is, what we do with, and in the environment has consequences, some of which we cannot foresee.

Temporal considerations can be distinguished in terms of environmental effects, environmental impacts and social impacts. The short-term effects of environmental degradation include such things as the release of chlorofluorocarbons into the atmosphere, the long-term effect being the accumulation of greenhouse gases and ultimately climate warming. Environmental impacts begin with global warming as a manifest consequence of planetary change, and results in the latent consequences of changes in sea levels and changes in regional temperatures and precipitation (among other things). The social impact of environmental change is both immediate, as in the case of respiratory problems or increased probability of disease outbreak, and long-term (e.g. lower quality of life, alteration of physiological functioning).

Temporal considerations also are relevant to analysis of discrimination relating to environmental harm. For example, environmental justice researchers deal with temporal issues by considering when and why poor or minority communities end up living near toxic waste facilities. A key question is whether or not the proximity between pollution and certain communities is the result of the placement of the facility in that community (direct discrimination), or whether the placement of the facility attracts these communities because housing values become depressed (indirect discrimination). By physically mapping out environmental harms, over time, and in relation to population characteristics, it is possible to determine what kind of discrimination is in fact at play (see for example, Stretesky and Hogan 1998; Stretesky and Lynch 1999; Lynch *et al.* 2002). Did the pollution come to the people, or did the people come to live near the pollution? This is answerable through temporal analysis.

The overall impact of environmental crime can be examined in terms of environmental impact (e.g. dead fish from polluted water), social impact (e.g. food poisoning from eating dioxin-laden fish) and economic impact (e.g. banning of commercial fishing, replenishing of fish stocks). The timeframe for providing remedies to environmental problems will depend upon the nature of the harm. Responses in the short-term and the long-term will vary depending on whether we are dealing with oil spills, over-fishing, loss of habitat or finding a home for radioactive waste.

The detection and origins of some types of environmentally-related harm may be unclear due to significant time-lags in manifestation of the harm. Here it is important to acknowledge the notion of cumulative effects. For example, this could refer to the way in which dioxins accumulate in fish flesh over time. It could also refer to the cumulative impact of multiple sources of pollution as in cases where there are a high number of factories in one area (such as places along the US–Mexican border). Diseases linked to asbestos poisoning may surface many years after first exposure, and this, too, provides another example of long-term effects of environmental harm. Persistent use of pesticides in particular geographical areas may also have unforseen consequences for local wildlife, including the development of new diseases among endemic animal species (as has been suggested has occurred in the case of facial tumour disease now rampant among the Tasmanian devil population in Australia).

From the point of view of ecophilosophy, the tendency has been for anthropocentric perspectives to dominate when it comes to answering the questions, *what to do, over what period of time?* And yet, protection of the environment very often requires criteria that go beyond a human-centred approach. To put it differently, the appropriate timescale for understanding resource and population stability is generally much longer than we are used to:

> Different systems move along different timescales. Geology works in the millions of years; economics in the tens of years; biology from a few minutes to a few centuries; evolutionary biology from a few years to millions of years. Appropriate time-scales depend on how long it takes for things to happen in the subject area (Page 1991: 64).

The importance of temporal concerns is reflected in cultures that view the relationship between people and the environment in holistic, reciprocal terms. The concept of 'balance' in some indigenous communities, for example, remains of vital significance (Robyn 2002). Here we see a value system and code of ethics that embodies living within one's means and living within and as part of nature (see also Langton 1998). It is an ecocentric approach to life.

The philosophy of living in and with nature is empirically reflected in two phenomena: one relating to 'place', the other to 'time'.

> The diversity of Native cultures and kinds of social organisations which developed through time represent a high degree of social/ political complexity and are varied according to the demands and necessities of the environment. For example, American Indian nations organised at the band level of social/political development have used effective strategies to take advantage of marginal habitats such as the Arctic and deserts of the Americas where resources are limited (Robyn 2002: 198–199).

Importantly, such systems are usually decentralised, communal and self-reliant: 'These societies live closely with and depend on the life contained in that particular ecosystem. This way of living enabled indigenous communities to live for thousands of years in continuous sustainability' (Robyn 2002: 199).

The point of this discussion is that evaluation of environmental issues needs to consider the element of time: negatively, from the perspective of short- and long-term consequences of environmental harm; positively, from the perspective of 'what works' in protecting and preserving environments.

Measuring crimes, measuring consequences

There are, then, a number of intersecting dimensions that need to be considered in any analysis of specific instances of environmental crime. These include consideration of who the victim is (human or nonhuman); where the harm is manifest (global through to local levels); the main site in which the harm is apparent (built or natural environment); and the timeframe within which harm can be analysed (immediate and delayed consequences). In actual cases, issues of movement, space, time and harm are inevitably mixed up and intertwined. Who gets harmed, when, where and how depends upon the specific nature of the environmental harm. An indication of the need for specificity of analysis as well as flexibility in conceptualisation of harm is provided in Box 4.2. This story illustrates the dynamic nature of environmental harm, and the shift from being a particular problem to one of more general public and political importance.

Box 4.2 Dioxins and the spatial dynamics of environmental harm

Environmental harm can be simultaneously specific and general in its concrete manifestations. In other words, the distributions of harm can have both a 'universal' and a 'differential' character. Indeed it is precisely this dual character that sometimes spurs governmental action around particular problems. Where you live is of crucial importance to those who investigate the nature of toxic waste dumps and issues surrounding contamination of local neighbourhoods. Yet, the static nature of habitation can be contrasted to the dynamic movement of the toxic contaminants.

In February 2006, the New South Wales government announced the banning of commercial fishing in Sydney Harbour. Authorities ended commercial fishing after tests showed that the level of cancer-causing dioxin in fish was almost 100 times the World Health Organisation recommended maximum levels. They also warned recreational anglers not to eat too much harbour fish, and that a multi-million dollar clean-up operation would take place (Perry 2006).

An expert panel was put together under the auspices of the New South Wales Food Authority in late December 2005. The panel found that seafood and fish caught in Sydney Harbour/Parramata River (Port Jackson and its tributaries) posed a possible health risk and should not be consumed on a regular long-term basis. The main problem was the

---

high level of dioxins in the waterways. Dioxins refer to the generic term for a group of environmentally persistent toxic chemicals that can concentrate in body fat and accumulate as they move through the food chain. The panel pointed out that:

> Dioxins have earned a reputation as being among the most toxic of organic compounds with acute and chronic effects including skin lesions (chloracne) in humans, and reproductive and immune disorders and some types of cancers in animal experiments. Given the potential for accumulation and the occurrence of toxicity at very low levels of intake in animals, the main health concerns for humans are likely to be associated with long-term intake through food. It is thus desirable to keep the food supply as free from dioxins as possible (New South Wales Food Authority 2006: 4).

The main sources of the dioxins were areas around Port Jackson that were used as industrial production sites for many years. These included chemical plants, which typically contaminated the waterways through their industrial activities. Union Carbide, situated on the Rhodes peninsula at Homebush Bay, was one of the plants producing

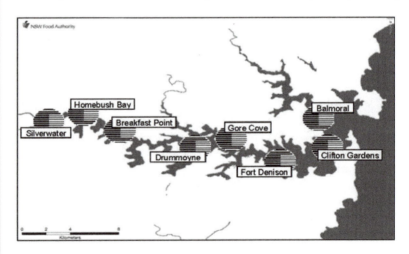

Map 4.1 Port Jackson sampling sites for dioxins in prawns and bream in 2005.
Source: New South Wales Food Authority 2006: 14.

pesticides, including Agent Orange, which contributed to the large scale production of dioxins. Indeed, between the late 1940s and the mid 1970s, Homebush Bay was used regularly as a dumping ground for dioxin. Fishing has been banned in this Bay for several decades. The chemical plants were closed down in the mid 1980s.

A survey of the main sample sites related to the toxicity of Port Jackson found that Homebush Bay was a major hotspot. Homebush Bay is located at the far western end of the Port Jackson waterways system. An indication of the level of pollution in the bay is provided in the accompanying chart, which shows the levels of dioxin recorded in bream samples harvested from eight different locations in Port Jackson.

What this phenomenon illustrates is the way in which distributions of environmental risk shift over time from the *particular* (e.g. the specific locality of Homebush Bay) to the *universal* (e.g. the whole of Port Jackson). It also demonstrates a movement, in social terms, away from the lower income areas vis-à-vis geographic location to the higher income districts with close proximity to the heart of Sydney city. Accordingly, the toxic pollution of the waterways becomes transformed from a problem of locality per se (and hence YOUR problem), to a problem that affects all of our homes (and thus OUR problem). This transformation process is twofold: sectors of the urban environment are degraded via the transportation of poisons through the medium of water, while simultaneously the harm itself crosses socially constructed boundaries that demarcate poor from rich, disadvantaged from advantaged.

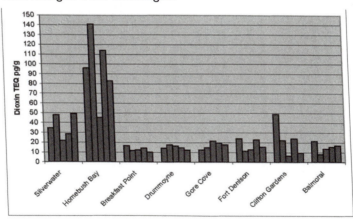

Chart 4.1 Levels of dioxins recorded in 36 composite prawn samples harvested from eight different locations in Port Jackson. *Source:* New South Wales Food Authority 2006: 16.

We also have to be aware of the methodological difficulties and opportunities associated with investigation of environmental harm. For example, on the one hand, the mainstream press under-reports the incidence and seriousness of environmental harm, particularly those linked to big business interests (Simon 2000) and this can inhibit public knowledge of the harms. Corporate offenders also have the legal and political resources to shield their operations from outside scrutiny and to ward off prying eyes. On the other hand, criminologists are utilising alternative sources of information – such as evidence drawn from medical literature and from environmental protection agencies – rather than relying solely upon conventional criminal justice sources or information supplied by perpetrators (Lynch and Stretesky 2006; Lynch *et al.* 2002).

Given that certain harms are undetectable to the human senses, issues of measurement and knowledge also loom large from a technical point of view. For example, analysis of the harms associated with the use of depleted uranium (DU) weapons in war-torn countries such as Iraq highlight important uncertainties and difficulties. As mentioned in Chapter 2, DU in its gas form is basically undetectable to unaided human senses. This means that there is greater reliance upon technical expertise and technological capacity for the measurement and recording of DU levels and impacts compared with other types of environmental harm. The role of the scientist in ascertaining the nature and level of harm therefore becomes paramount.

The dynamics of environmental harm are such that discussions surrounding definitions, deliberations and typologies will be ongoing. While these discussions are crucial to informing our thinking in the here and now about environmental issues, work undertaken in this area also conveys a sense of urgency and priority vis-à-vis preventing harm. Regardless of disputes and contested ideas, there is ample documentation of environmental harm across many different domains of human activity.

Extent of environmental crime

Environmental crime is socially constructed both through definitional processes and by the ways in which environmental law enforcement is carried out in practice. As noted elsewhere:

> The ways in which we 'measure crime' are thus intertwined with both 'how crime is defined' (and what is deemed to be serious and harmful) and 'how it is responded to by institutions

of criminal justice' (through specific campaigns, programmes, and interventions) (White and Habibis 2005: 10).

What is of concern to green criminologists is how best to measure the dark figure of environmental crime – those harms presently unreported, undocumented or unacknowledged as environmental crimes. Also of concern is how best to gauge institutional biases in what is deemed to be worthy of official attention and what is not. It is important, as well, to consider the question of victims and to establish some kind of baseline criteria that can be used to measure who or what suffers which kinds of environmental victimisation.

From a statistical data collection point of view, the measurement of environmental crime is difficult for a range of reasons. This initially relates to lack of consolidated data collection on environmental crimes. For example, there has been little sustained effort to bring together official and alternative sources of information, much less data between different government departments and criminal justice agencies (such as police files, data collected by non-government organisations and activist groups, animal welfare service providers, journalist accounts and so on). Who is collecting what, for whom, and why are essential questions when it comes to data on environmental crime.

Even if such data were readily available, the offences would need to be clearly defined, and categories of offence would have to be standardised across jurisdictions in order to allow for comparability (e.g. wildlife offences can be grouped separately from pollution offences). More sophisticated analysis would allow researchers to count the number of offences (the incidence of crime), as well as the number of offenders (the prevalence of crime). Probably the best sources of data on environmental crime is that provided in annual reports of environmental protection agencies (or their equivalent), and in court reports (including environmental law courts). However, such sources tend to report solely on particular jurisdictions (such as Victoria as a state within Australia, or England and Wales as distinct from Scotland in the UK) or on individual cases only.

Compilation of adequate statistics on environmental prosecutions and convictions is still in its infancy in many jurisdictions around the world. Part of the difficulty lies in determining which offences will be dealt with via regulatory agencies, such as licensing bodies and local government authorities, and which through formal courts or specific environmental protection tribunals. Moreover, depending upon how cases are proceeded against, different agencies will keep different records, have different types of follow-up procedures, and will vary in whether or not the information is easily and publicly accessible.

The countries that have better reporting and tracking systems tend to be those that are economically most developed, and that simultaneously produce the most amounts of waste and pollution. Data on environmental crime and harms, for example, is compiled by such agencies as the US Environmental Protection Agency, the Environment Agency in the UK, and similar bodies in other countries. Relevant information, especially of a comparative and regional nature, can also be garnered from organisations such as the United Nations Environment Programme and the Organisation for Economic Cooperation and Development (OECD). The amount and quality of data collected is influenced by the capacity and resources available to agencies and/or countries for its collection, as well as by the political priority attached to the gathering and disseminating of such data.

The inadequacy of environmental crime data can be reflected in what data there is. For instance, in 1998 in New South Wales Local Courts there were only 129 charges for environmental pollution. The figure for 2002 was 595 (New South Wales Bureau of Crime Statistics, 2003). While the number of pollution offences has grown from 1998 to 2002, these remain small compared with other types of offences. Moreover, no person was imprisoned for pollution offences over the years 2000 to 2002. In the state of Victoria, there were only 34 major prosecutions in 2002–2003, down from a previous high of 46 in 2000–2001. Most of the work of the agency takes the form of infringement notices, vehicle enforcement actions and provision of information (Victoria, Environmental Protection Authority 2003).

It is evident, therefore, that detailed study of specific offences and particular agency responses is required in order to both obtain a better picture of environmental harm and to monitor how institutionally the State and community is responding to this type of harm.

Figure 4.4 outlines a series of areas that might assist in guiding the process of gathering more data on environmental offences. The collection of this data would enable the construction of a baseline model from which the nature, extent and dynamics of environmental harm over time can be gauged.

- Define the scope of the research area (harm to the natural environment, to humans, to nonhuman animals, etc.);

- Identify:

  - Relevant legislation;
  - Relevant penal provisions;
  - Relevant civil enforcement proceedings;
  - The responsible government agencies.

- Ascertain whether each relevant agency collates data in relation to the following:

1 Number of prosecutions or other enforcement proceedings undertaken by the agency;

2 Data on conferences, mediation and agreements undertaken by the parties under the various Acts;

3 Extent to which points 1 and 2 above are recorded, monitored and/ or followed up by agency;

4 Number and nature of enforcement proceedings undertaken by third parties in relation to relevant legislation;

5 Identification of the enforcing parties (if not the agency itself).

- Obtain data/statistics where available;

- Compile an analysis identifying:

  - Existing statistical data bases;
  - Who maintains the above and on what basis (statutory obligation, departmental policy, voluntary);
  - Areas where it is desirable that such databases should be established.

Figure 4.4 Strategy for exploratory research on environmental offences
Source: White and Habibis 2005: 147.

The problem of data collection is compounded by difficulties in ascertaining the nature of the harm itself. In other words, the definitions and experiences of environmental crime can also be linked into different kinds of expertise and experience.

Knowing environmental harm

The measurement of environmental harm is not just about gaining access to criminal justice statistics or those supplied by regulators such as environmental protection agencies. It also involves weighing up different kinds of evidence, produced in different social spheres. If we want to learn about the prevalence and profile of sexual assault, for example, one source of information might be official police records. However, this could be supplemented by case file materials and record keeping on the part of non-government sexual assault centres. In a similar vein, tapping into the nature and extent of environmental crime is best served by having multiple sources of information.

As with alternative information sources in regards to conventional crimes, there is always going to be some questioning of the credibility of informants. Some are generally deemed to be more credible than others. For example, when scientists from around the world concur that big problems are looming environmentally, and there is sustained scientific evidence in support of this, this provides a useful tool by which to confirm and investigate diverse forms of environmental harm (see United Nations Environment Programme 2007). Even with this kind of evidence, however, there are those who strategically wish to deny or downplay the results by hiring their own scientist so as to produce a counter-truth (see Beder 1997; Athanasiou 1996).

There is also no doubt that scientific knowledge claims must be critically scrutinised, but then again this is in the nature of the scientific method itself. That is, science demands testing and re-testing of propositions in the light of evidence and ongoing theoretical developments. Determination of the extent and nature of any specific environmental problem demands, at some stage, scientific testing and diagnosis. The definition of 'clean air', for example, may be subject to legal and political wrangling in terms of which level of pollution regulators are willing to accept. But it is the scientist who will tell us what is actually in the air at any point in time.

Scientific knowledge thus also has a social context. It is produced in socially patterned ways, and is not socially neutral in application. Again, it is important to consider the ways in which scientific knowledge is applied in practice, and the effects of different applications on specific population groups.

Case study 4.1   Science-based risk levels

The risk assessment process by which 'safe levels' of exposure to chemicals and other pollutants are assessed is highly problematic, and incorporates a range of ideological and moral assumptions. As Field (1998: 90) comments, 'the use of the apparently reasonable scientific concept of average risk, for example, means that data from the most sensitive individuals, such as children, will not be the basis for regulation, but rather data from the "statistically average" person.' Thus, science provides grounds upon which we may base judgements, but these grounds are not necessarily neutral in terms of social impact. The interplay between scientific finding and social objective is of vital importance.

While one can be properly sceptical of 'science', especially when allied to particular social interests (e.g. the corporation medical officer or toxicologist), this does not mean dismissing science altogether. Rather, it means corroborating information from as many sources as possible, and making sure that the scientific method has been rigorously applied. The idea of peer review was introduced precisely to 'keep things honest', which is also why many science journals today also require disclosures by reporting scientists regarding who funded their research and whether it can be considered independent of the funding bodies.

It is also useful to acknowledge here that for many green criminologists not only is conventional scientific expertise essential to understanding what is happening to the environment, but, as well, there is recognition of 'expertise from below' – as in the case of farmers who 'know' their land, indigenous people who 'know' their country, and so on.

Case study 4.2   Indigenous knowledge and technologies

Some indigenous concepts of nature are informed by the notion of 'balance' in which 'the relationship between plants, animals, the elements, the air, water, wind and earth are all equally and evenly placed within the whole' (Robyn 2002: 202). This is accompanied by the practical concept that we should only take what we need in order

> to survive and leave the rest. The concept of 'Indigenous Knowledge' (IK) refers to the unique, traditional local knowledge existing within and developed around the specific conditions of women and men indigenous to a particular geographical area. Such IK systems, including management of the natural environment, have been a matter of survival to the peoples who generated these systems. Simultaneous to this is the concept of 'Indigenous Technology', which is defined in terms of hardware (equipment, tools, instruments and energy sources) and software (a combination of knowledge, processes, skills and social organisation) that focus attention on particular tasks (Robyn 2002). Fire burning amongst indigenous Australians, for example, constituted an informed and conscious means to work in and with certain types of local environment (Langton 1998).

Layperson, practitioner and indigenous knowledge is, however, also frequently subject to undue dismissal and even ridicule. This, too, is part of the 'politics of denial' mentioned at the beginning of the chapter. From the point of view of measurement, scientific and other sorts of knowledge is crucial to determining different kinds of environmental harm. The incorporation of a diversity of values and of different kinds of expertise into public dialogue is part and parcel of the democratisation of environmental issues, and is an important element in counter-hegemonic struggles against dominant socio-economic interests under late capitalism.

Conclusion: where to from here?

Both definitional issues and measurement issues require much more attention than has hitherto been the case. Environmental criminology needs the development of new and more extensive typologies. In particular, it would be very useful to undertake a sustained taxonomic process in relation to environmental harm. This would involve a systematic process of documentation and classification – a 'naming' of harms. Source materials could include not only existing criminal justice and allied types of data, but, as well, scientific reports that detail the changes in global environmental well-being and qualitative data based on interviews with practitioners (such as farmers and fishers) and indigenous peoples: the richer the sources of information, the richer the taxonomy.

Drawing upon specific data sets in order to present a picture of environmental crime in its aggregate form would also be useful. For example, data on hazardous waste in the US could be presented in ways that give ordinary people a better sense of the sheer quantity of waste that exists. This could be done in several ways. For example, the total waste could be calculated on the basis of the number of kilograms/pounds of toxic waste per capita (that is, for every 100,000 persons). Or the calculation could be based on the number of kilograms/pounds of toxic waste per square kilometre/mile. These kinds of analysis could also be used for the purposes of cross-national comparison (e.g. to compare the US with, say, Germany or Japan or Russia). As well, such comparisons would enhance trend analysis of toxic waste levels (that is, measuring changes over time), especially as this pertains to countries such as China and India which have experienced significant economic growth in recent years. This type of aggregate analysis has major implications for the need for and nature of environmental regulation and environmental law enforcement.

Another issue that is worth pursuing in greater depth is how the processes of criminalisation and decriminalisation impact upon perceptions and responses to environmental harm. While the naming exercise just mentioned implies an expansion of existing and potential harms in relation to the criminological agenda, there are countervailing processes at work as well. For example, the decriminalisation of environmental harm occurs when governments change legislation to allow previously illegal activities to now proceed.

An example of this is in the state of Tasmania where in 2007 following a 2006 Federal Court decision in *Brown vs Forestry Tasmania*, the State and federal governments allowed changes to the Tasmanian Regional Forestry Agreement (*RFA*), effectively nullifying the court's decision which sought to protect three endangered species from the operations of Forestry Tasmania in the Wielangta Forest. The then Australian Minister for Forestry and Conservation, Senator Eric Abetz, stated that these amendments 'will restore the policy intent of the RFA, and will continue to provide certainty to the forest industry in Tasmania while maintaining the protection of rare and threatened species'. Yet two months earlier, Justice Marshall, after having heard countless submissions from independent experts, stated that were the operations in the Wielangta Forest to continue these endangered species would be placed at unacceptable risk (see Pearce 2007).

Definition of harm is thus in the eyes of the beholder, and in the hands of the legislator. Environmental crime and questions of legality and illegality is always going to be a fluid process. Green criminologists have to be conscious of the history of particular legislative changes, as well as sceptical regarding who is saying what about the nature of environmental harm. Listening to different voices is an important part of being reflective and critical in this regard.

Chapter 5

Transnational environmental crime

Environmental harm occurs everywhere and anywhere, and there are often important continuities that provide common ground across the globe. Transnational environmental crime is that which is truly global in scope, and that reflects broad socio-economic processes and trends associated with globalisation. The diversity and complexity of such harm can be understood in terms of national borders and international social processes, and the pressures and limits of economic life as shaped by the dictates of 21st century capitalism.

Introduction

This chapter explores recent trends and issues pertaining to transnational environmental crime and how these are intrinsically linked to questions of global inequality. The chapter has two broad thematic areas: the globalisation of waste distribution, and; the dynamics of cross-border movement of flora and fauna. Under these two umbrellas, the chapter describes developments relating to the disposal of toxic waste, incidents of transborder pollution, transportation of hazardous materials, and illegal trade in flora and fauna. Notions of biosecurity and biopiracy are examined within the context of neo-liberal 'free trade' economic frameworks.

Underpinning the analysis is the contention that exploitation of humans, of nonhuman animals and of the biosphere is mutually reinforcing. A global political economy provides insight into the social and ecological inequalities associated with the making of, and responses to, environmental harms of a transnational nature. This is well summarised in the following passage:

> Many have noted that there is a direct relationship between the increasing globalisation of the economy and environmental degradation of habitats and the living spaces for many of the world's peoples. In many places where black, minority, poor or indigenous peoples live, oil, timber and minerals are extracted in such a way as to devastate ecosystems and destroy their culture and livelihood. Waste from both high- and low-tech industries, much of it toxic, has polluted groundwater, soil and the atmosphere. The globalisation of the chemical industry is increasing the levels of persistent organic pollutants, such as dioxin, in the environment. Further, the mobility of corporations has made it possible for them to seek the greatest profit, the least government and environmental regulations, and the best tax incentives, anywhere in the world (Robinson 2000).

The relationship between the local and the global can thus be collapsed into the category of the transnational. The movement between levels, and across geographies, is one of the hallmarks of environmental harm in the contemporary world.

The problem of waste

A recent United Nations Environment Programme conference identified three specific areas relating to hazardous waste that require urgent attention. The conference was held in November 2006 in Nairobi, Kenya and featured representatives from some 120 governments (VOA News 2006). The three issues of particular concern were:

- The proliferation of 'e-waste' generated by the disposal of tens-of-thousands of computers and other equipment;
- The safe disposal of old ships and aeroplanes, which likewise contain metals, chemicals and other contaminants;
- The illegal shipping and dumping of hazardous waste materials to countries made vulnerable by weak regulatory or enforcement systems.

Much of the transfer of waste has been from advanced industrialised countries to 'Third World' countries.

Consider, for example, the case of Somalia. The tsunami of Boxing Day 2004 uncovered serious environmental problems in Somalia:

[A]long more than 400 miles of shoreline, the turbo-charged wave churned up reinforced containers of hazardous toxic waste that European companies had been dumping a short distance offshore for more than a decade, taking advantage of the fact that there was not even a pretend authority in the African 'failed state'. The force of the tsunami broke open some of the containers which held radioactive waste, lead, cadmium, mercury, flame retardants, hospital waste and cocktails of other deadly residues of Europe's industrial processes. As the contaminants spread across the land and in the air, the United Nations said that an unknown number of people died from breathing in toxic dust and fumes. Subsequent cancer clusters have also been linked to Europe's special gift to the country, delivered by that tsunami (Bridgland 2006).

As Bridgland (2006) and others have pointed out, European companies have long been striking deals with Somali warlords to dispose of their waste. The warlords gained money for their arms, but of course no treatment process and no proper storage of the waste were ever really in the equation. The ongoing violence and political instability also precluded the chance of a future clean-up.

As waste management has become globalised, countries with civilian unrest, no environmental law enforcement or weak legislative frameworks have become prime targets for illegitimate hazardous-waste dealers, who are likewise globalised.

It is estimated that around 500 million tons of toxic waste is discharged worldwide each year, mostly by developed countries. In the US and Europe it costs around US$400 to treat one ton of toxic waste – it costs a tenth of that to treat that same waste in a developing nation (Chi 2006).

The biggest exporter of toxic waste is the United States. Hazardous residues and contaminated sludge are most likely to find a foreign home in a Third World country. The pressures for this are twofold. On the one hand, the US has seen the closing of many domestic landfills due to public health problems, and increasing public consciousness of the dangers posed by toxic waste. On the other hand, poor countries (and corrupt state officials) may find it financially attractive to offer their land as sites for US waste.

> When the cost of legitimately disposing of toxic waste in the United States was about $2,500 per ton, some impoverished countries, burdened by massive foreign debts, were accepting as little as $3 per ton to dispose of toxins within their borders. In 1987, for example, it actually was cheaper to ship waste by barge to the Caribbean than to move it overland just forty miles (Rosoff *et al.* 1998: 97).

Other European and North American rubbish is dumped in landfill sites and off the coastline of Africa. Plastic waste is buried in giant pits in the Egyptian desert. German and French radioactive waste finds its way to African states (Bridgland 2006).

The African Union (AU) has called for Western nations to help Africa tackle the impact of the environmental damage largely caused by the West. It argues that it is beyond the means of African states to address the problems generated by climate change and waste disposal in Africa because they lack the technology and financial capability (Iafrica 2007). The concerns of African leaders were heightened by the tragic events in Ivory Coast in August 2006 (see Box 5.1).

Box 5.1 Waste dumping in Abidjan

In August 2006 some 600 tons of caustic soda and petroleum residues were dumped at 18 open air public waste sites in Abidjan, the main city of the western African nation of Ivory Coast. Early news reports spoke of fumes from the waste causing nosebleeds, nausea and vomiting. A terrible stench permeated the city of around five million inhabitants, consisting of a rotten egg smell. Most of the waste was dumped in the poorer parts of the city. Dump sites included the lagoon-side city's main garbage dump, a roadside field beside a prison and a sewage canal.

To date, 16 people are acknowledged to have died as a result of this event. More than 100,000 people have sought medical attention, and around 75 people have been hospitalised. The source of complaint was 'slops' – a general term for cargo and tank-washing residues – which in this case contained substantial quantities of hydrogen sulphide,

---

sodium hydroxide (caustic soda) and chemicals called mercaptans that smell like garlic or rotting cabbage.

In a media statement on 13 September 2006, a United Nations representative expressed fears that the pollutants may have spread to the food chain. Youssouf Omar, a UN humanitarian coordinator, said that 'reliable sources indicate that a significant amount of waste was dumped in the sea and the lagoon as well as near the market gardening zones' (COSMOS Magazine 2006). The Ivory Coast government was to order the destruction of vegetable plots of bananas and tomato plants near the main rubbish dumps. It also banned fishing in Abidjan's vast lagoon in the light of contamination of the fish. In November 2006, it was reported that over 400 pigs were culled and incinerated by authorities, since they were suspected of being contaminated by the toxic waste (Amsterdam News 2006).

The dumping of these toxic slops involved a number of international bodies. The Dutch company Trafigura Beheer BV chartered the boat to carry its toxic cargo. Trafigura is a global oil and metals trading company. It has offices in London, its chief executives include French nationals and it has its headquarters in Lucerne, Switzerland. The tanker, *Probo Koala,* was Korean-built, is Greek-owned and Panamanian registered, and has a Russian crew. The final disposal of the waste was devolved to a local Ivorian company, Tommy.

A French clean-up company, Tredi International, was brought in by the Ivorian government to remove the waste, which could only be destroyed using European technologies. The company had to remove and transport to France not only the actual toxic waste, but the soil, rocks, water and concrete that was contaminated by the waste. More than 6,000 tons of contaminated soil and toxic liquids were removed (Red Bolivia 2006). It takes about two weeks of processing the waste before it is neutralised, then it has to be transported by freight train for incineration at another location.

The path to the Ivory Coast involved a series of choices and decisions – by Amsterdam Port Services, by Trafigura, by the captain of the *Probo Koala,* by authorities in Estonia and Nigeria, and by local élites in the Ivory Coast (see White 2008c). The disaster did not have to happen.

The concerns of African leaders are likely to increase rather than diminish. Illegal trade in waste is widespread and growing.

For example, a 2005 report by the European Network for the Implementation and Enforcement of Environmental Law indicates that illegal trade is on the rise. 'A joint enforcement operation carried out in 17 European seaports examined 3,000 shipping documents and physically inspected 258 cargo holds. Of these, 140 were waste shipments, of which 68, or 48 per cent, turned out to be illegal' (Environment News 2006).

Legal, but unequal, trade in waste is also evident. For example, the proposed Japan–Philippines Economic Partnership Agreement was set to include 'products' such as 'slag, dross and other waste from the manufacture of iron and steel; ash and residues containing arsenic, ash and residues from the incineration of municipal waste, municipal waste; sewage sludge'. Neither country had ratified the Basel Convention (see below). Yet, 'exporting the waste to the Philippines smacks of a business deal as most likely it is much cheaper for Japan to ship its toxic waste to the Philippines than to treat it and dispose of it at home in accordance with Japan's own environmental standards' (Stinus-Remonde 2006). Local commentators insist that the Philippines address their own, serious, waste problems before they get involved in handling the hazardous waste of other countries.

The legal trade in waste also takes the form of waste recycling. The notorious ship recycling yards of India and Bangladesh, for instance, provide an indication of the extent of the problem and the issues that arise from the doing of waste disposal (see Box 5.2).

Box 5.2 Recycle shipyards

Workers in Bangladesh currently break down more than half of the world's old ships (Mercury Newspaper 2006). Many people have also heard about the Indian shipyards of Alang, which are notorious for scrapyard activities that involve pulling apart huge ships that are no longer in active service.

In 2006, France was eventually forced to abandon its attempts to dispose of an outmoded aircraft carrier by sending it to Indian breaking yards. Campaigners argued that the Indian yards are poorly equipped and put the workers at immediate risk. Asbestos-laden vessels, such as the aircraft carrier, should, they argued, be considered toxic waste, and thus responsibility for disposal rests with the country that creates it (Edie News Centre 2007).

> What to do with the proliferating number of cruise liners and former military vessels is a conundrum that, so far, has been matched by the short-term profits, and short-term vision, of businesses and workers in places such as India. The breaking up, cannibalisation and disposal of unwanted freighters and liners brings with it profit and employment to locals. In places such as Alang shipyards it also brings huge health problems. A recent government-commissioned report found that one in six workers here carries signs of asbestos poisoning (Black 2006).
>
> Yet, recent UN figures tell us that the problem will get a lot worse, for a lot more people in Third World countries in Asia and Africa. According to the United Nations Environment Programme, almost a third of the 25,000 large civil aircraft now in service will be dismantled in the next 10 to 15 years. The number scrapped is expected to increase to more than 35,000 by 2035. Meanwhile, new tanker construction and maintenance rules means that about 2,200 ships will end service in Europe by 2010, while another 1,800 will be scrapped in North America, Brazil and China. Many of these will be carrying asbestos and other hazardous materials (Mercury Newspaper 2006).

When it comes to the disposal of waste, the distinction between legal and illegal is increasingly irrelevant from the point of view of human well-being and health, much less the impact on local environments.

As alluded to above, one of the key growth areas in terms of waste is e-waste. Electronic waste or e-waste consists of things such as discarded computers, TV sets and mobile phones.

> Just beneath the glamorous surface of the benefits and the wealth created by the information technology revolution looms a darker reality. Vast resource consumption and waste generation are increasing at alarming rates. The electronics industry is the world's largest and fastest growing manufacturing industry, and as a consequence of this growth, combined with rapid product obsolescence, discarded electronics or e-waste, is now the fastest growing waste stream in the industrialised world (Basel Action Network and Silicon Valley Toxics Coalition 2002: 5).

According to the United Nations, about 20 million to 50 million tons of e-waste is generated worldwide annually (United Nations Environment Programme 2006). The waste contains toxins such as lead and mercury or other chemicals that can poison waterways if buried or release toxins into the air if burned. Much of this waste ends up as transfers from rich countries to the poor.

Old computers and mobile phones are often not declared as waste but are shipped abroad as material for repair or recycling, according to bills of loading. Much of it ends up in Nigeria, where it is burned in huge garbage dumps. Under guise of recycling or charity donations, the process of moving waste from the US to Africa has been described as follows:

> American brokers and scrap dealers are paid to haul away useless computers, which they then ship along with used laptops, working computers, old televisions and other electronic equipment with some value to places like Lagos. The Americans avoid US dumping costs while the Nigerians find enough in the load to make a profit and then throw away or burn what's left (Lambrecht 2006).

Again, the overlap between legal and illegal, between useable and useless, ensures that environmental harm is inevitable.

Local and transborder pollution

The problem is not only the transfer of toxic waste; it is the generation of toxic waste in other countries by companies based in advanced industrialised nations. The classic case of this are the maquiladoras, American-owned factories set up across the border in Mexico. Here, environmental regulation is lax, with resulting high levels of chemical pollution, contamination and exposure to toxic materials. There are approximately 2,000 maquiladoras along the border and companies pollute freely, degrading the border environment and affecting residents and workers on both sides of the line (Robinson 2000).

Then there is the huge environmental damage caused to the Ok Tedi River in Papua New Guinea (PNG) by the activities of the Australian mining corporation BHP (see Low and Gleeson 1998). Because the PNG government was dependent on the earnings from the Ok Tedi copper mine it actively cooperated with BHP in the destruction of local rain forest and much of the river system. Many villagers have lost the entire environment that supported their way of life (Low and Gleeson 1998: 8). Similar events have occurred in West Papua (Irian Jaya, Indonesia), the other side of the Papuan island. Home to one of the world's largest copper and gold mines, the region had been closed off to outsiders as well as to the traditional landowners who were dispossessed. The mine has been accused of dumping tons of waste rock tailings into local rivers as a means of disposal. The military has been used to guard the mine and protect the resources by whatever means they feel necessary (Robinson 2000).

These examples highlight the fact that to understand the overall direction of environmental issues demands analysis of the strategic location and activities of transnational corporations, as supported by nation-states. Capitalist globalisation, bolstered via neo-liberal state policy, means that there is great scope to increase environmentally destructive activity.

> The structural difference of economic needs and government regulation between the developed and developing worlds, and the absence of any supra-national body to ensure consistency in environmental standards, has encouraged western industrial capital to shift unpopular and increasingly illegal hazard-producing activities and wastes across national boundaries to states which often define, and welcome, these transfers as 'investment' (Low and Gleeson 1998: 121).

We can add to the list of transborder problems the threats to health posed by smog. This is caused both by use of cars and factories (in places such as China and Hong Kong, as well as Sydney), and by specific incidents such as Indonesian forest fires that have caused havoc not only in that nation-state, but in neighbouring states as well. High levels of smog can lead to closure of businesses and schools as residents are advised to stay indoors until pollutant levels have peaked (see Edie News Centre 2007).

In 2006, the Blacksmith Institute initiated the first-ever list of the world's worst polluted places, those locations where pollution severely impacts human health, particularly the health of children. The list included:

Linfen, China
Dzerzhinsk, Russia
Ranipet, India
Haina, Dominican Republic
Kabwe, Zambia
Rudnaya Pristan, Russia
Norilsk, Russia
Mailuu-Suu, Kyrgyzstan
La Oroya, Peru
Chernobyl, Ukraine

The particular stories surrounding each site on this list makes for chilling reading. Each site is vulnerable economically, with the consequence of opening the door to profound environmental destruction.

Case study 5.1   Linfen, Shanxi Province, China

The Blacksmith Institute identifies 200,000 people who are potentially to be affected by pollutants such as fly-ash, carbon monoxide, nitrogen oxides, sulphur dioxide, arsenic and lead amongst other substances. These are outcomes related to nearby coal mines, steel factories and tar refineries, which have had a dramatic impact on the quality of air, land and water, including drinking water. It has been estimated that 16 of the 20 most polluted cities in the world are in China (Blacksmith Institute 2007).

Case study 5.2   Kabwe, Zambia

The Blacksmith Institute identifies 250,000 people who are potentially affected by pollution in the second largest city in Zambia. A history of the mining and smelting of lead has left a city poisoned from concentrations of lead in the soil and water. Local residents, especially children, are at risk of lead poisoning after exposure to contaminated soil through inhalation of soil ingested into the lungs. Playing in the dirt, bathing in a waterway linked to the former mine, and failing to rinse dust from cooking plates and food, all contribute to the hazardous effects (Blacksmith Institute 2007).

It is not only cities that are being polluted. Inland rivers and oceans and seas are also filling up with highly toxic pollutants. International waters that feature such pollution have no respect for national borders or national interests. The pollution affects all.

Case study 5.3   Plastic fills the oceans

There are five gyre or high pressure zones – slow, deep vortexes of air and water – in the world's oceans: in the North Pacific, the South Pacific, the North and South Atlantic, and the Indian Ocean. Together these cover some 40 per cent of the sea. What distinguishes these gyres is that they are places where plastic gathers in currents. The amassing of plastic waste across hundreds of kilometres of sea is having dramatic negative impacts. Thus, it has been pointed out that 'more than a million seabirds, 100,000 marine mammals, and countless fish die in the North Pacific each year, either from mistakenly eating this junk or from being ensnared in it and drowning' (Casey 2007: 3). The permeation of plastics throughout the food chain (including highly toxic chemicals) means that humans, too, are being affected by their ubiquitous distribution through land and sea environments.

Part of the problem with pollution is that it is extremely mobile. Consider for example what happened recently in China and how it was to later affect people in Russia. In 2005, an explosion took place at a chemical factory in Jilin, China. At least five people were killed and dozens were injured. The explosion released about 100 tons of toxic chemicals into the Songhua River. The chemical slick slowly travelled to Harbin, a Chinese city of some 3.8 million people, whose water supply was effectively destroyed by the chemical incursion. Without explanation, the city administration shut off the water supply, initially saying that this was for 'maintenance work'. Transparency and ecological consciousness have rarely been the strong point of Chinese bureaucrats and party leaders.

As the slick continued on down the river, it threatened the water supply of more than ten million people between the northeastern Chinese city of Harbin and Khabarovsk in Siberia, Russia (Lorenz 2005). As with the plastic in our oceans, the contaminated water does not recognise national or social boundaries. It affects all in its path. A national tragedy thus becomes an international incident.

Waste as a social phenomenon

The problems posed by waste generally are affecting greater numbers of people around the world as the global society shrinks. This section highlights several issues that warrant closer analysis and action in regards to waste issues.

Production and destruction are interlinked

Profit is to be had in setting up production in the most money-conscious and system-efficient manner. Profit is also to be had by building into the production–consumption process the most cost-effective form of waste disposal. What allows this to happen is the separation (theoretically and legislatively) of the inputs and outputs, and the combination (practically in terms of labour and local environments) of who actually does the work and suffers the consequences.

The impact of unsustainable environmental practices is that it puts more pressure on companies to seek out new resources (natural and human) to exploit as existing reserves dwindle due to over-exploitation and contamination from already produced waste. Nature itself is used as a dumping ground, particularly in the invisible spaces of the open seas and less developed countries. Waste is both an outcome and a driver of the production process.

Simultaneously, the social consequence of no work, no income, and no subsistence livelihood for significant numbers of people worldwide is that waste-producing and toxic forms of production (including recycling) are more likely to be accepted by the vulnerable. The imposition of such is embedded in the wider systemic pressures associated with global capitalism. Profitability very often means adopting the most unsustainable practices for the short-term gain.

Inequality not legality as the central problem

As indicated above, it is the poor and minorities worldwide who are copping the brunt of waste disposal practices, whether these are legal or illegal. There is ample evidence that globalisation is seeing the transfer of dirty industries and dirty waste to the Third World (Schmidt 2004; Harvey 1996). Characteristically, the biggest polluters and generators of waste – such as the US and the European Union – are also the most likely to export their waste to other less developed counties.

There is also strong evidence within particular national contexts, such as the US, and internationally, that those who are forced to live close to polluting industries and waste disposal sites are the poor and are frequently people of colour and indigenous people (Brook 2000; Bullard 1994; Simon 2000). This is known as 'environmental racism' (Pellow 2004; Julian 2004).

What is especially pertinent for present purposes is that the same people have to put up with the worst and most hazardous kinds of waste regardless of whether the waste comes to them legally or illegally. In other words, from the point of view of equality, equity and fairness, it is clear that waste is basically a problem for the poor, and something that is generally avoided by the rich. As with the Ivory Coast, the most disadvantaged sections of the community are the ones who live in closest proximity to legal landfill sites and garbage dumps. They are also the most susceptible to illegal dumping, whether it is in Abidjan or Chicago (see Pellow 2004).

Production of waste is a social process

Changes in the nature of production and therefore of waste, are in turn linked to a rising-costs model of waste disposal. The costs of recycling waste must be absorbed by business insofar as human activity must assume the recycling functions no longer assumed by nature (Deleage 1994). Pouring waste directly into the air, water or land is now increasingly regulated, and hence waste management more expensive, in the advanced capitalist countries. Legal provisions guaranteeing clean air and clean water have further transformed waste into basically a problem of land pollution (Field 1998).

The substantive nature of the waste has changed as well. The post World War II period has seen reliance upon and growth in chemical and synthetic products. This has been subsequently accompanied by new problems and complexities in waste disposal, especially in relation to toxicity as well as extent of waste (Field 1998). The emergence of e-waste has only added further to the existing waste management problems.

There is an emerging principle of international law called the principle of proximity. This principle says that hazardous materials should be disposed of in the place in which they are produced (Living On Earth 2007). However, the implementation of this principle is bound to be fiercely contested, given that the recent history of waste disposal has seen waste transformed from a particular to a universal.

Specifically, the regulation of waste and waste disposal methods has transformed waste into a 'commodity', something to be bought and sold on the market. Its economic manifestation as 'exchange-value' means that waste becomes an abstract tradable commodity. As such, it transcends its place of production to take its place in global marketplaces as a commodity. Large corporations have been built upon the back of waste disposal. These same companies derive their profit from the fact that waste has to be treated, transported, neutralised and disposed of, as set out in legislation.

> Commodified waste is disassociated from the particular plant or region which produced it and placed in commerce for handling by the now huge waste disposal industry. This directly impacts the spatial distribution of pollution. Since there is no tie between a given industry and the companies which handle waste, the treatment and disposal of waste can occur anywhere. Prior to the rise of the waste industry, a company would generally arrange for disposal at or near its plant. To this extent, the beneficiaries of the plant who generally lived nearest to it were also those who bore the problem (Field 1998: 87).

The reconstitution of waste as a commodity thus transforms the specific nature of waste into an 'unrecognisable' universal quality. Its origins no longer matter.

Control rather than prevention increases the value of waste

Responding to waste issues is acknowledged at the international political level in instruments such as the Basel Convention (see Box 5.3).

Box 5.3 International responses to waste

Under the terms of the 1989 international hazardous waste treaty, known as the Basel Convention, any nation exporting hazardous waste must obtain prior written permission from the importing country, as well as a permit detailing the contents and destination of the waste. If the waste has been transferred illegally, the exporter is obliged to take back the waste and pay the costs of any damages and clean-up process.

The Basel Convention was amended in 1995 to include a ban on toxic waste shipments from industrialised nations. However, some African states, including Ivory Coast, have failed to ratify the main amendment. Meanwhile, key nations like the United States – which produces the most hazardous waste per capita of any country in the world – have rejected it altogether. So, too, have Canada and Australia. Among those countries which have also not approved the amendment are India, Pakistan, Bangladesh, Philippines and the Ivory Coast.

Basel Convention signatories have also been called to ratify the convention's Liability and Compensation Protocol that creates a fund to help affected countries get compensation from illegal toxic waste dumping. As of December 2006, only 7 of the 20 nations needed to ratify the protocol had done so, and an emergency fund set up in the interim had only received US$270,000 in donations. Compare this to the US$30 million that Ivory Coast initially claimed it needed for the clean-up operation in Abidjan.

The European Union has around 30 special depositories for toxic waste, primarily in countries such as France, Germany and Belgium (Deutsche Welle 2006). Countries in Africa, such as Ivory Coast, simply do not have the legal and technical institutional capacity to monitor traffic in waste and to deal with waste disposal.

The European Union's Court of Justice ruled in 2005 that the European Commission has the power to draft criminal laws and decide what constitutes a crime, notably in the area of the environment. In February 2007, a draft EU law was proposed, one that would force member governments to make sure a list of environmental crimes – all already banned by national and EU law – are treated as criminal offences. It would cover releasing hazardous substances that pollute the air, water or soil; illegal shipments or treatments of waste; the unlawful trade in endangered species or ozone-depleting substances; and running a plant either involved in 'dangerous activity' or storing dangerous substances. Companies and individuals found responsible for environmental disasters would face punishment of up to five years prison or a US$975,000 fine (Associated Press 2007).

On 12 July 2007, the European Union introduced new rules on the shipment of toxic waste. The rules, which update a regulation from 1993, require EU governments to carry out inspections and spot checks of ships in their territory. They also give governments the right to open up containers to check their contents. The new regulation also lays out rules for shipments within the 27-country bloc, including requirements for detailed information to accompany cargo with hazardous waste (Reuters 2007).

Present concerns about waste regulation and control, as evident in EU moves to tighten monitoring and adherence to rules, substantially reinforce the notion of a 'waste crisis' and that waste is and ought to be continued to be treated as a 'commodity'. The problem, in this framework, is not the waste itself, but the ways in which waste is treated and disposed. The source of waste still remains 'hidden' in the sense that it is not identified with a particular plant or source. Private companies are thus absolved from having to deal with the 'waste crisis'. Instead, it is the State, in this case either specific nation-states or supra-national bodies such as the EU, that take responsibility for waste issues. Thus, 'waste disposal becomes a locational problem for the State rather than a production problem for capital' (Field 1998: 88).

Indeed, study of contamination, waste disposal and pollution as social processes reveal a constant shift in how the problem is socially constructed. For example, the recent contamination of Sydney Harbour in Australia was caused by industrial waste produced by factories further up the river system at Homebush Bay (see Chapter 4). In the discursive domain of politics the general problem of the pollution of Sydney Harbour – which is seen to be universal and catastrophic in nature, especially given the iconic status of the Harbour – was translated *back* into the specific problem of Homebush Bay. The environmental problems at each location were then linked in the public eye in ways that reconstruct them as matters of public interest. Viewed in this way, rather than through the lens of diverse private occupational, industrial and financial interests (e.g. fishers, manufacturers, developers), the problem is seen to reside in the hands of government first and foremost. In a nutshell, the history of the toxic creation is ignored, and the main beneficiaries of any remedial action are freed of the costs of land and water improvements, while the taxpayers of New South Wales have to shoulder the financial burden of fixing someone else's problem.

Disasters such as what occurred in Abidjan tend to call forth even greater regulation and tightening up of formal controls over waste disposal. This then feeds into the spiral of rising waste management costs. The net result is profit for those who trade in the commodity of waste. Rarely, if ever, however, is prevention on the agenda. This is because prevention goes to the heart of the production process itself, and as such challenges the right of capital to produce what it wants, how it wants, how much it wants and under what conditions it wants. In other words, the issue of prevention opens up the

Pandora's box of the foul nature of the mode of production itself (Harvey 1996; Field 1998).

Nexus between corporations, states and organised crime

The lucrative trade in waste means that people in positions of power and influence are more likely to want to receive their cut as waste is transferred around the globe. Corporations such as Trafigura shop around to get the best deal in waste disposal. Corrupt and/ or inept government officials take the money and turn a blind eye. Criminal organisations move in to take advantage of new markets for clandestine illegal dumping (Schmidt 2004; Simon 2000; Block 2002).

Ever stricter European environmental laws mean increasing costs of cleaning up and disposing of waste – therefore, criminal middle-men step in and offer low-cost solutions in places like Africa. Similar developments have been documented in regards to organised crime and waste disposal in the US (Simon 2000). Meanwhile, Bridgland (2006) describes how the seas off of Gibraltar are believed to be a gathering point for 'garbage cowboys'; where ships with unwanted poisonous cargoes transfer them to other vessels specialising in the illegal dispersal of waste in Third World countries. It has been estimated that illegal dumping generates up to US$12 billion worldwide in criminal revenues annually (see Schmidt 2004).

A distinction can be made between organised criminal activity and organised criminals. Many 'legitimate' companies are frequently involved in criminal and illegal activity as a matter of course. The history of the corporation is in fact a history of repeat offending (see Glasbeek 2004) and what has been described as the pathological pursuit of profit (Bakan 2004). Nevertheless, in areas such as waste disposal, and more recently tuna fishing in the Mediterranean, it has been suggested that organised crime syndicates are also directly engaged in illegal fishing practices (West Australian 2007). In each case, the driving force is private profit in what are seen as increasingly lucrative industries. Changes in supply and demand generate the potential for enormous windfalls for those willing and able to ignore international conventions, national legislation, ecological limits and moral prescriptions. As further discussed in Chapter 6, there is frequently overlap between licit and illicit markets.

Scale of bribery

It is not only ideology and corruption that drives environmental injustice and inequality. It is also the sheer scale of the bribery and economic transactions that make it attractive for poor people and poor countries. For example, writing in 2000, Simon (2000: 638) made the extraordinary observation that 'Guinea-Bissau, which has a gross national product of US$150 million, will make US$150 million to US $600 million over a 5-year period in a deal to accept toxic waste from three European nations'. Whether it be direct bribery of officials, or the offer of revenue to penniless states, or the prospect of income for chronically unemployed workers, money from the West is hard to resist for those enduring Third World conditions.

The costs of doing business are even further reduced where you have so called 'failed states' such as Somalia, or nations at civil war, such as the Ivory Coast. Lack of adequate legislation, regulatory measures, law enforcement, technical training and skill development, and a culture of compliance all contribute to loose borders and the greater possibility of illegal dumping. So too, poor countries are susceptible to legal and illegal bribes from powerful corporations, and many of the poorest of the poor are willing through circumstance to trade health for cash-producing activities, including recycling hazardous waste (Schmidt 2004). Environmental racism does not mean that inter-racial divisions are not possible – corrupt officials can and do collude with outsiders to dump toxic waste in the backyards of their own people (see also Pellow 2004). This is not just a problem of 'colour' per se, but of class and corruption.

The NIMBY effect on energy policy

There are major debates taking place worldwide over the impact and nature of climate change and what kinds of energy sources are available now and into the future. One of the preferred options, by conservative governments and by some prominent environmentalists such as James Lovelock (2006), is nuclear energy. For example, Lovelock has praised the fact that France has essentially 'proven' that nuclear power can be a clean and safe source of energy. The problem remains, however, of what to do with nuclear waste.

In this case, and as befits the general pattern of waste disposal discussed throughout this chapter, the answer is Africa and the Third World. The export of radioactive waste, while regulated by international treaty and national legislation, continues to be a vexing question. It also continues to happen, and 'out of sight, out of mind' in France translates into waste being disposed of in someone else's backyard.

The problem of waste production and disposal is basically a problem of the transference of environmental harm. Transnational environmental crime also includes activities relating to the movement of plants and nonhuman animals across national borders.

The problem of biodiversity

Most discussions of transnational environmental crime portray the issues in terms of the illegal trade in wildlife, illegal fishing and illegal logging. Added to this list are the transportation of hazardous waste, persistent organic pollutants and ozone depleting substances, all of which are deemed to be worthy of sustained licensing and surveillance systems (see for example, Elliot 2007). A range of international protocols and conventions have been put into place to cover topics such as these, as well as endangered species and genetically modified organisms. Among the better known of these are the Montreal Protocol guiding responses to ozone-depleting substances, the Basel Convention on hazardous wastes, and the Convention on International Trade in Endangered Species or Wild Fauna and Flora (CITES).

For present purposes, the main concern is the movement of plants and animals (or parts thereof) across national borders. A central concern of this section is to explore the dynamic interrelationship between 'biopiracy' and 'biosecurity' as a way to frame transnational environmental issues.

Biopiracy is linked to exploitation of Third World resources and Third World peoples and knowledge. Under the banner of free trade and the global (competitive) commons, the race to patent is the one that counts for many transnational companies. Biopiracy can be understood in relation to 'traditional knowledge of the uses of plants' (TKUP) and the usurpation of ownership and control over plants using Western legal and political institutional mechanisms and forums.

> ... biopiracy may be defined as the unauthorised commercial use of biological resources and/or associated traditional knowledge, or the patenting of spurious inventions based on such knowledge, without compensation. Biopiracy also refers to the asymmetrical and unrequited movement of plants and TKUP from the South to the North through the processes of international institutions and the patent system (Mgbeoji 2006: 13).

As explained by Mgbeoji (2006), corporate interests have used two methods to take what they want: institutional and juridical mechanisms (such as patents) and gendered and racist constructions of non-Western contributions to plant development and use (such as 'traditional' methods versus 'scientific').

> Most important, the legal and policy factors that facilitate the appropriation of indigenous peoples knowledge operate within a cultural context that subtly but persistently denigrates the intellectual worth of traditional and indigenous peoples, especially local women farmers. Cultural biases in the construction of knowledge provide the epistemological framework within which plant genetic resources developed by indigenous peoples are continually construed as 'free-for-all' commodities – commodities that are just waiting to be appropriated by those with the cunning and resources to do so (Mgbeoji 2006: 6).

Biopiracy is facilitated by World Trade Organisation agreements relating to Trade-Related Intellectual Property Rights (TRIP) that regulate things such as patents on drugs. It is further enhanced by the ways in which corporations are putting in TRIP stipulations inside bilateral trade agreements. For example, treaties routinely include stipulations which bind countries to standards higher than those specified in TRIPs (i.e. patent protection). Normally TRIPs allows members to exclude plants and animals from their patent laws. However, under bilateral agreements with industrialised countries, less developed countries such as Jordan, Mongolia, Nicaragua, Sri Lanka and Vietnam are being required to provide patent protection on plants and animals. Importantly, the negotiation of bilateral treaties is a generally confidential affair. The texts are kept secret until they are agreed on. Parliaments and congresses are not consulted. Public opinion is kept out of the deal. The winners are the corporations exerting the patent protection.

Biosecurity, on the other hand, is linked to preservation of advantages within specific geographical domains that preclude competition from the outside. The threat is not only from foreign business interests. It also includes potential losses associated with lack of species variety and diversity.

Ironically, one of the greatest threats to biosecurity is in fact the industrialisation of agriculture (incorporating the use of seed and other patents) since this is one of the greatest causes of erosion of plant genetic and species diversity. This is reflected in the following observation.

Today, a mere four crops account for two-thirds of the calories humans eat. When you consider that humankind has historically consumed some 80,000 edible species, and that 3,000 of these have been in widespread use, this represents a radical simplification of the food web (Pollan 2007: 47).

In other words, there is a tendency toward monoculture, since uniformity means ease of cultivation and harvest, which translates into higher profit. However, the simplification of production, in turn, generates potential problems.

> One consequence of the erosion of plant genetic diversity is that the capacity of the economically preferred plants to resist pests and diseases is compromised. The marketability of plant produce is not necessarily coterminous with the inherent superior quality of the plants to be marketed or selected for mono-cropping. Given the potential utility of plants that market forces may erroneously dismiss as economically useless, the short-sighted depletion of the plant genetic pool can be both costly and dramatic (Mgbeoji 2006: 181).

At a political level, concerns about biosecurity incorporate this sense of unease at being vulnerable to pests and disease. For instance, there is great resistance in Australia to the entry of New Zealand apples (due to the perceived threat of the fire blight disease) and Canadian wild salmon (due to the perceived threat of specific salmon-related diseases to the salmon aquaculture industry in Australia).

Related to the issue of patented biotechnologies is the phenomenon of *terminator technology*. This technology is about market exploitation. It simultaneously threatens biosecurity for local producers. The technology prohibits farmers from growing second-generation crops from the same seed. Also known as 'genetic use restriction technology', terminator technology involves the use of chemicals that after one season block genetically altered seeds from germinating.

> Considering that at least 1.4 billion people rely on farm-saved seed for their annual crop and farming activities, the implications of the terminator technology are devastating and irreversible. For example, unsuspecting farmers whose farms are near farms planted with terminator technology plants may have their crops ruined by escaped genes from the patented seeds. In other

words, the impact may not be limited to farmers who purchase artificially sterilised seeds (Mgbeoji 2006: 183).

Patent protection ensures that the big agribusiness companies are able to control markets and production processes. This is based upon patents of existing organic materials (that is, through biopiracy) and technological developments (that is, through genetic modification of organisms). The point is to make direct producers – the farmers – reliant upon commercially-bought seeds (and related products such as fertiliser and pesticides).

The interests of agribusiness are also reflected politically in terms of how some governments are responding to issues such as climate change. For example, the push toward biofuel production reflects the interests of large agricultural businesses, who can patent the monocultural crops designed as 'energy crops'. Restoring and protecting trees, while ecologically more sound and efficient, would be less profitable (Munro 2007). Moreover, keeping the ball in the court of the 'new technologies' of genetically modified organisms (GMOs) means less attention to the devastation wrought by current legal and illegal logging, which is likewise profitable for the businesses and organised criminal syndicates involved in both First and Third World countries.

Case study 5.4 Biofuel versus food

Powerful interests, including car manufacturers and grain farmers, have benefited from the search for energy alternatives to fossil fuels. The shift to biofuel is seen as a key source of green fuel supply for the world's car manufacturers. Greater demand for biofuel crops such as corn, palm oil or soya also means that farmers are finding the growing of such crops very lucrative economically. However, the trend toward biofuel is generating its own problems (Reuters 2008; Reliable Plant 2007; The Scotsman 2008). First, the use of crops for fuel is leading to food price rises and food shortages – so much so that Mexicans have protested in the streets about the price of cornflour that makes tortillas, a situation brought about by US corn growers selling an increasing portion of their harvest for the purpose of making corn-based ethanol (a diesel-type fuel made from plants). Less corn for food equals higher food prices. Secondly, the profitability of biofuel production is leading to the establishment of large-scale plantations in places such as Indonesia and Brazil. This process has seen the clearing of rainforests and in some instances the forcing of indigenous people off of their lands. Thirdly, there is evidence that the nitrogen-based fertiliser used in (the increasing) corn production is causing environmental harm in its own right. Millions of kilograms/pounds of those nitrates end up in the Gulf of Mexico each year, where it is causing a massive algae bloom. This bloom impacts negatively on the ecology of the Gulf: 'when the algae dies it sinks to the bottom, where it absorbs oxygen as it decays. In recent years that oxygen depletion has created an aquatic "dead zone" covering about 8,000 square miles in which shrimp, fish, oysters and crabs cannot survive' (Reliable Plant 2007). Biofuels are thus not quite the panacea to environmental and energy crises that some supporters claim.

While 'legal' practices can be conceptualised in terms of biopiracy, and 'legal' production can be demonstrated to lead to significant environmental and social harms, illegal trade in plants and wildlife represent their own kind of threat as well. The threat here is to biodiversity in relation to endangered species, as well as to the economic viability of industries such as agriculture, forestry and fisheries.

> Illegal exports of wildlife and wildlife products from Australia pose a threat to the protection of endangered species. Illegal imports are accompanied by the potential for the introduction of pests and diseases which could have a dramatic impact on agriculture, conservation of the environment, and specialist industries, such as aviculture. (Halstead 1992: 1).

How threats posed by legal and illegal trade are dealt with have implications for overall environmental well-being. Here it is useful to discuss recent changes to 'biosecurity' philosophy and arrangements in countries such as Australia.

What is deemed to be legal or illegal trade in plants and animals is institutionally determined by state agencies such as Biosecurity Australia (and their equivalents in other jurisdictions). Animal Biosecurity, for example, develops quarantine policies that are meant to protect Australia's farmed, domestic and wild animals and their natural environment from exotic pests and diseases. Activities include such things as import risk analysis of chicken meat, deer genetic material, dogs and cats, freshwater crayfish, honeybee semen, and zoo primates. These import risk analyses are intended to allow for the safe importation of animals, their genetic material and other products. In a similar vein, Plant Biosecurity aims to protect Australia's horticultural industries through import risk analysis of things such as bananas from the Philippines, avocados from New Zealand, and table grapes from the US.

Global trade in plants and animals, and quarantine rules, are guided by international treaties such as the International Plant Protection Convention and the World Trade Organisation Agreement on the Application of Sanitary and Phytosanitary Measures. According to the Biosecurity Australia website, 'The *major obligation* on members (including Australia and most of our trading partners) under these treaties is not to restrict trade more than is necessary to maintain quarantine security' (emphasis added). Indeed, it is pointed out that 'As a signatory to these agreements, Australia stands to gain increased market access opportunities because specific import conditions must be removed if a scientific analysis shows that they are unnecessarily restricting trade' (Biosecurity Australia 2008). The link between free trade and biosecurity considerations has had a significant impact on the movement of plants and animals across borders. This has not been uncontroversial (see for example, Bambrick 2004).

For instance, the importation of apples from New Zealand has generated much consternation among Australian apple growers. When Biosecurity Australia began the process of removing trade restrictions on apples because its expert advice was that pests and disease risks are manageable, Australian producers begged to differ. They were especially concerned about the possibility of importing fire blight, also known as the foot and mouth disease of horticulture, which is present in some 40 apple producing countries, including New Zealand.

According to Darral Ashton, chair of Apple & Pear Australia Limited, the bulk of growers are sceptical about the safeguards and about the whole import risk assessment process. The scientific issue of risk assessment is being subsumed under the trade issue, and the same organisation is regulated by the one and same body, namely Biosecurity Australia. Hence, 'It keeps coming back to the processes Biosecurity keep coming up which are seen as the "least trade restrictive" – it doesn't stand up to being the most scientific justified to ensure the well-being of the Australian apple and pear industry' (quoted in Lewis, 2004). Biosecurity Australia is the author of the import risk analysis, they also judge appeal submissions that go in, and they also make the final recommendations to the Secretary of the Department of Agriculture. In essence, trade and science issues are conflated, and the overall process of assessment has become highly politicised because of the 'free trade' agenda.

Meanwhile, scientists complain that there are not enough experts to guard Australia's borders from biological invasions – basically because government agencies do not want to pay for trained scientists such as taxonomists (i.e. those who put names to organisms and/ or identify new species and genera). The need for such experts is illustrated in the following example.

> The problem of salvinia – a floating fern from South America that completely choked tropical waterways, including many in northern Australia – was solved only through the recognition that two species complexes were involved: one in the plants and one in the weevils that were the bio-control agent. Until this taxonomic tangle was unravelled by CSIRO (Commonwealth Scientific and Industrial Research Organisation) scientists, the causes of success and failure of control were a mystery, and salvinia destroyed local economies in Africa and Southeast Asia, and killed people by preventing fishing and essential river transport systems (Rowe 2007: 26).

Rowe goes on to argue that 'In coldly economic terms, a doctor would be hard-pressed to kill more people than the local road toll; a quarantine error can easily kill thousands or destroy industries and wipe out livelihoods for tens of thousands' (Rowe 2007: 26).

On the one hand, then, there are pressures to 'open up' borders due to the influence of free trade ideology by dominant market powers such as the United States. The free trade agenda includes toxic waste, as well as conventional goods and services.

On the other hand, there are also emergent pressures to 'tighten up' border security due to the ill effects associated with unsafe products. This has become a huge issue of concern for consumers, especially in countries receiving products from China. For example, the US accounts for one-fifth of all Chinese exports. In recent times the US government has ordered the recall of various goods from China, including cat and dog food, toothpaste, toys and tyres, all of which were deemed to be poisonous, unsafe or potentially hazardous (Thottam 2007).

The importation of food is especially worrisome for some US producers and consumers. For example, China is the foremost exporter of seafood to the United States. However, in 2006, nearly two-thirds of the seafood shipments that were turned back due to public health violations came from China. Chinese fish products reportedly contained residues of antibiotics widely used in aquaculture in that country, as well as malachite green which kills fungus on fish (Weisskopf 2007: 27).

Another factor influencing border security is the presumed threat of terrorism to the food supply.

> In addition to the impact on health and safety, bioterrorism against the food supply would also directly harm the US economy. US agriculture contributes $1 trillion to our gross domestic product (GDP) annually and provides 22 per cent of all jobs in this country. The food production industry exceeds $200 billion, with over $55 billion worth of products exported each year. The production of food is so extensive (most of it comes from 500,000 farms and is handled by 57,000 food processors and 6,000 meat, poultry, and egg product processors) that if even a small number of contaminants were intentionally introduced to some part of the food chain, such an incident could seriously damage public confidence in the safety of the nation's food supply and could result in staggering economic losses for the agriculture industry (US Food and Drug Administration 2007).

Whether contaminants enter into the food production system through conscious terrorist act, illegal importation of banned organic substances or the legal use of patented materials, the result will be the same – devastation to the basic requirements of life.

Finally, in considering the movement of plant and animal materials across borders we need to consider the impact of illegal, and unsustainable, activities on local peoples. In areas such as logging and fishing, for instance, the issue is one of both legality and sustainability. It has been estimated that the illegal wildlife trade generates at least $10 billion a year (Schmidt 2004). This makes such industries lucrative from the point of view of organised cartels and business operators. It also means that the damage will be extensive and far reaching.

Speaking about the situation in Honduras in the mid-2000s, Duncan Brack from the London-based Royal Institute of International Affairs has been quoted as making the point that: 'Illegal logging, fishing, and wildlife trade are almost invariably carried out at unsustainable levels, running down the natural capital from which poor people derive their livelihoods' (Schmidt 2004: A97). Transnational environmental crimes of this kind thus negatively impact upon local workers and residents, as well as animals and environments.

The flip side of this process of dispossession, alienation from nature and economic loss, is reflected in how these same people bear the brunt of the waste explosion. Thus, in Asia, 'recycling' of e-waste presents certain types of opportunities:

> The open burning, acid baths and toxic dumping pour pollution into the land, air and water and exposes the men, women and children of Asia's poorer peoples to poison. The health and economic costs of this trade are vast and, due to export, are not born by the western consumers nor the waste brokers who benefit from the trade' (Basel Action Network and Silicon Valley Toxics Coalition 2002: 1).

For that which is not 'recycled' the solution is simply disposal, however and wherever local conditions allow: 'Vast amounts of e-waste material, both hazardous and simply trash, is burned or dumped in the rice fields, irrigation canals and along waterways' (Basel Action Network and Silicon Valley Toxics Coalition 2002: 2). The problems of waste and of trade thus feed into each other, compounding already difficult circumstances.

As indicated above, the concentration of power and ownership of production into a handful of large corporations leads to simplification. The answer to wider health and environmental problems lies in rekindling, cherishing and protecting diversity. But this, in turn, would force a challenge to the monopolies that simplify what is produced for human consumption.

> Biodiversity in diet means less monoculture in the fields. What does this have to do with your health? Everything. The vast monocultures that now feed us require tremendous amounts of chemical fertilisers and pesticides to keep from collapsing. Diversifying those fields will mean fewer chemicals, healthier soils, healthier plants and animals and, in turn, healthier people. It's all connected, which is another way of saying that your health isn't bordered by your body and that what's good for the soil is probably good for you, too (Pollan 2007: 70).

The economic forces that underpin biopiracy and biosecurity alike are precisely the forces that work most assiduously against biodiversity.

As such, they operate against the interests of humans, environments and nonhuman animals. Profits come before people. Profits come before ecological sustainability. The outcome is perpetuation of transnational environmental harm.

Conclusion: where to from here?

This chapter has provided discussion of the problem of waste and the problem of biological diversity. Framed in these ways, transnational environmental crime can be seen as stemming from essentially the same kinds of political economic processes. The main human casualties in each area of harm also tend to be the same. Further work on transnational environmental harm ought to pursue these matters in greater depth, through intensive case studies and elaboration of those technological and political processes that are creating new kinds of risk and threat to environmental well-being.

However, we also need more work on those transnational environmental harms that, while global, are not necessarily localised. Specifically, we could look at global climate change in terms of consequences (e.g. climate-related disasters) and causes (e.g. carbon emissions and polluting industries). Where does the potential for criminalisation of certain types of production fit into the climate change scenario? Given the proliferation of multilateral agreements on everything from transportation of chemicals to protection of endangered species, one could also ask whether global responses to climate change will be adequate to the task, given the politics of self-interest and the dominance of neo-liberal free trade ideology.

Transnational environmental crime is as much as anything defined by the concept of borders. As this chapter has demonstrated numerous times, borders do not mean much in the case of many instances of environmental harm, especially those pertaining to contamination, pollution and movement of materials/particles through water and air. From an analytical point of view, this implies development of new ways of thinking about crime, harm and criminology itself. In particular it suggests that more needs to be done in both comparative criminology and a global criminology (see for example, Larsen and Smandych 2008).

As part of this, greater attention could be placed on tracking corporate wrongdoing that cuts across national borders and that spans great geographical territory. Earth is the target and the planet is the prize. We need to appreciate that international competition among capitalist sectors (and among communities) for access to healthy resources, including clean water, is also intensifying due to the overall shrinking of the natural resource base. The search for new waste sites goes hand-in-hand with the search for pristine environments. This is a key paradox of late capitalism.

Chapter 6

Explaining environmental harm

The perpetrators of environmental crime include individuals and groups from a wide range of backgrounds and socio-economic situations. However, the greatest harms are committed by those who have the power to do the greatest damage, the transnational corporations and other large business organisations. The actions of these entities are bounded by a political economic context that is fundamentally crime-producing. There are systemic imperatives to harm the environment.

Introduction

This chapter provides a perspective on environmental harm that seeks to explain it by reference to global political economy. Discussion is based on the premise that adequate study of environmental harm must proceed from sustained analysis of the basic institutions and structures of contemporary capitalism. The central question at the core of environmental degradation and destruction is the organisation of human subsistence and the relationship of this to nature. The chapter thus demonstrates the centrality of capitalist political economy to the construction of the substantive problem (environmental harm), while also discussing the limitations of some proposed solutions to this problem.

The chapter covers a range of substantive concerns. These include the relationship between production and consumption; the developments underpinning the extension of 'consumerism' in capitalist society (e.g. privatisation and commodification);

the symbolic place of consumption and its association with the realisation of surplus value by capital (e.g. production of meaning, identity and desire), the mechanisms of environmental harm in the form of the interrelationship between licit and illicit markers; and system contradictions and limits. Each of these areas has implications for the conceptualisation of environmental problems, and how to regulate or respond to environmental harm. We begin, however, with consideration of key players.

Class and corporations

Some would argue that the most criminogenic agents of environmental harm within a global capitalist political economy are members of the capitalist class, operating within the institutional context of transnational corporations (see for example, Lynch and Stretesky 2003). This is because it is the most powerful groups and institutions in society that have the capacity to engender the most harm. It is also because the power and wealth associated with contemporary ruling classes is precisely tied to the exploitation of nature and of humans. A global economy characterised as capitalist is one that is populated by certain key classes.

In a capitalist society, the defining classes are the capitalist class and the working class, although these are not the only classes that are present. While other classes are present in the capitalist mode of production, they are not *fundamental* classes; that is, those whose relationship defines the mode of production. In any class society (e.g. ancient, feudal, capitalist), the fundamental classes are the class of direct producers (e.g. slaves, serfs, workers), and the ruling ownership class that appropriates the social surplus of the direct producers (e.g. slave owners, land owners, factory owners). In the more concrete terms of historically existing class societies, however, there is always some 'slippage' at the boundaries of class, insofar as individuals can occupy positions that shade into or oscillate between more than one class situation (see Meiksins 1986). Nevertheless, it is the specific predominant class relations that individuals enter into that are central from the point of view of shaping material interests and structural position. Class is fundamental to how people access societal resources, whether these are economic, social, cultural or political.

Typically, the organisational forum within which the ruling classes rule is that of the corporation. As indicated in Box 6.1, this particular institution has been designed from the very beginning to create distance between those who make decisions and the taking of responsibility for these decisions.

Box 6.1   Legal fictions relating to corporations

1) The registered corporation is deemed to be a separate legal person, acting in its own right.
This corporate 'person' is separate from the shareholders who stand to benefit from its profit-chasing activities. Shareholders are protected from fiscal losses. They are also rendered legally immune from any wrongful, illegal and criminal acts the corporation might commit in their search for profits.

Sometimes directors/managers are held responsible if it can be determined that their thoughts and acts are their own, rather than those of the corporation. But the starting position is that senior managers have a measure of immunity, although not quite the privilege of total legal irresponsibility enjoyed by the shareholders.

2) Because the corporation needs others to think and act, it cannot be guilty of a criminal offence.
There is no wrongdoer whose intention to commit an illegal act can be proved. No one seems responsible – not the senior management, not the shareholder, not the corporation. To get around this, the law is forced to use another pretence: it holds the corporation 'criminally responsible' when its acting mind and will exhibit wrongful intention. In a large corporation, this is immensely difficult to provide.

3) Corporate wrongdoing pays, because the structured criminogenic nature of the corporation is almost always avoided in cases where real people are actually prosecuted.
Corporations commit an enormous number of offences, and they reoffend regularly. That is, they have high recidivism rates.

Corporate evildoing is not exceptional behaviour: rather, it is the norm. The corporation has been legally designed as a criminogenic creature – in other words, prone to compulsive criminal behaviour. The law has devised a scheme of business regulatory rules that penalises offenders without criminalising them.

Source: Glasbeek 2003, 2004.

The corporate form is thus itself criminogenic in nature. For example, it is difficult to secure meaningful convictions for corporate wrongdoing due to the complications surrounding the status of corporations as legal persons, and because corporate crime tends to be socially defined as less harmful (see Glasbeek 2003; Bakan 2004). This fosters a culture of impunity and self-righteousness. Moreover, the complexities and nuances of the crimes of the powerful, involving corporations and the State, demand even greater than usual investigatory sophistication and a steadfastly critical theoretical orientation if they are to be fully appreciated and unravelled (see Tombs and Whyte 2004). Powerful social interests not only perpetuate great harms, they also obscure and mask the nature of the harm production. They are also best placed to resist the criminalisation process generally.

Class has a profound shaping influence in the lived experiences of people. For example, the capitalist class cannot be understood only in terms of who actually comprises it (for example, in the West, predominantly wealthy white men), but in terms of the relations it embodies (that is, ownership, control and exploitation of non-owners). If we see things this way, then the issue becomes one of how particular social relations are produced and reproduced – including crime and criminality.

Class situation is linked to specific types of criminality. Thus, where you are located in the class structure will influence the kinds of criminal activity you engage in, the propensity to engage in such activity, and the intensity of that involvement (and, of course, whether it will be identified by the State as criminal, and whether it will be policed or punished).

The capitalist class is comprised of the owners of capitalist enterprises and those who control and manage the capital accumulation process on their behalf (who themselves overwhelmingly own shares in the enterprises they manage). It is the dominant class economically, but the smallest numerically (van der Velden and White 1996). The initial difficulty in determining criminality within the capitalist class is that State laws reflect the very interests of the capitalist ruling class that controls the State. As such, many types of social harm may not be incorporated into the criminal law if to do so would go against capitalist interests generally. Hence a central focus of environmental criminology must be to make this transparent through reference to specific harmful activities (for example, the [legal] clearfelling of forests, the [legal] acceptance of certain poisons in drinking water, the [legal] production of toxic landfill).

The problem for criminologists in trying to tackle corporate crime is that virtually every act of the corporate sector is deemed, in some way or another, to be 'good for the country'. This ideology of corporate virtue, and the benefits of business for the common good, is promulgated through extensive corporate advertising campaigns, capitalist blackmail (vis-à-vis location of industry and firms) and aggressive lobbying. Anything which impedes business is deemed to be unreasonable, faulty, bad for the economy, not the rightful domain of the State, to undermine private property rights, and so on. In other words, the prevailing view promulgated by government and business is that, with few exceptions, the 'market' is the best referee when it comes to preventing or stopping harm and potential harm. Powerful business interests (which, among other things, provide big financial contributions to mainstream political parties) demand a 'light touch' when it comes to surveillance of, and intervention in, their activities. In this framework, the State should not, therefore, play a major role in regulation of corporate activities beyond that of assisting in the maintenance of a general climate within which business will flourish.

The 'naturalness' of capitalist crime – the way in which social harms, economic exploitation and environmental destruction is built into the fabric of everyday, ordinary life as a 'normal' feature of how we produce and consume – makes it that much more difficult to challenge. This is compounded by the fact that much of what occurs, does so in a fully 'legal' way (regardless of actual harm). Moreover, where external controls (materially and ideologically) on profit maximisation are weakened, then we can reasonably expect to see an increased incidence in illegal corporate activity and, more generally, greater propensity for social harm regardless of legal definition.

On top of this, the close ties between economic élites and political leaders, in terms of shared ideology, contributions to campaigns and interchangeable personnel, manifests itself in governmental platforms that can entrench an anti-environmental agenda. This was especially apparent in the US under the regime of George W. Bush (see Weidner and Watzman 2002). Interlocking directorates among corporations are complemented by active engagement in policy discussion groups and government advisory groups (Beder 2006; Murray 2006). Governments are heavily influenced by corporations, through concerted corporate lobbying efforts, their backing of think tanks and the funding of corporate-friendly research, and by the flow of top-level officials through the 'revolving door' between government and business. The private interests of the corporations translate into massive environmental degradation (see Beder 2006).

To address this kind of criminality, then, requires a political understanding of class power, and a rejection of formally legal criteria in assessing criminality and harm. It is therefore from beginning to end a political process. As such, it implies conflict – over definitions of behaviour and activity (e.g. as being good or bad, harmful or not so harmful, offensive or inoffensive), over legitimacy of knowledge claims (e.g. media portrayals, expert opinion), and over the role and use of State instruments and citizen participation in putting limits on corporate activity (e.g. via regulations, through public access to commercial information). In other words, the basis for such criminality lies within the social structure itself, in the very nature and imperatives of capitalist forms of production, consumption and distribution.

Instances of harming the environment have usually been subsumed under the broader categories of 'white-collar' and 'corporate' crime which cast environmental harm as something that results from the particular actions of specific companies. The scope of these studies is somewhat limited, however, in that environmental harm is by no means reducible solely to the (negligent) actions of corporations or the individuals within them. People who drive to work each day, reside in dwellings which undermine the natural water flows of the land, or who consume non-recyclable products, all contribute to environmental problems en masse. This suggests that environmental harm is in fact ubiquitous – a structural or systemic phenomenon – rather than exclusively contained within the operations of specific corporate giants or certain 'careless' individuals.

Capitalism, population and technology

To fully appreciate the causes of environmental crime it is essential to locate such harm within the context of the dominant mode of production on a world scale, namely, capitalism. The capitalist mode of production is defined by particular patterns of ownership and control over the means of production (e.g. private ownership of factories, media, agribusiness, chemical companies), particular relations of production (e.g. wage-labour rather than subsistence production) and particular forces of production (e.g. use of modern techniques and technologies rather than traditional). It is based on specifically bourgeois concepts of private property (see Fine 1984) and propelled by the logic of profit. The long-term trend under the capitalist mode of production has been for the concentration of ownership of the means of production, signalled by the shift from competitive capitalism to monopoly capitalism (Mandel 1975).

The search for profits demands exploitation of humans at the point of production (through struggles over wage costs, production methods, welfare benefits), exploitation of nature (in the form of using up 'natural resources' and commercialising exotic environments) and pursuit of new consumption markets (so that the extent and flow of money exchange is kept at high levels). It also encompasses the formation of certain types of human nature – acquisitive, possessive, individualist, self-interested (see Macpherson 1962) – that best suits the capitalist production–consumption cycle. This can be achieved, at least in part, through changes in the material supports provided by States (via privatisation and diminishment of publicly provided health, education and welfare), and by ideological offences that place the onus and responsibility for well-being squarely on the backs of individuals (via neo-liberal 'free market' policies). The emotional and affective aspects of human life are impacted upon by constant and systemic propaganda campaigns (i.e. advertising) that delimit social life mainly in terms of certain types of capitalistically-defined consumption.

Global capitalism redefines and reshapes the fish in the sea, the birds in the air, the animals in the forest and plant life everywhere. It reaches into the very essence of the land, the air, the water and leaves no place and no person untouched by its pervasive influence. Yet, even in the midst of acknowledged ecological crisis, many writers turn to population or to technology as the source of the problem, and its solution. The tendency is to assume 'business as usual', and to tweak the system around the edges. The fundamental character of global capitalism is left unchallenged (see Foster 2007), and the 'solutions' put on offer seem to inevitably rest upon a platform of social inequality.

Consider for example the notion that population pressure is a driver of environmental harm. While refuted in both technical demographic terms (Jackson 2004) and causal terms (Gosine 2005), the myth of over-population plays a powerful ideological role in deflecting attention from core structural issues at the heart of global environmental degradation. Furthermore, 'reducing much of the ecological-environmental problem to a simple population problem' (Harvey 1996: 381) generally leads to conclusions that scapegoat the world's poor and dispossessed (Mass 1976; Gosine 2005).

The seeds of present concerns over 'surplus populations' were present in the writings of Thomas Malthus, who wrote his treatise on population some two centuries ago. The treatise is worth revisiting for illustrative purposes. Malthus (1798/1973) wanted to establish the scientific validity of three propositions related to population: that population is necessarily limited by the means of subsistence; that it will increase with increases in the means of subsistence, unless prevented by powerful checks; and that these checks on population were all resolvable into moral restraint, vice and misery. In examining these questions, Malthus provided a detailed guide of population checks around the world. He also strongly argued against those who view 'systems of equality' as a solution to the population dilemma, as well as criticising the English 'Poor Laws' because of their consequences for population growth.

The political bottom line in the Mathussian scheme of things is summed up best in the following passage:

> That the principal and most permanent cause of poverty has little or no direct relation to forms of government, or the unequal division of property; and that, as the rich do not in reality possess the power of finding employment and maintenance of the poor, the poor cannot, in the nature of things, possess the right to demand them; are important truths flowing from the principle of population, which, when properly explained, would by no means be above the most ordinary comprehension (Malthus 1798/1973: 260).

Such self-evident 'truths' have consistently been used to convince people of the horrors of over-population, to target the vulnerable and marginalised sectors of world humanity, and to abrogate any responsibility for environmental problems from the system and from the rich. This is one 'science' that has failed miserably to address key issues of social and ecological justice. Yet the advent of *environmental refugees* – beginning with the island peoples of the South Pacific and quickly enjoining the lowland peoples of Bangladesh and other at risk regions – will once again raise the spectre of population as a populist evil to be fought using ever more draconian methods of containment.

Population control is not the solution to a problem that has its origins in the capitalist mode of production. Nor is technology, as such, the answer. Indeed, as ably argued by Davison (2001, 2004), technology is a social practice that is both product and producer of social order and cultural meaning. For business interests, technology is now frequently touted as the key means to overcome the 'limits to growth' so worried over by the populationists. In this view, it is the state of technology that counts, and it is in and through technological advancement that ecological well-being is to be assured (see Davison 2001). Against this is the acknowledgement that technologies create risks as well as possibilities, that the technology question is inherently about the human character of social practice. Thus, as Davison (2004: 144) points out:

> Technologies of genetics, biology, energy, matter and information cannot be neatly sorted into good and bad, or sustainable and unsustainable, piles. Produced within militaristic – or unjust or colonising or wasteful or racist or patriarchal, etc. – social practices, renewable energy technologies, sustainable forms of agriculture and other 'green' techniques may reduce some forms of ecological risk, but they may also help to prop up, to sustain, an unsustaining social whole.

The social context of technological use and development is therefore crucial.

The notion that technology is socially 'neutral' and that it is the answer to environmental problems can be used to obscure the substantive social, environmental and military differences in the 'choices' being made. Consider for example the application of technologies to agriculture (and, indeed, aquaculture – see Chapter 9). Athanasiou (1996) argues that modern biotechnology is today presented as a true environmental alternative, but that basically it entrenches the existing agrochemical industry. Reference to technological expertise and advancement is used to dismiss alternatives, in part due to the political economy of agricultural production. For instance, 'rotational grazing' is a simple method of managing pastureland that, by giving it periodic chances to recover, increases total 'productivity' as much as by injecting dairy cows with bioengineered bovine growth hormone (BGH). However, BGH is seen as scientific and therefore more attractive from a political point of view. It also promotes larger herds, rather than small-farm economy, and thus leads to a concentration of ownership. Similar kinds of social impact from biotechnological 'solutions', especially in the Third World, are evident in other ways as well: 'Already ag biotech is accelerating the shift from small farms to large plantations by promoting techniques that smallholders simply cannot afford, such as the mechanised harvesting based on bioengineered vegetables that all ripen in machinelike unison' (Athanasiou 1996: 255). The technological and the social are inseparable parts of human practice.

The search for a technological fix provides an easily suggested, if dangerous, way out for those who cannot find answers except from within the present political economic framework of late capitalism. Thus, James Lovelock, creator of the concept of Gaia (the concept of Earth as a living organic system), recently wrote of the extreme nature of the present-day environmental crisis (Lovelock 2006). Yet his only 'solution' is not social or political, it is technological. He argues for a huge expansion of nuclear power facilities around the world as a limited substitute to the present energy economy. Arguments about how, and where, to dispose nuclear waste and the link between uranium mining and nuclear weapons, are casually dismissed. Others, however, are very critical of such answers, and raise major concerns about safety, security and storage in regards to nuclear power (Caldicott 2006; Athanasiou 1996). Come what may, as Foster (2007) observes, any framing of the solution must at some point consider how best to transcend business as usual if environmental catastrophe is to be averted.

Sustainable development and commodity production

For governments, denial of harm is usually associated with economic objectives and the appeal to forms of 'sustainable development' which fundamentally involve further environmental degradation (for examples, see Harvey 1996).

At the heart of these processes of denial is a culture which takes for granted, but rarely sees as problematic, the proposition that continued expansion of material consumption is both possible and will not harm the biosphere in any fundamental way. Some aspects of denial are consciously and directly linked to instrumental purposes (as in firm or industry campaigns to de-legitimate environmental action surrounding events or developments that are manifestly harmful to local environments). At a more general level, however, denial is ingrained in the hegemonic dominance of anthropocentric, and specifically capitalist, conceptions of the relationship between human beings and nature. Basic assumptions about economic growth and commodity production – central components of the dominant worldview – make it difficult for many people to accept that the essence of the problem lies in the system itself (see Halsey and White 1998; Harvey 1996).

Environmental harm is about what human beings do to and with nature. How we do so is fundamentally a social process. It involves the actions of human beings working in concert with each other to meet their needs in particular ways. To understand environmental harm, therefore, it is essential to ask basic questions about the mode of production in any given society.

In the present era, this means that we must examine the nature of capitalism, as capitalism is the central defining feature of production in the world today. While much of the contemporary environmental and criminological literature alludes to the fact that 'regulation' or 'environmental crime' or 'consumption' take place in the context of global capitalism, it is rare to find analyses which attempt to theorise what this might actually mean for analysis of specific issues and trends. In the main, concern has been directed at study of the undesirable *effects* of the dominant capitalist mode of production, rather than the dynamics and operation of it. Yet, if we are to discern the limits and possibilities of dealing with environmental harm, then it is essential to delve into the political economic structures of capitalism. It is these which dictate much of the public perception about and definitions of environmental harm, and which likewise provide the basic frameworks for existing 'management' practices in relation to this harm.

Built in to the logic and dynamics of capitalism is the *imperative to expand*. Increasing the production of surplus value by labour – the source of profit – demands constant changes in ways in which labour is exploited, and in the things which can be transformed from simple use-values (i.e. objects of need) into exchange-values (i.e. commodities produced purely for exchange). This can be achieved by changes in the organisation of work, by manipulation of the conditions within specific workplaces, and by transforming previously unproductive or non-capitalist forms of activity into sites of productive labour (e.g. family farming into agribusiness). The extended reproduction of the system rests upon the expansion of commodity production, since only labour hired by commodity-producing capital is directly productive of surplus value (van der Velden 1998).

Capitalism in essence means expansion. And this expansionary dynamic – the extended reproduction of capital accumulation – has several major implications for the environment. First, it implies that 'natural resources' are themselves subject to varying processes of commodification, that is, the transformation of existing or potential use-values into exchange-values (for example, transformation in the nature of water utilities). The distribution of goods and services through market mechanisms (rather than, for instance, on the basis of communal assessment of need, as in some forms of allocation of public housing) can take different forms. Use of market mechanisms is central to the capitalist firm (where the return is to the private investor), as well as to some State agencies (where the return is to the public entity, although use of this mechanism may be for either distributive or profit-making purposes). Institutionally, specifically capitalist forms of market distribution can be represented in the form of corporatisation (where public institutions sell their product for profit on the market) and privatisation (where public institutions are sold off to private companies). In many cases, the former is the precursor of the latter.

Secondly, the appropriation of nature does not merely involve the turning of it into commodities; it also frequently involves capital actually remaking nature and its products biologically and physically. It has been observed, for instance, that 'A pre-capitalist nature is transformed into a specifically capitalist nature' (O'Connor 1994: 158) in the form of genetic changes in food crops, the destroying of biological diversity through extensive use of plantation forestry, and so on. The generative principle behind such transformations is the search by capital to lower costs, to create new markets and to reconfigure the productive use of diminished natural resources. The issue here is not whether 'nature' should be transformed. As Harvey (1996: 147) points out, 'What exists "in nature" is in a constant state of transformation'. Rather, the issue is ultimately about the preservation of a particular social order, than about preservation as such (Harvey 1996: 148).

It is important to view specific forms of production and consumption as articulated elements in a larger production unity – the mode of production in general (Marx 1973). *The nature of consumption under capitalism is inseparable from the nature of production.* It creates the material for consumption. It determines the manner of consumption. It creates the product in the form of a need. What is consumed and how it is consumed thus stem from the manner in which production is organised and carried out by the owners of the means of production. The raw materials that go into making goods and in the provision of services, for example, are fundamentally determined by the producers, not the end consumers. Similarly, the waste by-products of production and the refuse left over from consumption are ultimately determined in the production process itself, according to the dictates of private profit-making. If we are to understand consumption as a social relation, it is essential to consider both the objective developments underpinning the extension of consumption in capitalist society (i.e. the process of commodification), and the symbolic place of consumerist ideology as part of the capitalist realisation of surplus value (i.e. the production of meaning).

Resource colonisation and new market creation

The exploitation of the world's natural resources by the major transnational corporations is matched by expanding the world's 'needs' via consumerism. This will be considered in greater depth shortly. For now, the focus is on different ways in which capitalism as a system manifests in specific kinds of activities. For example, exploitation occurs through the direct appropriation of lands, plants and animals as 'property' (including intellectual property as in the case of patents). It also occurs through the displacement of existing systems of production and consumption by those that require insertion into the cash-buyer nexus, in other words, the purchase of goods and services as commodities.

Biopiracy and exploitation of indigenous lands

The great voyages of discovery and grand days of European imperialism (from around the late 1400s onwards) were times when the planet as a whole was carved up and plundered by the technologically dominant nations. Central to the colonial and imperialist projects has been resource colonisation (Robyn 2002). Around the world – in places such as North and South America, and Australia and New Zealand – indigenous territories were considered frontier lands. These were places that were (apparently) un-owned and under-utilised, and therefore open to exploitation. The prior ownership rights, interests and knowledges of indigenous inhabitants were, and in many cases still are, ignored or treated as irrelevant by both the (colonial) State and invading individuals. As discussed in Chapter 5, the phenomenon of biopiracy continues the exploitation of indigenous peoples even if land itself is not subject to expropriation.

Case study 6.1 Claiming ownership of indigenous plants

South (2007: 239) recounts an increasingly familiar story pertaining to biopiracy involving indigenous people:

> ... in 1986 Loren Miller obtained a US patent on a purported variety of an Amazonian vine also known as Ayahuasca. In 1994 the existence of this patent was discovered with some dismay by the body representing the organisations of indigenous peoples of the Amazon Basin. Ayahuasca has been cultivated and used for medicinal and religious purposes throughout this region for centuries so the evident question was how a stranger could 'discover' its properties and claim ownership? A long dispute followed with the patent first being overturned in 1999 but then reinstated in 2001. Future continuing dispute is likely.

In this way, indigenous knowledge and technology is ignored or subjected to rules and procedures foreign to their cultural, social and economic context.

Notwithstanding the intrusions and disputes generated by bio-prospectors, the appropriation of nature on indigenous lands continues in other ways beyond that of outright expropriation or biopiracy. For example, contemporary colonialist intervention has meant that even with treaties and land rights in places such as British Columbia and Alberta in Canada, governments and companies are free to exploit indigenous lands for timber and water resources (Rush 2002). In many cases there are clear instances of environmental racism, as evidenced in the systematic efforts by companies to exclude indigenous people from participation in decision-making processes (for example, by narrowly defining issues that can be raised in environmental impact statements) (Brook 2000; Rush 2002; Langton 1998).

The complete disregard for the physical and cultural well-being of indigenous people, and their connection to 'country', is evident in other ways as well. We might consider, for example, the indigenous homelands of the Tjarutja people at the site of Maralinga (located in South Australia). These lands were grossly affected by the British nuclear testing programme between 1955 and 1963.

Case study 6.2   Radioactive homelands

The British government, with the approval of Australian authorities, exploded seven nuclear bombs and conducted numerous other experiments and trials at Maralinga from the mid-1950s. This area was chosen because it was presumed to be uninhabited and provided for an easily secured area. The reality was that it was criss-crossed with dreamtime tracks used by the Tjarutja people. Attempts were made to forcibly remove the indigenous people from their lands, but it was clear that they continued to travel through contaminated lands. The lands and the people were violated, and the nuclear tests damaged their culture and their environment. Yet, due to the fact that information about the tests was classified as top secret it was decades before detailed knowledge about what had happened saw the light of day (White and Habibis 2005: 170–171).

When indigenous people have contested the power of corporations and nation-states to do certain things on their lands, they have frequently been met with coercive responses. Thus, in North America, 'Indian people who have challenged multinational corporate giants and the government through political activism in an effort to halt environmentally destructive projects on their lands have been criminalised and arrested to silence their claims' (Robyn 2002: 198). Indigenous people nevertheless insist that they ought to have decision-making powers and not simply be 'consulted' about decisions that affect themselves and their environments. Establishing tribal control over their own natural resources would mean being able to use their own indigenous knowledge and techniques to deal with environmental issues. Biopiracy, and corporate disrespect for indigenous beliefs and relationships to the land, undermine this possibility.

Bio-imperialism and the creation of new markets

Many of the contemporary environmental harms are related to how the basic means of life of humans is being reconstituted and reorganised through global systems of production. For example, the 'globalisation of food production and manufacture and the use of new technologies and chemicals in farming and food processing have created a variety of risks to humans, nonhuman animals, the environment and health' (Croall 2007: 206) and in many cases we still do not know the longer term effects of new developments in the food area. What is happening to food generally is symptomatic of how commodification is taking place vis-à-vis all aspects of human life and in all parts of the globe. The global political economy of genetically modified organisms (GMOs) provides a case in point.

According to New Zealand's Royal Commission on Genetic Modification (quoted in Walters 2004: 152), genetic modification can be defined as the use of genetic engineering techniques in a laboratory that involves:

(a) The deletion, multiplication, modification, or moving of genes within a living organism;
(b) The transfer of genes from one organism to another;
(c) The modification of existing genes or the construction of novel genes and their incorporation in any organism;
(d) The utilisation of subsequent generations or offspring of organisms modified by any of the activities described above.

The application of GM technologies to food production is perhaps one of the most publicly recognised, and fear-inspiring, uses of such technology (Croall 2007; Walters 2004, 2005). As indicated in Box 6.2, countries that have been reluctant to adopt GM crops have been subjected to intense pressures to do so.

Box 6.2   Zambia rejects GM crops

The promotion of GMOs by large transnational corporations has continued apace regardless of serious reservations being raised about significant potential risks to human health and safety, antibiotic immunity and contamination of the environment (Walters 2004). The rejection by Zambia, a Southern African landlocked country, of GM food brought to the foreground the efforts of hegemonic states, such as the United States, and monopolistic companies, namely the GM-producing corporations, to put pressure on countries worldwide to adopt GM food.

Zambia rejected the introduction of GM food on the basis of concern about potential harm to its population and biodiversity. As Walters (2005) details, grain is a cornerstone of Zambian society,

---

especially cassava and maize, and holds substantial social, political and cultural value that goes back thousands of years. In adopting a precautionary approach to GM food, Zambian authorities, with widespread popular support, were safeguarding the biological integrity of locally grown grains and the production independence of local grain growers. GM maize, for example, was considered harmful to human health and as potentially contaminating natural maize varieties. The Minister of Agriculture told Walters that:

> We are adopting the precautionary principle on GM food and until we have more accurate scientific facts that clearly show that it is safe, we will not introduce it into our environment ... I am wanting to explore the potential of our biodiversity before we destroy what we already freely have, what God has given us for free. How can we accept GMOs when I know that such technology could destroy our biodiversity, the possibilities of which are still unknown (Walters 2005: 29).

Huge pressures were exerted on Zambia to allow the introduction of GM crops. The US distributes food aid through the United Nations' World Food Programme, and this continues to contain GM maize. Economically, it is to the advantage of US farmers that surplus GM crops be distributed in this way (Walters 2005). In a range of political and media forums, US officials roundly criticised Zambia's stubborn resistance to the introduction of GM crops, and have manipulated aid funding and used research funding to try to promote GM technologies and crops.

In essence, food aid itself was being used to advance private business interests in the US by being so inextricably linked to the promotion of GM crops. The pressures on poor, developing countries to adopt GMOs has, in turn, been construed as being in contravention of international environmental law that is meant to safeguard the autonomy of biological diversity of individual nation states and to protect them from the exploitive and aggressive trade policies of powerful Western states (Walters 2005: 39).

The reason why GMOs are pursued so relentlessly is that their introduction and establishment is extremely profitable for powerful corporations. It also suits particular national economies that are the main source points for the production and distribution of GM crops. The prising open of new markets also means that excess GM crops that otherwise would put downward pressure on local prices can be offloaded overseas. Such is the case with US farming and its abundance of GM crops (Walters 2005).

Pressures to change production methods and consumption habits are generated by those who have the most to win in shifting global marketplaces. Specifically, in the case of GM food, the overwhelming majority of such food (and its accompanying fertilisers, seeds and herbicides) are produced by four chemical corporations – Monsanto, Syngenta, Du Pont and Bayer (see Walters 2005). These companies not only control GM crop production through share of market. They also control the GM technologies, built into the crops, through the use of patents. Under the guise of 'free trade', and with the support of the US and the World Trade Organisation, these companies are ruthless in their efforts to monopolise crop production around the globe. This is a form of bio-imperialism involving the further concentration of power, wealth and resources into fewer and fewer hands on a world scale.

Privatisation, commodification and consumption

Capital is constantly seeking new areas for investment and consumption in order to maintain and increase profit. A driving aspect of this process is to offset declining profit rates. Thus, every aspect of human existence is subject to transformation insofar as capital seeks to create new forms of consumption (e.g. fads, fashions) and the transformation of existing or potential use-values into exchange-values through commodification of all types of human activity and human requirements (e.g. water, food, entertainment, recreation). For example, what may have been formerly 'free' is now sold back to the consumer for a price (e.g. paying for things such as private music lessons or paying levies to private security firms or garbage collectors, when previously such services were offered as tax-funded, socialised services available at school and local neighbourhood levels).

Consumerism, as a materially 'lived' ideology, is thus the name given to a process in which certain habits of consumption are intertwined with the pursuit of profit. The process involves the transformation of the production of goods and services according to the dictates of exchange, rather than simply immediate use. It also involves the incorporation of certain kinds of consumption into the (over time, unconscious) routines of everyday life. The desire to consume, particularly in relation to satisfaction of basic human needs, is not the main issue. Rather, it is the structured patterns of consumption, and how these intertwine at an existential level to promote a deep desire to consume in particular ways (see below), that is the key question.

Importantly, the process is driven by private interests, rather than communal or State concerns (Bocock 1993). From a systemic perspective, the patterns of investment and the constitution of 'new' forms of consumption are endemic to the capital accumulation process. The privatisation of State services and goods is largely explainable in terms of the dynamics of capitalism to incorporate and subsume all parts of daily life into the web of accumulation (Mandel 1975; Jalee 1977). It is evident in the corporatisation of public institutions and in the direct transfer of such institutions into private hands (e.g. telephone, utilities, banks). Similarly, the introduction of user-pays as a form of cost recovery (e.g. medical and educational fees) represents steps toward the commodification of goods and services, which in turn lend themselves to further privatisation of provision over time.

The extension of the market for 'consumer' goods and services is historically based upon the massive extension of money wages, and changes in the working and social life of wage-labourers. The social determination of wages beyond that of simple physical subsistence engendered the rise of the 'consumer society' as we know it. This, in turn, has been linked to major transformations in the nature of the family as a unit of consumption. Thus, for example, the 'reproduction of the commodity of labour-power is increasingly achieved by means of capitalistically produced commodities and capitalistically organised and supplied services' (Mandel 1975: 391) in the form of pre-cooked meals, ready-made clothes, electrical household appliances and so on, which previously would have been produced by family members as immediate use-values. The movement of women in great numbers into the paid workforce further deepens the dependency of workers on mass produced 'household' commodities, and hence expanded capitalist reproduction. Similar trends are apparent in the sphere of recreation and leisure, where the cultural needs of workers are met through commercial enterprises and outlets.

The sphere of consumption has been dramatically altered under the force and persuasion of capitalistically produced commodities. Consumption plays a vital role in the realisation of surplus value. As such, emphasis is on continually expanding the quantities of consumer goods and services through creating new needs, and through ensuring the rapid turnover of commodities on the basis of planned obsolescence, fashion trends or accelerated technical innovation. This form of consumption is, in turn, sold back to the private individual as a form of 'freedom', one that requires a minimum of effort or conscious reflection.

In structural terms, the rationale behind consumption is not the meeting of human needs, or making the constitution and satisfaction of these a central question of politics (Deacon 1983). Rather, it is about meeting the needs of capital. Effectively, consumption has been put at the service of production, rather than vice versa. Gorz (1989: 114) describes the transition towards this relationship between production and consumption as follows:

> *Unlimited* maximum efficiency in the valorisation of capital thus demanded *unlimited* maximum *in*efficiency in meeting needs, and *unlimited* maximum wastage in consumption. The frontiers between needs, wishes, and desires needed to be broken down; the desire for dearer products of an equal or even inferior use value to those previously employed had to be created; what had merely been desirable had to be made necessary; wishes had to be given the imperious urgency of need.

The obvious implication of this relationship is for constant and escalating pressures on the world's non-renewable resources, huge waste of existing human and natural resources and potentials, major issues of disposal and clean-up, and a 'demonstration effect' which is distorting world production-consumption patterns (Bocock 1993; Szentes 1988).

The nature of work itself has had a major effect on consumption patterns (see Mandel 1975: 394). For example, statistics on the hours of work of full-time employees in Australia demonstrate that a large proportion of such workers are now working for longer hours (and, relatively speaking, less pay) than has been seen for several decades (see Buchanan *et al.* 1999). This fact alone suggests a greater reliance upon mass produced commodities and services to accommodate the physical needs of these workers. There is thus a structural imperative to engage in particular forms of consumption. These reinforce the reliance upon, and profitability of, capitalistically produced consumer goods and services. Even where specific workers are working less than may previously have been the case, there is no guarantee that their consumption patterns would vary to any remarkable degree from those around them (depending upon financial resources). This is due to the place of certain forms of consumption in broader cultural life.

Desire and alienation

Doing environmental harm may be construed as a 'pleasurable' activity insofar as pleasure provides the emotional subjective state within which harmful activities may be justified, not thought about, or neutralised in some way. In abstract formulation one might agree that 'not only is it profitable to be environmentally destructive (in the sense of mining, manufacturing cars, clearfelling forests), it *feels* good too (in the sense of purchasing a gold necklace, driving on the open road, looking at a table, chair, or house constructed from redwood, mahogany, mountain ash or the like) (Halsey 2004: 844, emphasis in original). Yet, this in and of itself implies too much agency, too much distance between the affective and the structural. It also makes little of the distinction between environmental harm stemming from production, and that related to consumption, although there is indeed a link between the two.

Pleasure and pleasure-seeking are themselves constructed through the prism of structural imperatives associated with the market. The sense of belonging and social integration 'takes place through the "seduction" of the market-place, through the mix of feeling and emotions generated by seeing, holding, hearing, testing, smelling, and moving through the extraordinary array of goods and services, places and environments that characterise contemporary consumerism...' (Macnaghten and Urry 1998: 24). Trying to achieve pleasure through consumption forms part of the basis of contemporary capitalist society. As such, consumption of this sort has to be understood as a *social* phenomenon with social causes and social contexts.

Today, consumption has dramatically transformed social identity, and it is not based simply upon need, but desires. The sheer volume of consumer goods and services has signalled a qualitative change in how humans see themselves and relate to others. Indeed, it has been argued that no longer is social identity derived first and foremost from one's position in the occupational structure. Rather, it is consumer goods and household patterns of consumption which are now seen as crucial markers of specific kinds of identity and social belonging (Bocock 1993). This needs some qualification, however. For example, consumption-in-practice is not shared equally; not everyone in the West, nor many people in the developing countries, have the same capacities to consume as do the affluent.

An example of the interface between production and consumption is found in the advertising industry, an industry which is worth many billions of dollars. The whole point of advertising is to ensure that what is produced is consumed. It is necessarily premised upon unlimited growth. This is both extensive and 'an intensive process as well, an expansion into life, culture, and the mind' (Athanasiou 1996: 43). Writing about the basically 'necessary' things we have today that were unnecessary just a short time ago (such as mosquito vacuums, mini jetskis and mini compressors to blow up bicycle tyres), Maxwell (2007: 98) talks about how retail firms make it so easy for ordinary consumers to be unsustainable. He points out that people assume we need to do certain things as part of the sustainability equation, but the current base of consumption is now way out of proportion to what is truly sustainable. What we feel we need is, of course, heavily influenced by things such as regular advertising flyers – 'there's the Canadian Tire flyer, singing its siren song of sweet temptation' (Maxwell 2007: 98).

Advertising represents the public face of 'consumerism'; whereas capitalisation and privatisation represent the underlying process of 'commodification' to which advertising bears a symbiotic relationship. It is increasingly more sophisticated and far reaching in its efforts to influence consumer buying patterns and desire for commodities. For example, an article in *Time* magazine described the ways in which companies and marketeers are searching for new and novel ways of promoting a product. Some of these include the use of designer smells to create optimal shopping environments, or the micro-targeting of consumers through building profiles of specific individuals by tracing their digital footprints across the Web (Time 1999). While the specific ways in which advertising affects audiences is an open question (we cannot assume that there is a one-to-one relationship between what advertisers advertise and what consumers consume), the weight of advertising in general delimits the apparent choices and decisions available to consumers (notwithstanding the active rejection of such 'choices' on the part of some people). Advertising 'works' (although to what extent, and precisely how, are subject to debate) – otherwise, it would not constitute the major industry it is today.

The social construction of need is not only related to the powerful influence of advertising on spending patterns and buyer preferences. It is also tied to the extension of consumer credit on a mass scale. This has facilitated the accelerated circulation of commodities and enhanced the realisation of surplus value for commodity producers. It allows the purchase of private consumer goods and services on a scale hitherto not possible. It also has a disciplining role vis-à-vis the workplace insofar as workers who buy commodities 'on credit' are thereby more conscious of their financial obligations and the importance of secure employment even in the face of deteriorating working conditions and declining wages. Consumerism is thus a materially embedded ideological reality. As such, it has become a mode of life that is inseparable from the sphere of production in many different ways, and continues to be shaped by and contingent upon innovation in the realms of technical production and financial services.

The conditions of labour under capitalism transforms human labour power into an external and alien force – in which the goals and purposes of capitalist production predominate. This production relationship has significance in other ways as well, which directly pertain to the sphere of consumption. For the alienation of workers from the production process, and the products of their labour, is also associated with a general devaluation of the human world in favour of the world of things (see Swingewood 1975: 99). Human beings increasingly are defined by what they possess, by the quantities of money they can amass. Under the system of private property, 'need' is structured around money, which in turn is linked to paid work. In order to increase satisfaction outside of the realm of production the primary goal becomes acquisition. This is seen not only as an objective dynamic of capital accumulation, but forms part of the subjective dimensions of existence under capitalism generally (see, especially, Marx 1975: 361). In the end, the production relationship is such that 'the worker is only permitted to have enough for him (sic) to live, and he is only permitted to live in order to have' (Marx 1975: 361). The growth in 'desire' for commodities matches the systemic pressures to deny any limits to growth generally. This is reinforced by the ways in which 'progress', 'success' and 'the good' are predominantly conceptualised and measured (see Gorz 1989: 120). There is, then, a certain coherency to the manner in which growth has become entrenched in the minds and hearts of many a private consumer, individual worker, economic planner and corporate boss.

Consumption and meeting consumer needs

It has been pointed out that 'the conversion of many former luxury goods into mass consumer goods generally leads to a systematic reduction in the quality of these commodities', and that furthermore there are constant pressures on capital to ensure rapid turn-over of commodities (through poor quality or constant marketing of 'innovative', 'new' commodities) in order to shorten the period of consumption (Mandel 1975: 394). While the quality and cost of some goods has no doubt improved over time (e.g. motor vehicles, computers), constant change over is encouraged through 'new model' campaigns and accelerated technological development, particularly in regards to micro-electronic devices. Meanwhile, other goods (such as food, water and clothing) are declining in quality as they are inserted into new forms of global mass production processes dominated by private corporations. Again, the pressures to consume are driven by capitalist imperatives to produce, and to realise the surplus value embodied in the commodity via consumer purchases. This precludes the notion that there can be the rational development of consumption under capitalism, one which is subordinated to different conceptions of human needs and collective interests (see Mandel 1975; Deacon 1983). For the system ultimately depends upon the generation of 'profitable' consumption, regardless of health, cultural or social consequences.

Where there is a monopoly situation in which the producer has exclusive rights to produce the commodity (as in the case of long-term contracts of supply), and where simultaneously the actions of the producer are not subject to close public scrutiny and review, there is less pressure on companies to provide a product that exceeds bare minimum quality and safety requirements. A culture of secrecy and decreased levels of public accountability are frequently intertwined with the notion of 'commercial confidentiality' (see Freiberg 1997). At the same time, efforts will be made to reduce costs associated with production.

If we take the case of water treatment as an illustration (see White 1998), this can be achieved by such measures as not investing in new equipment or plant technology (e.g. replacing water mains), and/ or by reducing the overall labour force while continuing to supply the same quantity of product (e.g. through employment of fewer maintenance workers). In the end, the 'consumer' loses out on at least two fronts. First, given the profit motive behind water supply and treatment, there is every likelihood that cost-cutting pressures at the point of production will lead to poorer quality in the commodity made available. The point of commodity production is not to produce a good, useful or quality product; it is to sell the commodity. If there exists a 'captive market' for the commodity, this reduces the impetus to improve the quality of the product. Secondly, there may be an increase in prices for the supplied commodity (perhaps justified in terms of the necessity to put more money into new technology, etc.), insofar as pricing controls are driven by profit considerations of the company, rather than actual costs of production per se. Notions of 'best practice' and more 'efficient' production methods are in essence a cover for the underlying rationale – which is to make money for the private provider. Another dimension to questions of price is that concerns about the quality of the main product also open the way for increased sale of alternative sources of water (i.e. bottled water), a process which further penalises consumers generally on the basis of capacity to pay.

Box 6.3 Environmental harm, water and transnational corporations

Water is vital to human life. Yet, thousands of human lives are lost each day, each week, and each month, due to inadequate supply and the poor quality of drinking water in many parts of the world today. There are three important developments in relation to drinking water: the transnational privatisation of water and the concentration of control over water resources into private hands; the trend toward the 'profitable' use and management of water; and the presence of toxic delivery systems (in this instance, related to privatisation processes) that ultimately pose major threats to the health of water users in a variety of different ways.

There are now privatised water concessions in cities on every continent (see Boykoff and Sand 2003; Barlow and Clarke, 2003; Beder 2006). In every region of the world, the great majority of these concessions are run by only three giant global corporations, namely Viola Universal (previously known as Vivendi and Generales des Eaux), Suez (also known as Ondeo) and RWE (which also purchased Thames Water). In the past fifteen years these corporations have assumed control of the water supplied to millions and millions of people worldwide (see Whelan and White 2005).

Under present tendencies of the global capitalist economy, resources essential to human needs, such as water, are increasingly being sold as commodities. Thus, drinking water has, in recent years, been increasingly valued for its 'exchange-value' rather than 'use-value'. It is not the usefulness of water that counts, but its sale as a commodity. The selling of water as a commodity means that it is first and foremost treated as a source of profit. The actual scarcity of fresh, clean water means that there are lucrative profits to be made by privatising water (and water-intensive industries), and delivering it only to those who can pay for it.

In poor areas where privatisation has been implemented millions of people have been cut off because they cannot afford to pay water bills that often make up 30 per cent of their incomes. For example, as many as 10 million South Africans have had their water cut off for various periods of time since 1994, according to a 2002 national survey by Municipal Services (Pauw 2003: 3). In effect, the water companies are pillars of a user-pays policy that imposes high rates with little concern over people's ability to pay. These rates are enforced by water cutoffs, despite evidence of serious dangers to people's health that these actions create (Marsden 2003: 3).

As pointed out by the Public Citizen Organisation (2004) in the US, the private control of drinking water generally leads to:

• Higher water bills for consumers and supply cut-offs due to rate hikes;
• Reduced water quality;
• Reduced local control;
• Less accountability to local citizens and local community needs;
• Weak regulation and oversight leading to lower quality service;
• Complex contract disputes (such as legal suits by companies for 'lost profits').

The conjunction of these factors has enormous implications for the health status of diverse populations, in many different parts of the world.

To take just one illustrative example, we can consider what happened in Canada at the beginning of the new millennium. In 2000, seven people died and 2,700 were poisoned in the town of Walkerton, Ontario. This has been blamed on privatisation of testing, in which the town's water testing for Esherichia coli was outsourced to a local firm, which failed to do the testing (Bond and Bakker 2001; Snider 2002; Christensen 2002). The initial cause of the outbreak was triggered by heavy rains and flooding during which livestock waste (E. coli is found in the gut and intestine of cattle) from nearby farms contaminated the town's groundwater supply. The incident has been attributed to a number of specific faults – such as inadequate monitoring and operation of surface catchments, deficient chlorination practice, inadequate regulatory oversight, insufficient operator training, and lack of corporate commitment to safety. But the main problem was the privatisation of segments of Ontario's public water system, which included the disbanding of specialist teams responsible for collecting and testing water supplies (Snider 2002).

Many of these kinds of incidents and events were and are preventable. In most cases they are attributable to changes in the tariffs placed upon drinking water (issues of access and affordability), changes in the philosophy of water management (from public need to commercial profitability), changes in operational practices (linked to corporatisation and privatisation, and away from structures that allow greater public scrutiny and accountability), and changes in quality control practices.

The question of distributive justice is also linked to capacity to pay. It has been argued that low income consumers (predominantly the poor and working poor) get less or worse quality goods and services than people with bigger disposable incomes. This is due to factors such as an inability to buy in quantity, distance from cheaper shopping districts, being forced to plan spending over short time periods, and having access to only the most expensive forms of credit (Williams 1977). There are direct parallels between the unequal distribution of consumption and the unequal distribution of exposure to environmental risks, such as location of toxic waste sites (Harvey 1996). For the people, invariably poor and often minority communities, the parallels are basically the same. And they suffer the social disempowerment and health problems generated by capitalist organisation of production and consumption in each case.

The distributional aspects of consumption relate to not only the divide between rich and poor. They also bear a relation to different sectors and forms of consumption. Consumption as a structural process can be thought of as comprising two distinct spheres: business consumption; and private consumption (on the key departments of capitalist production, see Onimode 1985; Mandel 1975). A large part of consumption in society takes place in the interchange between different sectors of capital. The scale of consumption is quite different in this instance, as is the primary purpose of consumption. Whereas private consumption generally relies upon aggregate consumption by large numbers of individuals, business consumption generally involves sales based upon large quantities sold in large allotments to a small number of clients. Firms rely upon other companies as the suppliers of 'raw materials' which are then 'consumed' for production purposes by the consuming firm.

Consumption in this sense refers to something that is consumed in order to make something of exchange-value. Farmers who deliver to their cows particular kinds of feed are both consumers (of feed additives and grain products) and producers (of particular kinds of meat, or dairy products). Aquaculture involving the feeding of salmon (on frozen pilchards imported from overseas) likewise embodies this dual relationship. The specific character of corporate consumption is dictated by the larger transformations occurring in particular industries. For example, there have been major transformations in the meat industry, with important health and environmental side-effects. As Franklin (1999: 168) points out:

> Larger agribusinesses involving more intensified production and utilizing cheaper high protein animal by-product feeds, in combination with deregulated, centralised and continuous production-line slaughtering and processing plants, have measurably raised the risk of meat contamination. This has resulted in significant increases in cases of food poisoning and reduced consumer confidence.

How 'consumption' takes place in the production process thus has major consequences for how consumption takes place for the private individual consumer.

Mad cow disease (bovine spongiform encephalopathy), and the death of pilchards off the southern coast of mainland Australia, provide graphic illustrations of environmental harm directly associated with these particular kinds of consumption–production relationships. However, the 'harm' in this instance is not perceived as 'consumer' harm for the *producer* as such – unless the productive activity (meat farming, fish farms) is affected directly. For the producer/consumers the basic issue is production efficiency and the realisation of surplus value through private consumption. If allegations about aspects of the former affect the latter, then changes will be foisted upon a particular company or industry. If the connection between a particular environmental or health issue and a particular production process is not rendered an issue of public concern, then, regardless of scientific evidence or small-scale consumer complaints, there is little impetus to change methods of production which enhance the surplus-value extraction process.

Licit and illicit markets

The search for profit takes different forms. It can involve extending commodification processes into new areas of human life. It can involve the extension of patent regimes into new regions and new applications. It can involve engaging in activities that bring the greatest return relative to inputs and market opportunities. The dynamics of the profit motive also intrinsically lead to corrupt, unethical, criminal and deviant behaviour.

When it comes to environmental crime, profit-making is frequently made possible and/or enhanced through the overlapping relationship between licit and illicit markets, and the close connection between legal and illegal practices. A licit market is one that is State-regulated, open to public scrutiny and based upon legal activities. An illicit market is one that is unregulated, untaxed and is part of a subterranean or 'black' economy. Licit and illicit markets basically share the same practices, the same people and are driven by the same economic imperatives. Illegal activities can easily sit within the parameters of a licit market, either on the fringes or as a central part of that market, depending upon the nature of the commodity. This is illustrated in the following case studies.

Case study 6.3   Illegal logging

There is often overlap between legal and illegal logging operations. For example, commercial-scale illegal logging in Indonesia is widespread and involves a range of actors. The illegal activity of greatest concern in the province of Papua 'occurs in areas where logging is not permitted (e.g. watershed protection forests, protected areas) and is linked to companies with licenses to log areas nearby. Those companies may carry out the logging themselves, subcontract to smaller local companies, or simply buy logs without obtaining appropriate papers to demonstrate legality' (Akella and Cannon 2004: 16).

Case study 6.4   Illegal wildlife exports

The smuggling of wildlife across national borders has the potential to threaten the viability of endangered species, whether flora or fauna, as well as to provide a potential vehicle for the introduction of pests

---

and diseases into formerly unaffected areas. It has been argued that one way in which to effectively control the movements of creatures across regions is to allow commercial export of wildlife. However, the experience where legalised trade is allowed has been that this opens up opportunities for forging permits and other documentation, as well as other types of enabling activity. For instance, 'opening up a legal export trade in captive-bred birds would provide opportunities for laundering wild-caught birds, and concealing rare species of similar appearance' (Halstead 1992: 8).

Case study 6.5   Lobster poaching

The interface between legal and illegal practices, players and purchasers in the lobster industry means that a hidden economy flourishes. In the Atlantic provinces of Canada, for example, sellers and purchasers of illegal lobsters engage in a win–win situation for themselves, but that is to the disadvantage of governments in terms of tax revenue. Thus, 'outlaw poachers enter into alliances with hotels, restaurants, community groups, and private citizens to dispose of their illegal catches, and business poachers sell their illegal catches through the normal distributors and retailers. These arrangements amount to an underground economy, in that restaurants and hotel operators, for example, buy lobsters cheap from outlaw poachers and sell them at a greater profit. Lobster pounds and fish companies purchase lobsters from business poachers on a cash-only basis without providing receipts' (McMullan and Perrier 2002: 710). Profits are there to be made from activities that span the legal and illegal divide.

Part of the success of business done at the licit/illicit interface is that it can embody several different types of organisational relationship and entrepreneurial activity. That is, environmental crime can involve large enterprises, which sub-contract out work to smaller operators, as well as allowing space for private criminal outfits of a more modest size. The nature of environmental crime, as indicated in the case studies, lends itself to activities that each in their own right may be relatively discrete in impact, but that collectively can generate great harm. Or, it may be organised on a much larger scale, equivalent to assembly-line production methods.

For example, illegal fishing may involve huge factory-ships that operate on the high seas, and which process thousands of tons of fish at any one time. Alternatively, it may be organised around dozens of smaller vessels, each of which is contracted to provide a catch that ultimately brings reward to the originating contractor. In other words, illegal production can be organised according to the economies of scale (e.g. factory ships) or the economies of scope (e.g. small independent fishers). In each case, however, there has to be a link to legitimate markets (e.g. for abalone, for lobsters, for logs) for the value of the commodity to be realised in dollar terms. In each case, as well, the damage is manifest in phenomenon such as over-fishing and destruction of habitat that, in turn, affect subsequent market prices for the commodity in question. Scarcity is a major motivator for illegal as well as legal forays into particular kinds of harvesting and production activity. Field (1998: 84) makes the point that:

> It is no longer sufficient to assume, as did the writers of our environmental laws, that environmental risks come only from major sources. Instead, in the same way that textile and shoe companies have contracted out to independent sweatshop operators, major industrial sectors increasingly contract out the dirty and toxic operations to small contractors who are often least able to handle these toxic chemicals safely. Electroplating companies or computer component manufacturers which often use extremely toxic chemicals can exist literally in someone's garage.

These observations are important not only from the point of view of scale and scope of environmental crime. They also pertain to the feasibility of engaging in particular crimes in ways that reflect the specific context for its commission. For example, the nature of offender groups has implications for the visibility of the activity and its capacity to go under the radar of regulatory agencies. In the case of fishing, for instance, the sheer number of operators, the distances involved, the availability of isolated spots in which to trade or to fish, the availability of fishing gear and other basic instruments of the crime mean that pecuniary benefits may well outweigh the threat of being caught and punished. As mentioned, the connection between legal and illegal activities also serves to disguise or obscure the criminal nature of the environmental harm from a regulatory point of view.

Moreover, as demonstrated in cases such as the lobster industry in Canada, there may be strong cultural support and popular engagement in activities that are at a formal level illegal (McMullan and Perrier 2002). Traditions of hunting and fishing that have become embedded in local communities and cultures can thus facilitate the continued transgression of environmental and criminal laws.

Nor should we underestimate the impact of poverty, unemployment and disadvantage on the ability of businesses to draw upon a ready source of exploitable labour. Illegal fishing and logging, and harmful forms of industrial production and disposal of waste, involve layers of workers – some of whom benefit substantially by their engagement in illegal activity, others of whom gain bare subsistence income. The effect of social inequality is such that those who live and work in the most atrocious and harm-producing conditions do so whether such practices and conditions are legal or illegal (see for example, Pellow 2004). From the point of view of economic well-being and life prospects, what counts is the work that is available not the legal content of that work. If trawling for fish (a traditional task) translates into a product destined for illicit markets, then so be it. The activity is the same, whether defined as legal or illegal, and in the end it is the income that matters to those who have no other means of subsistence. Business operators who promise cash-producing activities that economically benefit individuals and communities in desperate circumstances, thus have easily exploitable labour power with which to make their profits.

System contradiction and limits

The destructive relation of capitalism to the environment surfaces in the form of a basic contradiction between economy and ecology. The main elements of this contradiction have been described by Foster (2007: 9–10) as follows:

- The *treadmill of production* – capitalism necessarily and constantly increases the scale of the throughput of energy and raw materials as part of the quest for profit and accumulation (e.g. putting pressure on the earth's absorptive capacity);

- The *second contradiction of capitalism* – capitalism undermines the human and natural conditions of production on which economic advancement ultimately rests (e.g. removing forests creates scarcity);

- The *metabolic rift* – capitalism creates a rift between society and nature and in so doing severs basic processes of natural reproduction (e.g. ecological sustainability is made impossible).

Foster (2007) goes on to describe the necessity of metabolic restoration, a process that must be based upon sustainable production. This is not possible under capitalism. Thus social tensions and ecological crisis are inevitably outcomes of the dominant mode of production globally.

Conclusion: where to from here?

This chapter has provided a brief overview of the reasons why capitalism is the culprit when it comes to understanding the nature of environmental harm on a global level. This is well summarised in the following passage:

> ... the fundamental problem is that of unrelenting capital accumulation and the extraordinary asymmetrics of money and political power that are embedded in that process. Alternative modes of production, consumption, and distribution as well as alternative modes of environmental transformation have to be explored if the discursive spaces of the environmental justice movement and the theses of ecological modernisation are to be conjoined in a programme of radical political action. This is fundamentally a class project, whether it is exactly called that or not, precisely because it entails a direct challenge to the circulation and accumulation of capital which currently dictates what environmental transformations occur and why (Harvey 1996: 401).

Future work in this area could be directed at more detailed and sustained analysis of who is doing what and why. Specifically, and firstly, analysis is needed of how global capitalist institutions engage in environmental crime as a matter of course, and how the institutional forms of capitalism have changed over time.

Secondly, as the global mode of production has changed (and here we need more investigation of the techniques and relations of production), so too, the types and extent of harm perpetrated in and through the capitalist mode of production have changed.

Criminality is thus grounded in substantive changes in production and consumption, and this needs ongoing scrutiny.

Thirdly, the relationship between national bourgeoisies and transnational corporations, between local élites of failed States and company bosses in Western countries, and between capitalism and organised crime/corruption, also emerge as issues of concern.

Finally, there is a need to keep shifting the analysis between considerations of structure (e.g. systemic features of the global political economy) and considerations of agency (e.g. decision-making and action taken within institutions), and in so doing to ground the more abstract pronouncements concerning economy, ecology and the human experience in concrete case studies and systematic field research.

Part III
Responding to Environmental Harm

Chapter 7

Environmental law enforcement

It is essential to respond to environmental harms, whatever their specific nature, origins and dynamics. How best to do this is always going to be contentious however. Nevertheless, there is place for a wide spectrum of interventions, ranging from persuasion through to use of criminal prosecution. Environmental law enforcement will become increasingly important as the incidence and consciousness of environmental harm grows.

Introduction

There are three main approaches to the analysis and study of environmental criminalisation and regulation (see Figure 7.1). One is to chart existing environmental legislation and to provide a sustained socio-legal analysis of specific breaches of law, the role of law enforcement agencies, and the difficulties and opportunities of using criminal law against environmental offenders (del Frate and Norberry 1993; Gunningham *et al.* 1995; Heine *et al.* 1997; Situ and Emmons 2000). This is the key focus of this chapter, with a particular interest in the role of the police in environmental law enforcement.

Socio-legal approach

- Emphasis on use of criminal law as presently constituted.
- Attempts to improve quality of investigation, law enforcement, prosecution and conviction on illegal environmentally-related activity.

Regulatory approach

- Emphasis on social regulation, using many different means, as the key mechanism to prevent and curtail environmental harm.
- Attempts to reform existing systems of production and consumption through adoption of constellation of measures, including enforced self-regulation and bringing non-government groups directly into the regulatory process.

Social action approach

- Emphasis on need for fundamental social change, and to challenge the hegemony of transnational capital and dominant nation-states in setting the environmental agenda.
- Attempts to engage in social transformation through emphasis on deliberative democracy and citizen participation, and support for the radical as well as other wings of the social movements.

Figure 7.1 Responding to environmental harm
Source: White 2008a.

The main emphasis in the socio-legal approach is how to best utilise existing legal and enforcement mechanisms to protect environments and creatures within specific environments (e.g. illegal fishing). For those who view environmental harm in a wider lens than that provided by criminal law, this approach has clear limitations. In particular, the focus on criminal law, regardless of whether or not the analyst is critical or confirming, offers a rather narrow view of 'harm' that can obscure the ways in which the State facilitates destructive environmental practices and environmental victimisation. In other words, a strictly legal definition of harm belies the enormous harms that are legal and 'legitimate' but that nevertheless negatively impact on people, environments and animals (Lynch and Stetesky 2003).

A second approach to environmental harm shifts the focus away from criminal sanctions as such and toward regulatory strategies that might be used to improve environmental performance. Here the main concern is with varying forms of 'responsive regulation' (Ayres and Braithwaite 1992; Braithwaite 1993) and 'smart regulation' (Gunningham and Grabosky 1998). This approach is the subject of discussion in Chapter 8 and is also relevant to Chapter 9.

In the third approach, writers tend to be more sceptical of the previous perspectives and developments, arguing that many key elements of such strategies dovetail with neo-liberal ideologies and practices (especially the trend towards deregulation of corporate activity) in ways that will not address systemic environmental degradation (Snider 2000). Rather than focusing on the notions of effectiveness, efficiency and the idea of win–win regulatory strategies, this approach is concerned with social transformation (Chunn *et al.* 2002). As such, it proceeds from the view that critical analysis must be counter-hegemonic to dominant hierarchical power relationships, and that present institutional arrangements require sustained critique and systemic change. This will be discussed further in Chapter 10.

The main interest of this chapter is with environmental law enforcement. This is especially so in regards to the role and activities of police in regards to interventions pertaining to environmental crime. Environmental harm, as construed by law enforcement agencies, is basically about the violation of national and international laws put in place to protect the environment. What is legally deemed to be 'bad' or criminal, therefore, is the main point of attention, whether this is illegal trade in wildlife and plants, or pollution of the air, water and land.

The chapter begins by discussion of the State's general response to environmental harm. It is rare that the State uses coercion solely or even as the key lever of compliance to environmental laws. Rather, a wide variety of measures are used, frequently in conjunction with each other, as a means to deal with environmental harm. Likewise, there is a range of agencies that are assigned the task of ensuring compliance and enforcing the law vis-à-vis environmental protection. Our particular interest, however, is with police as a criminal justice agency, and the increasing role that police are being called upon to play in this area.

Prosecuting environmental crime

In the legal framing of environmental crime, the nature of the harm is generally expressed in the following kinds of terms (Situ and Emmons 2000: 3):

> An unauthorised act or omission that violates the law and is therefore subject to criminal prosecution and criminal sanctions. This offence harms or endangers people's physical safety or health as well as the environment itself. It serves the interests of either organisations – typically corporations – or individuals.

Such crime violates existing environmental laws, and the victims can include people and the environment. It has also been pointed out that although corporations are the chief environmental offenders, other organisations (e.g. criminal combines or government agencies) as well as individuals can also commit environmental crimes (Situ and Emmons 2000).

Different countries have different laws and frequently quite different approaches to dealing with environmental crime. It is important, therefore, that socio-legal study be able to drill down to national and sub-national legislative and juridical particulars. Case law and legislation, as well as institutions and institutional processes, will vary depending upon whether one is talking about the US, Canada, individual member states of the European Union, Russia, India, Argentina, Ecuador, Angola or China (see for example, Boyd 2003; Burns and Lynch 2004). Detailed exploration of one jurisdiction can provide useful concepts and benchmarks by which to compare environmental laws cross-nationally. There are nonetheless concerns and issues that overlap jurisdictional differences and these are worth noting in socio-legal analysis as well.

For example, in many jurisdictions the primary regulatory authority for the control of environmental crime is the Environmental Protection Authority (EPA) (or equivalent: for example, the Environment Agency in the UK). These can operate at federal or State/provincial levels and their mandate generally includes such things as:

- Regulating environmental crime through administration of environmental protection legislation;
- Educating the community about environmental issues;
- Monitoring and researching environmental quality;
- Reporting on the state of the environment to State/provincial or national legislature and other relevant bodies.

Implementation of this mandate includes protecting and conserving the natural environment, promoting the sustainable use of natural capital, ensuring a clean environment and reducing risks to human health.

In countries such as Australia environmental protection is generally wrapped around notions of 'sustainable development'. This basically refers to the idea that economic activity can be carried out in ways that are sustainable environmentally into the future. The economy is central to this approach. Alternative ways of framing issues, such as recourse to concepts such as 'ecological sustainability', would lead to very different ways of producing, consuming and exchanging resources. Nevertheless, some notional adherence to environmental protection is a major plank in most Western governments' policy and legislative governance frameworks today.

The core principles relating to sustainable development in Australia have been identified as the precautionary principle; intergenerational and intragenerational equity; and the protection of biological diversity (Brunton 1999). In assessing whether or not governments are, indeed, engaging in sustainable development, they can be evaluated on the basis of how well they adhere to these basic principles. Even in the limited terms of sustainable development, however, criticism has often been laid that government action is inadequate, infrequent and inappropriate given the importance of the issues and the state of the environment generally (see for example, Brunton 1999). Government departments in general are ill informed, slow to act and fail to incorporate environmental principles into core business. Moreover, definitional issues and debates over specific policy (as in determining when and how to enact the precautionary principle) are accompanied by little concern to protect and conserve across the board. Selective enforcement and compliance activity seems to prevail.

This is not surprising given the economic imperatives that are at the core of sustainable development as an ideology and practice. The continuing degradation of the environment is also linked to the broad regulation and enforcement framework itself. Thus, there is preference for education, promotion and self-regulation (with limited success) rather than directive legislation and active enforcement and prosecution (Brunton 1999). For example, Environment Australia, as the lead agency in regards to contraventions of federal environmental and heritage legislation, states that to achieve its compliance and enforcement objectives, it uses a range of flexible and targeted measures to promote self-regulation (Environment Australia 2007).

'Compliance' means the state of conformity with the law. Agencies can usually try to secure compliance through two types of activity:

Promotion

- Communication (e.g. environmental registry);
- Publication of information (e.g. technical information);
- Consultation with parties affected by the Act;
- Creation of environmental codes of practice and guidelines;
- Promotion of environmental audits.

Enforcement

- Inspection to verify compliance;
- Investigation of violations;
- Measures to compel compliance without resorting to formal court action, such as directions by authorised enforcement officers, warnings, ticketing, and environment protection compliance orders by enforcement officers;
- Measures to compel compliance through court action, such as injunctions, prosecution, court orders upon conviction, and civil suit for recovery of costs.

The regulatory apparatus of the State, therefore, relies upon remedies such as administrative measures, civil proceedings and criminal prosecution as the ways in which to foster and enforce conformity to existing environmental laws.

Environment Australia (2007), for example, provides an outline of what it sees as the appropriate criteria to guide how the State ought to intervene in matters pertaining to suspected contraventions of Commonwealth (that is, federal) environment and heritage legislation:

- Objectives of the relevant legislation and the specific penalty provisions;
- Seriousness of the harm caused by the alleged contravention, both to other people and to the environment or cultural heritage;
- The level of malice or culpability of the suspect – was the contravention intentional, reckless, negligent, or a mistake;
- Whether the suspect has a history of prior contraventions;
- Whether the suspect has cooperated with authorities when the contravention was detected;
- The cost to the Commonwealth or general community of the contravention;
- The commercial value of the contravention to the suspect, the time elapsed since the contravention;
- The standard of evidence that has been collected;

- The likelihood of the contravention continuing or being repeated;
- The prevalence of the type of contravention;
- The likely public perception of the breach and the manner with which it is dealt;
- The most appropriate response to ensure an effective deterrent against continuing contravention or contravention by others;
- The cost of the proposed response option compared to the benefits of that option;
- Whether the proposed response option could be counter-productive in terms of maximising compliance with legislation; and
- Whether the use of the response option in a specific case would create a desirable precedent.

Jurisdictions such as Canada have also incorporated into legislation the circumstances under which mandatory prosecution of offenders is warranted; how and when to use such provisions is, however, a perennial issue for many regulators. This is because the mandate of most environmental protection agencies is not only to enforce compliance through use of criminal prosecutions, but to forge strategic alliances and working partnerships with industries, local governments and communities in support of environmental objectives. Often these are framed in terms of economic, and perhaps, social, objectives as well.

The multiple demands on environmental protection agencies from different sections of government, business and community, and the varied tasks in which they participate, may lead to a dilution of their enforcement capacities and activities. A review of the enforcement and prosecution guidelines of the department of environmental protection of Western Australia, for example, made a series of interesting and provocative observations (Robinson 2003):

> In summary, the Guidelines were found to be largely similar to those published in other states, but the language and tone could lead to an interpretation that the role of enforcement was de-emphasised in the Department's overall approach and that, in particular, the barriers to prosecution were overemphasised compared to the benefits (p. 3).

> While simple comparisons with other states can be misleading, the population based pro rata prosecution rate under the Environmental Protection Act 1986 (and indeed the rate of other punitive enforcement measures) appears to be below that which

> could be expected, drawing on the experience in the larger States, of what constitutes effective enforcement (p. 4).

> Scarcity of resources are recognised by all parties as providing a particular challenge to achieving significant improvement and this has been borne in mind in conducting the review (p. 4).

The review acknowledges the complexities of environmental regulation, including the central place of 'ecologically sustainable development' as a guiding philosophy for intervention. Regulation must be based upon cooperation, as well as use of coercive measures. Nevertheless, the review highlighted the importance of a 'bottom line' when it comes to compliance with environmental laws and rules.

> 'Speak softly and carry a big stick' is an appropriate aphorism for today's environmental regulator, but to be effective there must be certainty that the big stick can and will be used and the how, why and where of its use. It is the anticipation of enforcement action that confers the ability to deter (Robinson 2003: 11).

Accordingly, Robinson (2003: 23) argued that prosecution ought to be an equal partner in the enforcement tool box, and should be neither the first nor the last resort, but the appropriate response to a particular set of circumstances.

While Western Australia has attempted to change its enforcement culture by emphasising that *prosecution is an enforcement tool* to be used where appropriate and not only as a last resort, other states within Australia have relied less on the big stick than on different ways in which to undertake environmental prosecution. For instance, the state of Victoria has introduced 'alternative sentencing mechanisms' that allow the court to order a person to publicise the offence, to carry out specified projects for the restoration or enhancement of the environment and to carry out a specified environmental audit of the activities carried on by the person. It has been observed that alternative sentencing has been a success story insofar as those worst affected are compensated through action directed back into their local community.

> It may be that a defendant's (compulsory) contribution to an environmental project will also help to repair relationships (between the defendant and the community) damaged by loss

of amenity or more serious pollution events. Defendants and the community alike prefer to see the penalty directed into specific environmental projects, rather than disappearing into the mysterious pot that is 'consolidated revenue'. There can be no doubt that the publication order has a powerful deterrent effect, both specific (who would want to go through the ignominy again?) and general. There are many more readers of daily or weekly press than there are readers of EPA's annual reports. Those readers of *The Age*, or *The Herald Sun*, or the local newspaper well see strong evidence of an active environmental watchdog. Community confidence is given a boost (Martin 2005: 41).

Meanwhile, in the state of South Australia, 'civil penalties' have been introduced for lower breaches of the Environmental Protection Act (see Martin 2005). The perceived benefits from this are that it provides for more timely responses to the less serious contraventions plus the greater protection of the environment through the application of a lower burden of proof and efficiency of penalty application. Part of the appeal of this system is that it shifts the onus for calculating the penalty from the court to the enforcement authority (in this case, the EPA).

To illustrate the kinds of matters that come before the courts it is useful to consider the following examples of Prosecutions under the Environmental Protection Act 1970 in Victoria (see Jackson 2003).

Case study 7.1 Offensive odour

On 5 August 2002 at the Geelong Magistrates' Court, Shell Refining (Australia) Pty Ltd pleaded guilty to one charge of breach of license for the discharge of offensive odour beyond the boundary of its premises, contrary to section 27(2) of the Environmental Protection Act. The charge related to odours investigated by EPA Officers in the Corio residential area. The odours emanated from a waste water treatment plant and waste pits operated by the defendant at its Corio premises, and was described by the two investigating officers as the strongest they had ever detected. The defendant was convicted, and ordered to pay AUS$36,500 to the City of Greater Geelong for the completion of an environmental project, and EPA's costs of AUS$16,620. Maximum Penalty – A fine of AUS$240,000.

Case study 7.2 Dumping of waste

On 9 September 2002 at the Melbourne Magistrates' Court, Walter Construction Group Limited pleaded guilty to two charges under section 27A(2)(a) of the Environment Protection Act. The prosecution arose from the dumping of construction waste that came from works undertaken during the Docklands Infrastructure Project. The waste was dumped alongside and to some extent into the Moonee Ponds Creek in the Docklands precinct. Although the dumping activity occurred as a single, continuing course of conduct over nearly four months, two charges were laid because the offence period spanned the date on which the charge become an indictable offence, and the maximum penalty increased from AUS$40,000 to $500,000. The Court was told that about 90 per cent of the dumping occurred during the summary period. Charges were also pending against two other parties allegedly involved in the incident and, as part of its plea in mitigation, the defendant undertook to assist the EPA in those proceedings. No conviction was imposed, and the defendant was fined AUS$10,000, was ordered to pay AUS$10,000 to the Docklands Authority for an environmental project, and to pay EPA's costs of AUS$9,229.75. Maximum Penalty – A fine of AUS$20,000 for the first charge and a fine of AUS$500,000 for the second charge.

Case study 7.3 Storing of hazardous chemicals

On 4 December 2002 at the Dandenong Magistrates' Court, Miatech Pty Limited pleaded guilty to the charge of contravening a Notifiable Chemical Order, which prohibited the storing, handling, transporting and use of polychlorinated biphenyls (PCBs) without an Environmental Improvement Plan (EIP) approved by the EPA. The charge arose after the discovery of PCBs in approximately 4000 litres of waste oil at the premises of Master Waste Pty Ltd. Miatech was identified as having provided the contaminated waste oil, which had formerly been used in electrical transformers. No conviction was imposed, and the company was placed on an undertaking to be of good behaviour for 12 months with a special condition to pay AUS$1000 into the Court Fund. It was also ordered to pay EPA's costs of AUS$4,100. Maximum Penalty – A fine of AUS$240,000.

How regulation is constructed by governments, and how enforcement in particular is carried out in practice, is contingent upon what is occurring in the wider political economic context. It is also shaped by the nature of the offences, and offenders, themselves.

Limitations of criminal prosecution

One of the major stumbling blocks in using the 'big stick', much less other instruments in the law enforcement tool box, has been the difficulty in establishing liability in certain types of cases. To illustrate this, we can consider the banning of fishing in Sydney due to contamination of the Port Jackson waterways.

Recent years have seen high level of dioxins in the waterways of Sydney Harbour (see Chapter 4). The main sources of the dioxins were areas around Port Jackson that were used as industrial production sites for many years, including chemical plants, which typically contaminated the waterways through their industrial activities. The chemical plants were closed down in the mid 1980s.

For the actual originators of the harm, there has been no financial penalty for the harm they have caused or contributed to. This is so for several reasons. First, from the point of view of liability, the corporate form allows for 'no one' to be held responsible for the actions of a company that has been taken over by an even bigger corporate fish. It is already difficult to secure meaningful convictions for corporate wrongdoing due to the complications surrounding the status of corporations as legal persons, and how corporate crime tends to be socially defined as less harmful (see Chapter 6). In the context of company succession, over time, then the problem becomes even more difficult when it comes to assigning responsibility. This is further compounded when successive corporations are larger and more powerful than previous business formations.

In the end, the 'polluter-pays' principle only applies where the polluter can be found, and has legal standing. The issue has been too hard for the State government to resolve in this particular instance. Accordingly, the focus of government attention has been on the emergent problems of pollution in Sydney Harbour rather than the originating forces that created the problem in the first place. Action is taken, but the targets are those who are presently engaged in productive activity in the Harbour (i.e. the fishers), not those who produced the harm for these producers. The land around Homebush Bay remains in private hands, but the responsibility for the lands somehow evades questions of who ought to do what in addressing the issues of toxicity and pollution.

There are potential courses of action that could be taken in this instance to ensure prosecution of offenders. As recent work in environmental forensics demonstrates, there are ways in which to establish liability, even in cases that are removed in time and that involve multiple players.

> Certainly, it is not enough to find the pathways that chemicals have taken through the environmental media, nor enough to characterise the offending chemicals. In order to connect those findings to an existing party and to argue effectively that the party is responsible for paying some or all of the response cost incurred, the scientists and legal specialists also need to define the universe of past owners, occupants, generators, transporters, and/or arrangers. They need to be able to link the contaminants and the site conditions today somehow with the activities of the past (Brookspan *et al.* 2007: 24).

Typically this involves a narrative history based upon documents pertaining to company histories and corporate information, photos of an area, environmental assessments over time, letters of complaint from local residents, and the list goes on. Importantly, analysis of site history also includes multiparty sites, sites with previous uses and users to current parties, and sites in which wastes are commingled over a period of time. In other words, establishing liability is indeed possible – but demands political will, commitment to adequate investigatory processes, and employment of persons with expertise in developing the site history.

Moving from the specific to the general, it can be observed that there are limits inherent in the use of criminal sanctions against the more powerful groups in society (see Haines 1997). For example, corporations have considerable financial and legal resources to contest prosecution, making such prosecutions enormously expensive to run. Technical difficulties of prosecution (such as rules of evidence, multiple offenders, etc.), and the financial and human resource constraints of State legal machinery (e.g. regulatory bodies such as the police, environmental protection agencies and corporate watchdogs), preclude the use of criminal prosecution except in the most extreme or 'winnable' cases. There is, therefore, considerable discretion in prosecution and sentencing decisions.

Acknowledgement of these kinds of difficulties has fostered the development of new legal concepts relating to corporate liability and compensation (see Gunningham *et al.* 1995). Be this as it may, there are nevertheless persistent difficulties in prosecution of the powerful, whose use of the law is intrinsic to the maintenance of their dominant class position. The complexity of legal argument, and a political environment which sees environmental protection in the context of economic development, means that generally speaking the State is reluctant to proceed too far in either scrutinising or criminalising those sectors directly involved in productive economic activity.

The concentration of economic power at a global level, as manifest in the large transnational corporations, will obviously have an impact in the determination of what is deemed to be harmful or criminal, and what will not. It also means that, particularly in the case of environmental issues, the international character of capital and the transborder nature of the harm make prosecution and regulation extremely difficult. This is the case even where national legal mechanisms have been put into place to minimise environmental harm and to protect specific environments. Not only do the powerful have greater scope to shape laws in their collective interest, they have greater capacity to defend themselves individually if they do break and bend the existing rules and regulations.

The media have an important role in these processes. For example, they are key players in public understandings and portrayals of 'criminality' and law and order 'commonsense', which target the marginalised sections of the working class, and in particular ethnic minorities and indigenous people (Hogg and Brown 1998). Meanwhile, corporate control of the media, accompanied by the proliferation of public relations campaigns, conservative think tank 'analysis', professional lobby and advocacy groups, and manufactured 'grass roots' organisations, have been influential in 'greenwashing' the environment debate (Beder 1997; Athanasiou 1996). Such interventions on and behalf of corporate interests have a number of implications for the kinds of activities viewed as legitimate, regardless of real environmental effect, and for the regulatory role of both State and private institutions.

Where environmental harm has occurred, there are a number of issues which impinge upon the capacity and willingness of the State to enforce compliance or prosecute wrongdoing. Some of these include threats of litigation by companies against the State or third party critics on basis of 'commercial reputation'; a paucity of independent scientific expertise (related to cuts in the number of State regulators, the buying off of experts by companies, and funding crises affecting the research direction of academic institutions); the complexities associated with investigation and action in relation to transnational corporate environments (e.g. formation of international cartels, potential threats to future investment, monopolisation of particular industries, such as water); and State reluctance to enforce compliance due to ideological attachments to privatisation and corporatisation, and the notion of less State intervention the better (see White 1998).

Many businesses, for example, can gain protection from close public or State surveillance through the very processes of commercial negotiation and transaction. These range from appeals to 'commercial confidentiality' through to constraints associated with the technical nature of evidence required. For example, there is often difficulty in law of assigning 'cause' in many cases of environmental harm due to the diffuse nature of responsibility for particular effects, such as pollution in an area of multiple producers (e.g. mining companies). Furthermore, it has been pointed out that: 'evidence frequently can only be collected through the use of powers of entry, the ability to take, analyse and interpret appropriate samples and a good knowledge of the processes or activities giving rise to the offence' (Robinson 1995: 13). Such powers impinge upon the 'private' property rights and commercial interests which are at the heart of the capitalist political economy.

There are clear social differences in the ability of the powerful, in relation to the less powerful, to protect and defend their interests. This is evident in how the powerful are able to manipulate rules of evidence, frustrate investigatory processes, confuse notions of accountability and to forestall potential prosecution by ostensibly abiding by and complying with record-keeping procedures (see Gunningham *et al.* 1995). The expense of legal remedies in dealing with environmental harm is further complicated by the ways in which companies contest the domains of contractual and legal responsibility, and by the notions of 'privileged information' as a means to restrict access to needed evidence. Privacy, in this instance (and counterposed with that of the working class) is more likely to be assured.

Legal research has demonstrated that when it comes to prosecution of environmental crime it is small businesses that generally bear the brunt of State intervention. This is not only due to politics and the capacity to defend oneself. It is also related to organisational features. For example, Fortney (2003: 1620) observes that in the US 'generally the *mens rea* required for felony convictions is easier to prove in a small or close corporation setting, without resort to judicial strict liability constructs'. In other words, the mental element of criminal law is easier to establish in smaller firms. With already limited resources, it is not surprising therefore, that environmental law enforcement agencies concentrate on cases that they have a better chance of winning and that are less costly. Those most responsible for the vast majority of environmental violations, namely the large corporations, are also the least likely to suffer prosecution except in extraordinary circumstances.

Case study 7.4 The time and the money

In instances of dramatic and profound environmental harm, large corporations may well find it hard to escape public reprobation and criminal prosecution. Such was the case with French oil giant Total, that in January 2008 was ordered to pay several hundred million dollars in compensation after a Paris court found the company responsible for one of Europe's worst ever oil disasters (The Scotsman 2008). The company had chartered a 24-year-old rusted tanker that was to subsequently sink in the Bay of Biscay off of the Brittany coast in December 1999. This resulted in massive maritime pollution along the coast, with up to 75,000 birds dying and a crippling of local fishing, tourism and salt producing industries. The court also ordered that Total pay a US$555,000 fine, the maximum for marine pollution (Associated Press 2008). The verdict came after seven years of disputes and investigation, and a four-month trial. All defendants denied responsibility. An appeal was likely. After all, the American oil giant Exxon is still (as of January 2008) in the process of appealing an order by a US court to pay billions of dollars in compensation for the oil spill off Alaska from its tanker the Exxon Valdez in March 1989 (The Scotsman 2008). Regardless of final outcome, the fine and the compensation demanded of Total seem much less huge when put in the context of its reported US$4.64 billion in net profit in the third quarter of 2007 (Associated Press 2008). Having the time and money is the preserve of the large corporation.

Taking the influence of organisational factors into account, Fortney (2003) argues that what is needed is 'tailored enforcement', a form of environmental enforcement that ought to proceed according to organisation type. Thus, for instance, fines would be assigned on the basis of firm-type rather than offence committed, a fine-multiple system could be introduced for repeat offenders, and corporate leaders would be held personally liable for future offences once initial judgment has put corporate officers on notice that their company is in violation of the law. One could also envisage a combination of criminal, alternative sentencing options and civil penalties (as discussed earlier in the chapter) being used as part of such an approach. Similarly, a restorative justice approach to some types of environmental crime has been touted in New Zealand as a novel alternative to prosecution, one that nevertheless delivers benefits to local communities and that allows the offender to make right an environmental wrong (Verry *et al.* 2005).

A further complicating factor in regards to criminal prosecution of environmental harm relates to instances involving cross-jurisdictional matters. For example, the recent attempt by the European Commission to establish specific criminal penalties for those who pollute the environment was stymied by the European Court of Justice (Mahony 2007). In a ruling made on 23 October 2007, the Court reiterated its previous finding that the Commission can oblige member states to introduce common penalties for environmental pollution. However, the Court also ruled in this instance that the Commission may not determine what criminal sanctions should be introduced for different environment crimes in member states. In other words, there is recognition of the community-wide nature of environmental crime, but member states are given leeway to punish environmental polluters each in their own different way. The lack of uniformity in criminal sanctions thereby opens the door to country-shopping on behalf of potentially polluting activities such as disposal and transfer of EU waste shipments.

There are, then, important practical limitations in how the criminalisation and prosecution of environmental harm takes place. These include legislative barriers and cross-jurisdictional issues, through to difficulties associated with assigning liability. The power of companies and élite individuals to resist prosecution or to avoid criminal proceedings is a perennial issue. Another issue relates to the role and dynamics of the law enforcement process itself. This is worth discussing in greater depth, since it likewise highlights compliance and enforcement issues that will be of continuing relevance.

Policing and environmental law enforcement

Since environmental crime is now starting to garner much greater public and political attention as a distinct category of crime, it is starting to feature more prominently in the work of law enforcement officials such as the police (White 2007c). For many police, however, dealing with environmental harm is basically dealing with the unknown. It is a relatively new area of work for police, both individually and collectively.

The nature of environmental crime poses a number of challenges for effective policing. Such crimes may have local, regional and global dimensions. They may be difficult to detect (as in the case of some forms of toxic pollution that is not detectable to human senses). They may demand intensive cross-jurisdictional negotiation, and even disagreement between nation-states, in regards to specific events or crime patterns. Some crimes may be highly organised and involve criminal syndicates, such as illegal fishing. Others may include a wide range of criminal actors, ranging from the individual collector of endangered species to the systematic disposal of toxic waste via third parties.

These various dimensions of harm pose particular challenges for environmental law enforcement, especially from the point of view of police interagency collaborations, the nature of investigative techniques and approaches, and the different types of knowledge required for dealing with specific kinds of environmental harm. Moreover, many of the operational matters pertaining to environmental harm are inherently international in scope and substance.

As discussed in Chapter 4, the categorisation of environmental harm is varied in that there are different ways in which environmental crimes have been conceptualised and sorted (see for example, White 2005a; Beirne and South 2007; Carrabine *et al.* 2004). They include such things as air pollution, deforestation, animal abuse and so on, through to crime arising out of the flouting of rules that seek to regulate environmental disasters, including specific incidents such as the French government bombing of the Greenpeace boat, Rainbow Warrior, in 1985 in New Zealand, through to the dumping of toxic waste in Abidjan, the capital city of the Ivory Coast in August 2006, that led to the deaths of 16 people.

From the point of view of international law enforcement agencies such as Interpol (the International Criminal Police Organisation), the major issues relating to environmental crime are:

- The transborder movement and dumping of waste products;
- The illegal traffic in real or purported radioactive or nuclear substances;
- The illegal traffic in species of wild flora and fauna.

Issues such as illegal logging and illegal fishing are also starting to figure more prominently in discussions of transnational environmental crime (see Chapter 5). Interpol itself now has two key working groups that are actively involved in investigatory and operational work in regards to environmental crime: pollution and wildlife. These groups acknowledge that environmental crime has both national and international repercussions. The Pollution Crimes Working Group, for example, is an active forum in which criminal investigators from around the globe meet to discuss issues such as:

- Determining the role of organised crime in environmental crime;
- Identifying trends and patterns in transborder shipments of hazardous waste;
- Developing training and enforcement actions to combat illegal oil pollution into oceans, seas and inland waterways;
- Helping to develop a level playing field for law-abiding businesses by ensuring that penalties for pollution are sufficient to deter future illegal activity.

(Interpol 2007)

One of the key lessons from contemporary police studies is that it ought to be based largely on a problem-solving, rather than policy-prescribed model of intervention. In other words, specific problems demand specific kinds of responses, and a one-size-fits-all policy will not be adequate to the task. This applies to environmental policing as it does to other types. This means that in pursuing environmental law enforcement there is a need to include place-based and harm-based analyses that go to the heart of the issues at hand. A problem-solving approach to policing of environmental harm demands a certain level of specificity. That is, general pronouncements about the nature of harm need to be accompanied by particular site or harm analysis.

One of the initial questions to be asked of environmental crime is who is actually going to do the policing (Tomkins 2005)? Many jurisdictions have specialist agencies – such as environmental protection agencies – which are given the mandate to investigate and prosecute environmental crimes. The police generally play an auxiliary role in relation to the work of these agencies.

In some countries, however, members of the police service are especially trained up to be environmental police. In Israel, for example, an environmental unit was established in 2003 within the framework of the police. It is financed by the Ministry of the Environment and includes police officers who form the 'Green Police'.

These police carry out inspections, enforcement and investigation under a variety of laws in areas such as prevention of water source and marine pollution, industrial and vehicular pollution, hazardous substances, and prevention of cruelty to animals. Each year they carry out thousands of inspections of factories, landfills and sewerage treatment sites, in the process liaising with regional offices of the Ministry of the Environment (see Israel Police and the Israeli Ministry of Environmental Protection websites).

The police service in the Netherlands has been actively involved in enforcing environmental laws since the early 1990s and a significant proportion (over one-third) of police officers have had specific environmental law enforcement training (Tomkins 2005). In addition to general duties officers receiving training in regards to environmental matters, there are also specialised units within the police service, whose intensive specialised training enables them to identify and act upon environmental offences and offenders.

Within a particular national context, there may be considerable diversity in environmental law enforcement agencies and personnel, and police will have quite different roles in environmental law enforcement depending upon the city or state within which they work (see Tomkins 2005; Situ and Emmons 2000). In a federal system of governance for example, such as with the US, Canada and Australia, there will be great variation in environmental enforcement authorities ranging from police operating at the local municipal level (such as the Toronto Police Service) through to participation in international organisations (such as Interpol or Europol). The nature of the crime will determine the nature of the law enforcement, including who collaborates with whom (see Box 7.1).

Box 7.1 Strategic law enforcement approaches to abalone theft

In recent years the stealing of abalone has come to prominence and, indeed, is touted as one of the key areas in which environmental crime, as crime, is being addressed in a concerted way in Australia (see Chapter 4). The abalone industry is highly regulated, with strict quotas enforced, limited numbers of licensed divers and extensive documentation of each catch required. Part of the reason for this high level of regulation is that the industry is a major export earner, bringing in over AUS$100 million a year. Australia produces about

---

one-third of the global wild abalone harvest. Global demand for abalone and high profits from abalone sales have contributed to the growth in illegal harvesting.

The illegal abalone market has been described in terms of five categories of offender. In summary, these include:

- Organised poachers who operate in crews and harvest large quantities;
- Licensed divers who engage in over-quota fishing and docket fraud;
- Shore-based divers who access certain poaching spots;
- Extended family groups who engage in double-bagging;
- Individuals who take over-bag limit.

The main interest here is with the organised stealers of abalone (although there is some overlap with licensed divers, who may use the same networks for processing and distributing the catch). Organised poachers frequently have sophisticated infrastructure to facilitate the theft – boats, infra-red night vision equipment, scuba gear, hired transport vehicles, light aircraft and so on. Illegal processing of the abalone may also be quite sophisticated, and involve canning, drying or cryovac (vacuum) packaging.

Abalone thieves of this kind are willing to cross state borders to harvest abalone. Increasingly, it appears that organised criminal groups are moving into the industry, including outlaw motorcycle gangs and Asian crime figures. The illicit networks extend across state boundaries (from Tasmania to Queensland, or Victoria to New South Wales, for example). They also cross international boundaries, as one of the more lucrative markets for illegally harvested abalone is Asia. It has also been suggested that there are links between trade in illegal Australian abalone and the illicit drug markets. Again, these links transcend state and national boundaries.

Concerted efforts have been made to counter the illegal industry. Illegal accessing and processing of abalone is criminalised, both in terms of the law and in terms of resources put into the law enforcement process. Thus, 'each abalone-producing state has legislation carrying high pecuniary penalties and custodial sentences for abalone offending, and has dedicated abalone-crime investigators' (Tailby and Gant 2002: 5). In Tasmania, for example, offenders may be prosecuted under the State's Criminal Code for offences such as lying to public officials and receiving or possessing stolen property, or they may be subject to two indictable offences under the *Living Marine Resources Management Act 1995* that refer to illegally taken fish and falsifying documents (Leonard 2004; Little 2004). Each area of law imputes that the illegal action is treated as a serious matter. This is also apparent in the penalties assigned to offenders. For example, as a result of the joint efforts of the National Crime Authority (now the Australian Crime Commission) and Tasmania Police in 'Operation Oakum', an investigation into abalone theft, several people were sentenced to prison, including a two-year term of imprisonment in one particular case (Australian Crime Commission 2004; see also Tasmania Police 2004).

Investigation of abalone-related criminality features the use of a broad spectrum of police powers, including phone taps, dedicated surveillance, monitoring of documentation, and surprise inspections of processing facilities (Little 2004; Leonard 2004; Tailby and Gant 2002). The cross-border elements of the crime mean that it is of interest and concern to national law enforcement agencies such as the Australian Crime Commission, to State police services, to relevant fisheries bodies both at the national (National Fisheries Compliance Committee) and State levels (e.g. Fisheries Monitoring and Quota Audit Unit, Tasmania), to the Australian Customs Service, and to the Australian Quarantine Inspection Service. In other words, dealing with the crime necessarily involves a wide range of agencies at the local, regional, national and international levels. Cooperation amongst enforcement and monitoring agencies is essential, and agencies such as the ACC have played an important role in providing cross-jurisdictional coordination, access to substantial investigatory powers and use of advanced surveillance technologies.

Specific kinds of crime may involve different agencies, depending upon the jurisdiction. For example, the policing of abalone poaching in Australia is generally undertaken by civilian authorities, except in Tasmania and the Northern Territory where it is in the hands of the marine police (Tailby and Gant 2002). The transborder nature of illegal fishing operations – across state as well as international boundaries – means that often a local police service (such as Tasmanian Police) will necessarily have to work collaboratively with national agencies (such as the Australian Federal Police), that, in turn, will have relationships with regional partner organisations (such as Interpol). In some instances, as with the Task Force on Organised Crime in the Baltic Sea Region (which includes representatives from Denmark, Estonia, the European Commission, Finland, Germany, Latvia, Lithuania, Poland, Russia and Sweden), specific organisational structures are set up in order to share intelligence on environmental crime and to develop cooperative enforcement structures to deal with offenders (Tomkins 2005).

In jurisdictions such as Canada, the task of enforcing the law against poaching (for example, of lobsters) is in the hands of unarmed fishery officers (McMullan and Perrier 2002). The powers and resources available to specific law enforcement officials will vary greatly from jurisdiction to jurisdiction, and from agency to agency, depending upon whether or not the police are directly involved, and whether or not agents have been granted specific powers of investigation, arrest, and use of weapons to enforce environmental laws. Criminal enforcement of environmental law is basically shaped by specific national context, and the legislative and organisational resources dedicated to policing local environmental harms as well as those involving transborder incidents (see for example, Faure and Heine 2000).

Environmental crimes frequently demand a high level of collaboration with non-police agencies. For example, illegal fishing often involves customs officials, quarantine officials, federal and local police officers and sometimes the Navy. How best to organise law enforcement activities in regards to different environmental crimes is a perennial issue. Should specific environmental police units, within police services, be created, as in the case of Israel? Or, should 'flying squads' be created, that are comprised of personnel from different agencies and that reflect interagency collaboration and expertise (see Anderson and McCusker 2005) or, should it be the specific crime in question that ought to shape the organisational make-up and operational activities of law enforcement? It has also been suggested that there is a need to develop systematic environmental crime policing strategies to provide broad policy guidance to police jurisdictions and to ensure consistency in the expanded police interactions with non-police environmental agencies (Blindell 2006).

There are also major resource issues at stake here. This has a twofold character. First, governments will play a role setting priorities in regards to certain kinds of State intervention. For instance, the abalone industry in Australia is highly lucrative and generates millions of dollars in business each year. From a government point of view, this is a crime worth putting policing and other criminal justice resources into, including in the areas of prosecution and sentencing. On the other hand, there are cases in which environmental harm might be occurring, but in which governments are, for a variety of reasons, reluctant to act (for example, illegal logging). Secondly, senior police managers have to decide how best to allocate resources within their agency. Public opinion, media and political attention, and internal policing dynamics will all affect if, why and how specific types of environmental crime are addressed. How environmental issues are perceived within a police service will inevitably have an impact on organisational priorities.

Related to organisational matters, the dynamics of environmental crime are such that new types of skills, knowledge and expertise need to be drawn upon as part of the policing effort. For example, illegal land clearance can be monitored through satellite technologies (Bartel 2005). Toxic waste and pollution spills may require the sophisticated tools and scientific know-how associated with environmental forensics (Murphy and Morrison 2007). DNA testing is already being used in relation to logging, fishing and endangered species, that is, to track illegal possession and theft of animals and plants. Powers of investigation, particularly in relation to the gathering of suitable evidence for the specific environmental crime, will inevitably be shaped by State, federal and international conventions and protocols, as well as by availability of local expertise, staff and resources.

The place and role of civilian scientists and experts within police law enforcement agencies and the further specialised professional training of police staff are issues that will require ongoing review and assessment. Alongside a general familiarity with emergent technologies and techniques relevant to the detection, investigation, prevention and prosecution of environmental crime, police officers will need to be trained to be able to work in multidisciplinary, multiagency teams that also have the capacity to liaise with counterparts in other countries and jurisdictions.

Environmental law enforcement is a relatively new area of police work (Tomkins 2005; Blindell 2006) and is at a stage when perhaps more questions are being asked than answers can be provided. Certainly what would be useful is comparative assessment of local and nationally based 'good practice' in this area. So too, an assessment of how police work that 'gets a result' translates into prosecution processes and actual sentences for environmental offenders will provide insight into how the work of the courts impacts upon the morale and activities of those working in the field (McMullen and Perrier 2002).

Box 7.2 Social research into police work on environmental issues

One of the emerging areas where greater interface between researchers and police is needed is that of specific issues related to environmental law enforcement. There is a wide range of issues which both sociologists and police will be required to become familiar with in the coming years. For example, the policing of illegal fishing and illegal logging demands great sensitivity to different types of offending, different motivations for offending and different responses to address diverse social circumstances (e.g. large-scale versus traditional/indigenous fishers). The specificity of the crime will demand quite different kinds of law enforcement practices and interventions.

Social research can play a valuable role in informing 'good practice' when it comes to responding to environmental harms and crimes. It can also expose issues of concern, particularly issues pertaining to the police role and the occupational climate within which they operate. For example, lots of hard police work can go into gathering evidence and building cases against polluters, illegal fishers, transporters of toxic waste and so on. New technologies and new collaborations with non-police agencies may be required, as well as extensive police resources, time and energy.

However, what happens when cases get to court? Here there is scope to undertake research that examines which courts the cases are heard in (e.g. Magistrates' or a Superior Court), and the penalties assigned to offenders (which frequently seem rather 'light' given the nature of the crime). For police, a crucial issue might be the effect of perceptions that magistrates or judges do not provide adequate orders in relation to the nature of the offence. This is especially so when police spend a large amount of work in compiling their cases. A very practical research question here is what effect do court decisions have on the morale and work activities of enforcement officers, especially in new areas of policing such as that of environmental law enforcement.

Another crucial issue for police services, as well, relates to the dynamics of the interface between politics, the environment and law enforcement. Whose side are you on, should you take sides, and under what circumstances you need to take sides, are key questions for police when it comes to dealing concretely with environmental issues.

Case study 7.5   Protecting loggers, protecting protesters

McCulloch (2005) describes how civil action was taken by environmentalists in the state of Victoria against a number of loggers, the Construction Forestry Mining and Energy Union (Forestry Division) and the Secretary of the Victorian Branch of the Forestry and Forest Building Products Manufacturing Division of the union. The environmentalists alleged that during a protest action in the Otway Ranges State Forest in 1999, that they were prevented from leaving the forest by the defendants. The trial took over 64 days to be heard and involved considerable time and financial costs to all concerned. For present purposes, this case raises important issues relating to the practical role of the police in instances where there is conflict between protagonists at the ground level. Police have a duty to uphold relevant laws. They also have a duty to protect individuals from potential harm, including assaults and, in this case, alleged involuntary detainment of protesters by forestry workers. The tensions and passions of the moment place police in a precarious position, one that easily may be seen as partisan rather than 'neutral' when it comes to resolving the immediate situation.

Case study 7.6   Policing costs and forest protesters

Civil disobedience and public dissent are cornerstones of democracy (in that they reflect freedom of expression and the voices of the people) and have been at the heart of profound changes to present laws – from the unlawful actions of the suffragettes that led women to gaining the vote, to indigenous rights movements that have altered the relationship between colonial powers and Aboriginal peoples. In 2007, Allana Beltran was arrested for sitting silently on a giant tripod in the Weld Valley, dressed as an angel. She was protesting the logging of old-growth forests in Tasmania. What makes this case notable, is that the Tasmanian Police, in conjunction with Forestry Tasmania, lodged a claim for nearly AUS$10,000 in 'lost costs' for having to attend the artist's March forest protest (Worley 2007: 7). This was criticised by Green politicians as constituting interference in the political process. The editorial of local newspaper *The Mercury* was to advise that for the police, 'their job is quite simply to enforce the law. Protests are a legitimate form of activity in a free country'

(The Mercury 2007: 14). The costs of policing protests, therefore, are seen as part of the legitimate costs of ensuring democratic participation. For police managers, however, the policing of such protests nevertheless has an impact on other parts of operational police work. The issue is whether such considerations end up shading into matters of political interference and thereby constitute a stifling of the democratic process.

For police, conflicting views on the nature, and urgency, of environmental harm, especially where this involves protest action, poses great challenges in terms of professionalism, perceived neutrality in conflicts, and expenditure of time, energy and resources vis-à-vis public order policing. The same applies to state crime and other crimes of the powerful, which place pressure on police to act in non-partisan ways, and in a manner that upholds the rule of law universally.

It needs to be reiterated that dealing with environmental harm will demand new ways of thinking about the world, the development of a global perspective and analysis of issues, trends and networks, and a commitment to the 'environment' as a priority area for concerted police intervention. The challenges faced by police in affluent countries of the West will be even more difficult for their counterparts in Third World countries, in countries undergoing rapid social and economic changes, and in countries where coercion and corruption are generally unfettered by stable institutional controls. A scoping analysis of law enforcement practices and institutions in Brazil, Mexico, Indonesia and the Philippines found common problems across the different sites (Akella and Cannon 2004: 19). They included:

1. Poor interagency cooperation;
2. Inadequate budgetary resources;
3. Technical deficiencies in laws, agency policies and procedures;
4. Insufficient technical skills and knowledge;
5. Lack of performance monitoring and adaptive management systems.

These challenges are global in application, although the specific nature of the challenge will vary depending upon national and regional context. Basically the message is that more investment in enforcement policy, enforcement capacity and performance management is essential regardless of jurisdiction.

Disputes over definitions of harm, conflicts between different citizen groups and ambiguities associated with police practices in specific situations mean that environmental law enforcement will necessarily be complicated, contentious and, at times, contradictory. It will certainly be challenging.

Conclusion: where to from here?

The criminalisation of environmental crime does not necessarily equate with the prosecution and punishment of environmental offenders. This is because of a range of issues relating to detection, arrest, prosecution and sentencing of those who violate environmental laws. An indication of the kinds of factors that affect the determinants of the quality of environmental law enforcement is provided in Box 7.3.

Box 7.3 Determinants of the quality of enforcement

The enforcement chain has a number of interdependent links. The quality of enforcement depends on what is happening at each point, as indicated in the following examples (Akella and Cannon 2004: 10).

• Probability of detection is correlated to the incentives given to park guards, rangers, and forest and fishery environment protection agents (e.g. pay levels and other rewards); to availability of equipment; to number of personnel charged with detecting environmental crimes; and to technical knowledge and skill of personnel;

• Probability of arrest given detection is correlated to police pay and reward structure, to availability of equipment, to quality of evidence and to social perceptions about the crime;

• Probability of prosecution given arrest is correlated to rewards for prosecutors, to capacity of the justice system and those in it to prosecute environmental crimes, to whether the illegal act is a criminal or civil offence, to social attitudes toward the crime and to quality of evidence;

• Probability of conviction given prosecution is correlated to rewards for judges and magistrates, to capacity of the justice system, to nature of the crime, to social attitudes toward the crime and to quality of evidence.

Further work in the area of environmental law enforcement needs to examine closely factors as described above and throughout this chapter. Detailed analysis is needed of judicial decision-making processes and outcomes, the dynamics and structures of global policing, collaborative police work across borders and the role of local communities in assisting with compliance and enforcement activities. Legislative change and law reform may provide abstract solutions to environmental harm, but it is in the grounded activities of enforcement agencies that the law in theory becomes law in practice.

Chapter 8

Environmental regulation

Regulation in its various guises and involving a myriad of mechanisms is the general method used to control environmentally destructive activities and to limit the damage done. Prosecution of environmental crime is generally reserved as a means of last resort. Among the preferred contemporary methods it is self-regulation that has found most favour among governments and companies alike. Who is to regulate the regulators in this instance is a crucial question.

Introduction

The role of the State in dealing with environmental harm is much more circumscribed than the policing and regulation of street crime. The tendency has been to emphasise efficiency and facilitation, rather than control. At a practical level the costs of monitoring, enforcement and compliance, in relation to traditional regulatory standards setting and role of government, are seen as problematic. So too, the complexity of procedures and issues has been accompanied by efforts to streamline processes and by increased reliance upon expert-based advice, rather than full community discussion.

These trends fit nicely with neo-liberalism in that in supporting economic development the State can cut costs and encourage business growth by narrowing the scope of its purview and involvement in regulation. This reduction can take several different forms, such as cuts in State resources allocated to environmental audits (e.g. botany mapping), or the censoring of scientific information which may be publicly sensitive for specific industries (e.g. fishing, forestry, mining) or for private contract partners of government (e.g. water treatment plants, power station operators).

The State nevertheless has a formal role and commitment to protect citizens from the worst excesses or worst instances of environmental victimisation. Hence, the introduction of extensive legislation and regulatory procedures designed to give the appearance of active intervention, and the implication that laws exist which actually do deter such harms. The existence of such laws may be encouraging in that they reflect historical and ongoing struggles over certain types of business activity.

However, the regulation of environmental harm, whether it be in the areas of risk assessment, management of specific incidents or consumption-related activity, is inextricably bound up with capitalist accumulation. The most blatant or worst instances of environmental victimisation may be subject to State sanction; however, even this generally begs the issue of the capacity of, particularly transnational, capital to defend its interests through legal and extra-legal means (see White 1999).

This chapter provides an overview of environmental regulation. It begins by examining the main models and tools of regulation. This is followed by discussion of the political context of environmental regulation and the key influences on regulation-in-practice. The final section explore the politics of regulation and the ways in which contemporary regulatory models express systemic economic demands that mitigate against prevention of environmental harm in general.

Systems and models of regulation

There are diverse rationales for social intervention on environmental matters. There is, at times, a basic incompatibility of regulatory projects. Some of the motivations for regulation include:

- Evidence of extreme forms of direct and indirect environmental harm that makes it politically undeniable and problematic;
- A moral basis for action, especially around the themes of ecological justice and preserving or protecting nature;
- A concern stemming from consideration of local communities and equity, so that distributions of harm/safety are fairer;
- Protection of the 'value' of natural resources, from the point of view of economic baselines;

- The notion of universal human interests in the case of trends and processes that are seen to be a threat to global life;
- An agenda informed by social justice and equality considerations, focusing on the exploitation of humans and of nature.

The bottom line is that the task of environmental regulation is simultaneously analytic, political and moral.

There are several ways in which one can analyse issues pertaining to environmental regulation and the prevention of environmental harm. For example, there has been burgeoning interest in corporate regulation, including in relation to environmental matters, in the 'regulation' literature (see for example, Haines 1997; Braithwaite and Drahos 2000). At a theoretical level, much of this work has attempted to present regulation as lying on a continuum from direct command control on the part of the State through to voluntary compliance on the part of companies and individuals. The emphasis varies according to the theoretical position of the writer.

Three main approaches to responding to environmental harm have previously been identified – a socio-legal approach, a regulatory approach and a social action approach (see Chapter 7). The main concern of this chapter is the second approach, one that emphasises regulatory strategies that might be utilised to improve environmental performance, including 'responsive regulation' (Ayres and Braithwaite 1992; Braithwaite 1993) and 'smart regulation' (Gunningham and Grabosky 1998). These approaches attempt to recast the State's role by using non-government, and especially private sector, participation and resources in fostering regulatory compliance in relation to the goal of 'sustainable development'. Increasingly important to these discussions is the perceived and potential role of third party interests, in particular non-government environmental organisations, in influencing policy and practice (Braithwaite and Drahos 2000; O'Brien et al. 2000; Gunningham and Grabosky 1998).

The main concern of this kind of approach is with reform of existing methods of environmental protection. The overall agenda of writers in this genre has been summarised as follows: 'generally speaking, environmental reformers are optimistic about the possibilities of addressing environmental harms without fundamentally changing the status quo. Either implicitly or tacitly, minimisation ("risk management") rather than elimination of environmental depredation is conceived as the reformist object' (Chunn et al. 2002: 12).

The regulatory field is made up of many different stakeholders and participants. These include, for example, businesses, employees, government agencies, communities, shareholders, environmentalists, regulators, the media, trade customers, financial institutions, consumers and the list goes on. The role and influence of various people and agencies is influenced by factors such as resources, training, information, skill, expertise and legislation. These are also affected by the type of regulation that is the predominant model at any point in time.

It has been observed, for example, that the broad tendency under neo-liberalism has been toward deregulation (or, as a variation of this, 'self-regulation') when it comes to corporate harm and wrongdoing (Snider 2000). In the specific area of environmental regulation, the role of government remains central, even if only by the absence of State intervention. The general trend has been away from direct governmental regulation and toward 'softer' regulatory approaches. The continuum of regulation, from strict regulation through to no regulation, is illustrated in Figure 8.1. Measures include Environmental Impact Assessments (EIAs) and Environmental Management Systems (EMSs) through to voluntary adoption of good environmental practices.

Two general models stand out when it comes to regulation in general and environmental regulation in particular. The first is Ayres and Braithwaite's notion of 'enforced self-regulation' (1992). This is based upon a regulatory pyramid. The usual pyramid of sanctions has an extensive base with the emphasis on persuasion that rises to a small peak of harsh punishment. In the case of business transgressions, to take an example, the progression up the pyramid might include persuasion, a warning letter, a civil penalty, a criminal penalty, license suspension and license revocation. By combining different forms of regulation, Ayres and Braithwaite reconstitute the usual regulatory pyramid such that the bottom layer consists of self-regulation, the next layer enforced self-regulation (via government legislation), the

Strict regulation		No regulation
Command and control	*Self-regulation*	*Deregulation*
Strong codes of practice	*	Weak codes of practice
Licences and permits	Standard setting	Voluntarism
Setting of Standards	Industry-based compliance	Property rights
EIAs	EMSs	Incentive based

Figure 8.1 Environmental regulatory field

next layer command regulation with discretionary punishment, and at the top, command regulation with nondiscretionary punishment.

Building upon the insights of these and other writers, Gunningham and Grabosky (1998) argue that what is needed is 'smart regulation'. This basically refers to the design of regulation that still involves government intervention, but selectively and in combination with a range of market and non-market solutions, and of public and private orderings. The central thesis of 'smart regulation' is that recruiting a range of regulatory actors to implement complementary combinations of policy instruments, tailored to specific environmental goals and circumstances, will produce more effective and efficient policy outcomes.

Essentially this perspective adopts the position that it is possible to have a win–win solution to environmental regulation, one that promises improved environmental performance but at a price acceptable to business and the community. This means incorporating into the regulatory field the full schedule of regulatory options. These are presented in summary form in Figure 8.2.

Command and control regulation (direct regulation)
- Setting of environmental standards (technology, performance and/or process based);
- Licenses and permits;
- Environmental covenants;
- Land and water use controls;
- Environmental impact assessment;
- Site specific management plans.

Self-regulation
- Organised group regulates the behaviour of its members;
- Setting out of 'codes of practice' via rules and standards;
- Standard-setting and identification of breaches in hands of practitioners;
- Serves industry not public interest;
- Assessing and identifying non-compliant behaviour and punishing it.

Voluntarism
- Individual firm undertaking to do the right thing unilaterally, without any basis in coercion;
- 'Non-mandatory' contracts between equal partners;

- Encouragement and invoking of sense of responsibility;
- Public recognition of environmental achievements;
- Idea of establishing environmental protection as part of 'community norm'.

Education and information
- Education and training (specialist training, toll-free helplines);
- Corporate environmental reporting (eco-balance sheets);
- Community right to know and pollution inventories (especially in relation to disclosure of information on pollution control and chemical hazards);
- Related to establishment of 'good neighbour' agreements between companies and local communities;
- Product certification (eco-labelling);
- Award schemes (publicising of virtuous conduct).

Economic instruments
- Property rights (maintain value of what is owned in order to maximise profits);
- Market creation (tradable pollution rights or tradable resource rights that can be bought or sold like any other commodity via permits);
- Fiscal instruments and charge systems (taxes and charges on degree of harm caused, or in proportion to the amount of pollution activity – emission and effluent charges; subsidies via tax concessions);
- Financial instruments (green funds, subsidised interest rates, soft loans) for environmental activities such as sewage treatment, pollution control and reforestation;
- Liability instruments (threat of legal action to recover costs of environmental damages);
- Performance bonds (posting of security deposit which is redeemable upon satisfactory completion of a required task – such as mining);
- Deposit refund systems (such as beverage containers);
- Removing perverse incentives (subsidising of environmental 'bads' – such as traditional agricultural practices).

Free market environmentalism
- Allocating property-rights for natural resources to private interests;
- No government intervention, except to monitor and enforce the trading of individual property-rights;
- The market to determine the value people place on environmental goods, under a system of well specified property-rights.

Figure 8.2 Environmental policy instruments
Source: Gunningham, Sinclair and Grabosky 1998.

A number of issues arise in relation to how these measures are utilised in practice. Questions can be asked regarding the standards of what is deemed to be acceptable; the flexibility required in devising appropriate safeguards and strategies at local/site level; how to enact total management planning; what constitutes adequate monitoring; who is to do enforcement and compliance; what penalties and consequences are to consist of; how a plurality of instruments rather than a single approach is to be coordinated; how to deal with a culture of reluctance to use punitive measures against corporate misconduct; the general corporate immunity from prosecution and penalty; and why and how the extent of regulation varies according to size of firm.

The specifics of environmental regulation would entail such things as assessing a firm's environmental record; preparation of an environmental improvement plan; the conducting of periodic environmental audits; implementation of an EMS; examination of the intensity of the administrative and resource burden; analysis of the risks of regulatory capture by firms; consideration of the public right to know about contracts, and examination of the firm's history. Consider, for example, the notion of regulatory capture.

Case study 8.1 Regulatory capture

The concept of regulatory capture refers to the situation where a government agency is dominated by the very agencies it is meant to be regulating. For example, Simon (2000) details many instances in which the US Environmental Protection Agency (EPA) seemed to be more concerned with protecting corporate interests than protecting the environment. An example of this was a study that showed that the EPA devoted more of its resources in terms of time and money in the early 1990s to exempt corporations from its regulations than it did to enforce the regulations. EPA activity had also extended to opposing congressional attempts to pass tougher environmental regulations. Meanwhile, many former officials within the EPA ended up taking jobs as waste-industry executives. In terms of both activities and exchange of personnel, such situations serve private rather than public interests.

Case study 8.2 Light-handed regulation in the forestry industry

Research has shown that deliberately light-handed forms of regulation in the forestry industry in Tasmania have been accompanied by lack of transparency, absence of third party oversight and a privileging of the economic over the ecological (Hollander 2006; Pearce 2007). In part this approach stems from the fact that the regulator itself is intertwined with the commercial enterprise. The State has a financial interest in ensuring an economic return from logging in State forests, as managed under a corporatised State company, Forestry Tasmania. The regulators and the foresters are drawn from the same pool of people, and share a similar interest in enabling rather than fettering logging activity. Regulators who have tried to 'do their job' by enforcing rules and guidelines have been shifted out of their job and publicly denigrated by top politicians in public forums in which forestry regulation has been the key item (see Pearce 2007).

What detailed examination of particular forms of regulation show, and what explorations of different approaches to environmental regulation acknowledge, is that how regulation is carried out in practice, and whose interests are reflected in specific regulatory regimes, is basically an empirical question. That is, regulatory performance cannot be read off from an abstract understanding of regulation theory as such. Nevertheless, environmental regulation models directly influence the scope and possibilities of environmental regulation as it gets translated into practical measures at the ground level. The adoption of particular environmental models thus helps to shape the methods and behaviour of regulators. In ideal terms, the two key models of regulation would incorporate a range of actors and measures in order to 'keep things honest', presumably in ways that would be to the advantage of all stakeholders (see Figure 8.3). The limitations of this will be considered shortly.

Snider (2000) describes how in Canada, despite policy directives specifying 'strict compliance', a permissive philosophy of 'compliance promotion' has reigned. Given the tone of mainstream regulation literature (that offers a theoretical justification for enlisting private interests through incentives and inducements), it is hardly surprising that persuasion is favoured at the practical level. Close examination of self-regulation models, however, finds evidence of regulatory

Regulatory pyramid (structure)	Smart regulation (process)
Enforced self-regulation Hierarchy of sanctions Persuasion to coercion	Constellation of measures Harnessing of resources outside of public sector
Regulatory participants	
Growing importance of third parties such as public interest groups and commercial third parties	* Relies on recruitment of range of regulatory actors to implement complementary combinations of policy instruments

Figure 8.3 Environmental regulation models

failures, and this, in turn, indicates that governments cannot totally abdicate responsibility when a regulatory problem requires a State response (see Priest 1997–98). Certain conditions are necessary if self-regulation, as such, is going to offer an effective form of regulation. The tendency, however, is for governments to shed regulatory functions and responsibilities and to rely upon the rhetoric and savings afforded by self-regulation.

But, more than seeing this as simply a reflection of the new regulatory ideology, it is essential to consider the financial and political environment within which regulators are forced to work. For example, while never before in history have there been so many laws pertaining to the environment, it is rare indeed to find extensive government money, resources and personnel being put into enforcement and compliance activities. Rather, these are usually provided in the service of large corporations, as a form of State welfare designed to facilitate and enhance the business climate and specific corporate interests.

Political context of environmental regulation

The political relations of late capitalism are crucial in any discussion of environmental harm insofar as how, or whether, certain human activity is regulated is a matter primarily of State intervention. The ways in which nation-states (and varying other levels of government) attempt to deal with environmental concerns is contingent upon the class character of political power, and the interests bound up with different forms of class rule.

This general proposition applies as well to analysis of the former 'socialist' regimes of the Soviet Union and Eastern Europe, and to China. In these cases, however, the historical peculiarities of such regimes warrant careful analysis of issues such as the extent and nature of publicly provided services, the conflicts and interrelationship between capitalist and post-capitalist countries, the threats posed by imperialism that necessitated rapid industrial development of technologically backward countries, and so on (see Nichols 1999). To understand environmental destruction both post-1917 (the Russian Revolution) and post-1989 (the fall of the Berlin Wall) in places such as Russia requires close examination of Stalinism as a fundamentally anti-democratic social phenomenon, and of global capitalism as a compelling force in shaping 'development' in these countries. The collapse of the former 'socialist' countries (with a few exceptions, such as Cuba), has further reinforced the political and economic hegemony of the dominant Western capitalist states.

The instrumental and structural role of the State is intertwined with the maintenance and reproduction of capitalist class relations. Central to the State's role in protecting the interests of capital is ensuring that any monopoly on ownership of the means of production continues and is extended. Thus, as Onimode (1985: 204–205) observes:

> As an instrument of class domination, the primary and most important function of the State is the defence of private property. Because under capitalism, the system of property relations is synonymous with the class structure of society, the use of the state for class domination is the same as its use for the protection of private property. These property relations enable one class of owners to dominate another class of non-owners, to reap material, political and social advantages, while the other class suffers material and other disadvantages ... By guaranteeing the monopoly of the means of production by the ruling class, the State sustains inequalities in the distribution of wealth, the income from that wealth and in the distribution of social opportunities and facilities.

This is a crucial point. For if the State exists first and foremost as a protector of private property, and it is those with capital (as a form of private property) who are privileged by this, then State regulation from the very start basically reflects the interests of the ruling class.

This has a number of implications for environmental regulation in that the sacrosanct nature of private property under capitalism constitutes a major criterion against which State intervention in the 'private' affairs of capitalist business is measured.

The State also has a regulatory and management role directly in regards to the running of the capitalist economy. The precise relationship between the State and capital is driven by both general and specific concerns. The facilitative role of the State in respect to capital accumulation is demonstrated by the plethora of rules and regulations governing economic relations, in which the State exerts some partial autonomy relative to individual capitalists or even sectors of capital in order to ensure that the interests of capital as a whole are not impeded. In more specific terms, the State also plays a role in implementing the broad policy settings within which capitalist activity will take place. Thus, the shift from laissez-faire to Keynesian to economic rationalist policies occurred as the structural requirements of capital have changed over time.

The current policy context of State intervention is one marked by widespread adoption of 'free trade' ideology (Beder 2006). This ideology is premised on the idea that there is or ought to be an international level playing field, upon which individual corporations are to compete on the basis of best productivity, innovation, use of technology and service – all of which are linked to lowering the cost of labour. Such 'free trade' or neo-liberal policies are also linked to the commodification of a wider range of services and products which were formerly State-owned and operated ostensibly for public benefit. Education, water and power, for example, are now being sold in many advanced capitalist countries as profit-making enterprises. This is yet another instance in which the political relations of ordinary citizens are being transformed, in ways which reduce both the possibility of democratic participation in decision-making and in ensuring that there are public controls over how resources are managed and consumed.

The impact of globalisation, as administered via neo-liberal State policy, is to make ordinary workers extremely vulnerable economically. Under such conditions, there is even greater scope to either reduce environmental protection, or to increase environmentally destructive activity, to the extent that existing State legislation and company practices are seen to put fetters on the profit-making enterprise. Politically, the problems generated in and through capitalist restructuring are also reflected in the scapegoating of green activists, immigrants and indigenous people, who are frequently presented in the media as impeding the immediate job prospects of workers in industries associated with resource exploitation (e.g. logging, mining), industrial production (e.g. manufacturing) and project development (e.g. tourist resorts). Intensified competition between workers for jobs thus has major implications for environmental regulation and for environment related politics.

The political context within which economic growth and development (as narrowly defined) occurs has a major bearing on both the regulatory environment and the types of activities garnering State support. As Brunton (1999: 141) observes in relation to Australian regional governments:

> The States and Territories have restricted sources of revenues and thus are constrained and limited in their policy choice. One area under their control with the potential for expansion is natural resources. Thus the State and Territories understandably become committed to their exploitation, and consequently, generally hostile to conservation. They are always tempted to maximise resource throughput in the short-term rather than to husband resources for an optimal return over time. This results in a strong, at times authoritarian, commitment to 'development' at any cost.

After assessing the state of Australian environmental policy, Brunton (1999: 142) goes on to argue that, particularly in relation to biological diversity, greenhouse gas emissions and endangered species, voluntary and non-regulatory measures have not been very successful and should be rejected.

Regulatory approaches attempt to recast the State's role by using non-government, and especially private sector, participation and resources in fostering regulatory compliance in relation to the goal of 'sustainable development'. Analyses of new regulatory regimes, however, offer equivocal results in terms of effectiveness. For example, analysis of Canadian environmental law and policies reveals a patchwork of legislative and regulatory measures that fundamentally fail to protect the environment (Boyd 2003). At its broadest level, the ways in which regulation works or does not work is fundamentally shaped by systemic imperatives and philosophical vision. For instance, Boyd (2003) contrasts a model of regulation based upon an effort to mitigate the environmental impacts of an energy and resource intensive industrial economy, with that based upon ecological principles that are oriented to decreasing the consumption of energy and natural resources. However complex the laws and regulations in the first scenario, they cannot succeed in achieving sustainability because the system as a whole is inherently geared to growth in energy and resource consumption (see Chapter 6). In the latter case, the emphasis is on restructuring the economy to incorporate ecological limits, and thus to reduce environmental harm over time.

At a more mundane level, specific areas of regulation are now being subjected to empirical evaluation. For example, Stretesky (2006) points out that, while concepts such as corporate self-policing have been discussed at a theoretical level, very little grounded research has actually been undertaken. Yet, the shift from State command-and-control regimes to market-based regulation is a core concern of contemporary regulation theorists, especially in the area of environmental regulation (see Gunningham and Grabosky 1998; Grabosky 1994, 1995). In the study of self-policing in relation to the US Environmental Protection Agency, Stretesky (2006) found that there are a wide range of specific issues that require further examination, including how corporate culture impacts upon compliance with environmental regulatory efforts through to possible impacts of sanction severity on deterring potential offenders. A key point that is emphasised is that if the policy shift from direct regulation to market-based incentives is so important to policy makers then much more research about the dynamics and consequences of this shift is warranted.

Self-regulation and environmental management

The role of criminologists in providing a theoretical cover for questionable environmental practices is an issue warranting serious consideration, particularly in relation to contemporary thinking about corporate regulation. In general, the idea of encouraging trustworthiness ('virtue') by individual companies and by industry associations – of promoting regulation by 'consent' – has, unsurprisingly, garnered a modicum of support within official government circles and among business leaders.

The mainstream (and dominant) model of regulation is based upon the notion of a regulatory pyramid, with persuasion the favoured approach at the base moving upwards to coercion at the pinnacle (Ayres and Braithwaite 1992; Grabosky 1994, 1995). The basic argument has been that the most effective regulatory regime is one that combines a range of measures, most of which the targeted institutions and groups are meant to have some interest in participating in, or complying with (see Braithwaite 1993; Gunningham and Grabosky

1998). The implication is that corporate attitudes should be the focus for reform (including cases where third party input is encouraged in the regulatory arena). Arguments about whether to punish, persuade or do both, however, often separate the harm from its economic and political context – the implication being that somehow the structure of market competition and systemic expansionary pressures can be ignored or downplayed (for critique of this, see Haines 1997).

In the specific area of environmental regulation, there is likewise support for the idea that persuasion, not coercion, is or ought to be the key regulatory mechanism. This is usually associated with the ideology of 'self-regulation' (see, for example, Grabosky 1994, 1995). Here it is argued that corporate regulation should be informed by the idea of enlisting 'private interests' in regulatory activity via 'inducements' such as adopting waste minimisation programmes which translate into more efficient production, or earning a good reputation among consumers for environmental responsibility. Again, such proposals and strategies basically fail to acknowledge the structural imperatives of consumer capitalism, both in its general tendencies (i.e. to expand) and in the daily operations of specific capitals (i.e. to compete effectively in producing commodities and realising surplus value). Moreover, it downplays the active role of the corporate sector in 'greenwashing' the environmental debate (Beder 1997; Athanasiou 1996) in ways which are ideologically and materially advantageous to further commodity production.

Such perspectives also reinforce the notion that 'markets' are and should be a key component of any regulatory system. This simply taps into the dominant ideological framework of capitalism that 'the market knows best'. Analytically, the problem of regulation is divorced from structural analysis of political economic relations. Rather, great emphasis is placed on 'illustrative' examples and case studies in which specific forms of incentive and compliance appear to be 'working' in an environmentally friendly manner (see Grabosky 1994). Much is thus made of how 'market opportunities' can drive 'environmentally appropriate commercial activity'. Less is said about the overall expansionary pressures of consumer capitalism, or the immediate pressures on particular capitals to curb environmental controls precisely because of competitive costs (Haines 1997).

Specific forms of self-regulation

The privatisation of regulation has been accompanied by at least five different models of self-regulation, ranging from those reliant primarily on voluntary codes of conduct through to those that are strictly monitored via specialised government agencies (Priest 1997–98). Examples of self-regulation based upon 'codes of conduct' and customer charters are provided in Box 8.1, which describes how such measures work in relation to consumer protection.

Box 8.1 Self-regulation and consumer issues

The promotion of 'self-regulation' features strongly in the field of consumer protection. The trend in recent years has been away from rights-based regulation and toward market-based mechanisms. This is manifest in the proliferation of 'codes of conduct' across diverse commodity sectors.

Such codes have been criticised on a number of grounds. These include, for example, legitimation of harmful practices in the process of defining what is allowable, self-interested adjudication processes, non-transparent dispute resolution procedures, and lack of consultation with consumer groups and advocates (Field 1999). Similar kinds of concerns have been expressed with regard to the idea of 'customer charters', which are documents intended to provide consumers with information on the level of service or quality of products from agencies and business providers. Often premised on the idea of gaining an extra competitive edge by providing something special, customer charters are once again part and parcel of the 'new' self-regulatory approach.

In implementation terms, the key questions regarding these charters revolve around the obligation to consult, the obligation to inform and be accessible, the obligation to be accountable, and the obligation to provide redress (Smith 1997). More broadly, however, codes of conduct and customer charters still essentially entrench the key decision-making about what and how to produce, and which 'needs' to meet, in the hands of the industry or government departments.

The sphere of consumption has become a major site of dissatisfaction in recent years, whether this is over the shoddiness of durable consumer commodities, the quality of water, or inadequacies in energy supply. One of the material effects of the disjunctures between (manufactured or otherwise) consumer 'desire' and 'need', and actual commodity provision, has been increasing action and demands for better standards in both products and production

---

processes. One response has been to mobilise around selective buying of commodities, in order to ensure both quality, and to foster the production of environmentally friendly goods and services (Elkington and Hailes 1991). In view of the privatisation of basic necessities of life (such as water), there are obvious limitations to this strategy in some areas. So too, such strategies belie the lack of spending power of sizeable proportions of the world population, who must purchase whatever is cheapest on offer, by necessity.

Whereas issues of 'quality' lend themselves readily to a degree of favourable corporate and government responsiveness, issues of 'quantity' are a different matter altogether. Buying 'green' does little to reduce reliance on capitalistically produced commodities, nor does it offer a real range of choices in satisfying human needs (see Irvine 1991). Furthermore, the role of the State is now simply to inform the 'market' about what to look for from different producers, not to regulate production itself (see for example, Franklin 1999 in relation to the meat industry). In the end, green consumerism is a stop-gap measure at best, with little systemic consequences at the end of the day (Foster 2007; see also Buttel 2003). Aggregate consumption is ultimately not regulated by consumers, but by the rate of profit and accumulation, and the artificially constructed hierarchy of 'needs' fostered by capital (see O'Connor 1994; Pepper 1993).

Another popular form of self-regulation is adoption of Environment Management Systems (EMS). This describes attempts at the firm and industry levels to build environmental valuation and risk analysis into core activities (such as accounting practices, insurance, public image, standards, liability, audits and reporting). As part of this, emphasis will be placed on improving environmental awareness amongst employees, adopting clean technologies and engaging in activities such as recycling, and closely managing the supply and waste chain in order to minimise potential environmental harm.

In practical terms, a number of barriers to EMS have been identified (see Kirkland and Thompson 1999). Some of these include:

Awareness – lack of recognition of need, lack of awareness, lack of concern, belief of current adequacy, denial of need, avoidance of the unknown, reluctance to use relatively new solutions.

Perceived costs – related to lack of experience of firms and consultants, longer-term forward financial planning, underestimation of benefits via reduced waste, enhanced public image and avoidance of fines, civil damages etc.

Implementation – resistance to complexity, concerns about use of EMS in relation to legal compliance issues, resources (money, time, skills, knowledge), loss of commitment, inappropriate and/or limited application within organisations.

Personnel – lack of skills, knowledge, expertise and examples to implement process, reluctance to use external assistance such as consultants, no delegated responsibility or delegated responsibility with no resources or power to implement change.

A specific issue that stands out is that 'innovation may be particularly difficult in the case of small- and medium-sized companies where absorptive capacity is limited and where a failure in an innovation could result in the failure of the business' (Kirkland and Thompson 1999: 134). In other words, for such firms there may be neither expertise nor understanding, but lots of fear.

At a more abstract level, the embrace of EMS by many firms and corporations has been interpreted in several different ways. At the centre of changes to environmental regulation has been the movement toward 'corporate ownership' of the definitions, and responses to, environmental problems. This has taken different forms. One type of response has been to adopt the language of EMS and to assert that regulation is best provided by those industries and companies directly involved in production processes. This occurs at both particular firm levels, and in relation to the setting of international standards for environmental management, as in the case of the ISO 14000.

As explained, there are various dimensions to EMS, relating to environmental valuation and risk analysis, product design, corporate culture and environmental awareness, supply and waste chain management, and so on (see Kirkland and Thompson 1999). While EMS may be seen as progressive and a positive step forward in environmental regulation by some, embedded within EMS ideology are certain assumptions that imply 'more of the same' rather than system transformation. This is acknowledged in literature that is more sceptical and critical of what EMS appears to offer.

Traditionalist – as far as possible (in light of regulatory and compliance obligations) ignores impact of business activities on the natural environment or due to perceived barriers will not implement EMS procedures, or displaces activity to areas where unfettered firm activity is profitable/possible, i.e. decisions to not adopt EMS are economic-based and contingent upon immediate business strategic market concerns.

Reformist – sees value in development and implementation of EMS insofar as economic and environmental interests seen to be in harmony, attempts to offer a managerialist approach to limit human economic activity within bounds set by the ecosystem, framework of environmental sustainability, i.e. decisions to adopt EMS are economic-based and values-based.

Radical – dismisses EMS as tokenistic and as doing little to deal with the root causes of environmental degradation, in that dominant systemic pressures are inherently destructive to the environment in terms of ever-growing production, consumption, depletion of resources and waste generation, i.e. decisions to adopt EMS are essentially a form of ideological greenwashing that masks production and pollution as usual.

Strategic – sees EMS as addressing some of the worst environmental excesses (i.e. real material consequences in specific cases), but at ideological and symbolic level EMS serves to construct products and companies as 'green' and legitimises corporate management as the primary societal agent responsible for addressing environmental issues, i.e. decisions to adopt EMS are part of a political, practical and ideological response to the threat to corporate hegemony.

Figure 8.4 Differing views of environmental management systems
Source: drawing upon Levy 1997.

According to the critics, the key message of EMS is that corporations have the 'know how' to best protect the environment (on our behalf), in that they have the technical means and managerial strategies to do so. As Levy (1997) points out, and as echoed in the 'smart regulation' literature (see Gunningham and Grabosky 1998), EMS is presented as a win–win opportunity in which the potential structural conflicts between profit maximisation and environmental goals are avoided.

As well as not being demonstrated empirically, this provides yet another cover to circumvent government regulation. Much the same has been argued in relation to the 'standards' put forward by the International Organisation for Standardisation (ISO). That is, the ISO 14000 (relating to environmental impacts) constitutes a private sector initiative that allows for the State to divulge itself of regulatory functions and simultaneously remove regulation and standards-setting from the democratic process and beyond the reach of citizens and social movements (Wall and Beardwood 2001). The issue of who regulates what, and who controls the process, is central to any discussion of how best to respond to environmental harm.

The ways in which corporations communicate about environmental issues and concerns has also been touted as a positive example of the success of self-regulation. 'Corporate communication' can take many different forms. Some of these include:

- Annual reports and accounts;
- Specific corporate environmental reports;
- Statutory returns in the public domain;
- Statutory returns that are confidential;
- Product labels;
- Company surveys;
- Newsletters and videos;
- Press releases and media briefings;
- 'Open house' days and visits to company sites;
- Briefings and public meetings;
- Use of focus groups;
- Advertising.

Study of corporate reporting and communication strategies, however, point to great variability in how individual firms report – what they report, how they report it, and to whom they report (Topalov 1999; Hughes 2004).

It would appear that the variability in communication and corporate reporting stems in part from the fact that accountability relationships are still not clearly articulated and entrenched in legislation. To put it differently, at least in Australia, there are no uniform rules on the public disclosure of environmental matters and no legal requirement or process for the independent verification of the information reported (Hughes 2004). A further issue is that, even where the reporting is well structured and presented, this does not mean that the company in question necessarily translates environmental considerations into actual operating strategies.

The issue of corporate communication strategies also demands recognition of the ways in which firms engage in systematic propaganda campaigns. Inadequate corporate reporting mechanisms may be reinforced by concerted attempts to greenwash issues (this pulp mill will be the most environmentally-friendly ever built, claimed a prominent Tasmania-based company; which then proceeded to whittle away each safeguard that was central to the initial claim) and companies (we do everything in a sustainable and environmentally friendly way, says the same company). Greenwashing is basically about public relations, and is today a huge part of any corporate image-making (see Beder 1997; Athanasiou 1996; Hager and Burton 1999; White 2005b). To take just one example: 'When a scandal-ridden company called Nuclear Engineering Inc changes its name to U.S. Ecology, wins the contract to build a hotly contested radioactive waste dump, and distributes slick brochures explaining the dump's displacement of a threatened desert tortoise as 'A New Home for Endangered Friends', it is obviously the logic of appearance that sets the terms' (Athanasiou 1996: 232). Assessing environmental harm is difficult if the issues are clouded and obscured from the beginning.

Social power and environmental regulation

There is a need to deconstruct notions such as 'self-regulation' by examining the real world of corporate activity, and the persisting damage caused by systemic exploitation of humans and the natural environment. This involves identifying and explaining the transformations in regulation along a number of dimensions, taking into account the specific role of international capitalist institutions such as the World Trade Organisation, the International Monetary Fund and the World Bank, and accounting for the shifts in regulatory emphasis away from the State and toward private business interests (see for example, Goldman 1998b; O'Brien et al. 2000; Beder 2006).

In the context of neo-liberal policies and globalised capital relations, the relationship of the State to private interests is ultimately contingent upon baseline economic criteria. Recent arguments that what we need to do is to adopt forms of 'smart regulation' (that involve a wide constellation of policy measures) tend to assume that improved environmental performance is possible, at a price acceptable to both business and community. This can be achieved simply through adoption of the right mix of policy prescriptions (see Gunningham and Grabosky 1998). The emphasis is on efficiency and effectiveness of regulation; specific problems are presented primarily as technical matters rather than as residing in the realm of politics. In the end, the appeal to 'pragmatic' multi-dimensional sorts of regulation conflate the idea of feasible forms of regulation with forms of regulation that currently predominate in the here and now.

Yet, as Snider (2000: 172) points out with regards to corporate crime, of which environmental harm is one manifestation, the broad trend has been for it to 'disappear'. This occurs through decriminalisation (the repeal of criminal law), through deregulation (the repeal of all State laws, criminal, civil and administrative) and through downsizing (the destruction of the State's enforcement capability). A vital part of this disappearance has been the demise of 'command and control' legislation – that is, direct and systematic State intervention undertaken in the public interest in opposition to specific private interests. The contingencies of the regulatory pyramid are such that there is a lack of a pyramid as such if the peak is never attained (that is, if the 'big stick' is never or rarely used). Likewise, the contingencies of decision-making are such that the public interest is liable to disappear when the key voices in regulation are those of the industries themselves.

The mandate of most State-directed environmental protection agencies today is not only to enforce compliance through use of criminal prosecutions, but also to forge strategic alliances and working partnerships with industries, local governments, and communities in support of environmental objectives. These are often explicitly framed in terms of economic, as well as environmental, objectives. In many cases, the multiple demands on environmental protection agencies from different sections of government, business, and community, and the varied tasks in which they participate, may lead to a dilution of their enforcement capacities and activities. Important questions can be asked therefore in regards to the number of investigators and inspectors responsible for enforcing environmental law, and the philosophical framework that underpins their work. Budget cuts, reductions in personnel and loss of agency status all contribute to the diminish ability of State regulators to actually do their job. These are political decisions and deliberate policy choices.

The problems plaguing regulation at the local and national levels are even further compounded when pitched at the level of global relations. For example, BBC journalist Richard Black comments on the problems with regulation in practice:

There is corruption, there are the costs of enforcement, there is the lack of political will, there are opportunities for a fast buck. Two years ago, making an environmental documentary for BBC World Service, I set up a fake online identity, posing as an unscrupulous European computer businessman who wanted to export old equipment containing toxic materials without the hassle of the Basel bureaucracy. Negotiations proceeded far enough that two companies, both based in the US but with East Asian operations, were prepared to take containers of computer parts unseen into Hong Kong. As a party to the Basel Convention, China should not be allowing such materials entry to its ports without the appropriate paperwork. But both companies said they had 'ways' of getting material through customs without scrutiny. At the end of the trail lie Chinese villages where computers are disassembled using techniques unthinkable in the west. The environmental group Basel Action Network filmed circuit boards being processed in woks full of boiling acid (Black 2006).

Again, economic considerations appear to pre-empt the possibility of social and ecological bottom-lines in circumstances where State intervention is non-existent or light-handed.

There are false dichotomies in regards to some analyses of State and market-based regulation, such that each is seen to fail due to specific technical and resistance reasons, rather than as a reflection of essential power relations. As part of this dichotomisation, State intervention is usually miscast as 'big stick' and 'reactive', while market solutions are seen as 'incentive-based' and 'pro-active'. One form of regulation is thus seen as unnecessarily coercive, the other as necessarily facilitative – but neither view challenges the logic of the status quo, either in terms of present distributions of power, wealth and control, or in terms of the primary objective of environmental regulation in relation to economic development.

In this context, 'smart regulation' is therefore presented as a middle way, one that goes beyond either heavy State intervention or free market environmentalism. It is a 'pragmatic' response to what is essentially a political struggle over power, meaning and social interests.

The appeal of 'smart regulation' lies in its adherence to a particular ideological framework, one that says economic interests and environmental interests are compatible. Moreover, this is represented as a needed step beyond the 'standard view' of environmental management that proved to be woefully and obviously inadequate to address environmental problems (that is, scientific and popular concerns could no longer be ignored or avoided). But the dangers with this kind of pragmatism are those of political cooptation, sidestepping of central moral/ethical issues (in favour of a technical, 'neutral' approach with its emphasis on efficiency and effectiveness), facilitation of corporate sector 'ownership' of environmental responses, and enhancement of competitive advantage of those with the resources to use and/or sell more environmentally friendly technology (Harvey 1996; Sydee and Beder 2006).

Such an approach is therefore premised upon the idea of 'win–win' situations in which all players and participants are assumed to be winners. This, in turn, opens the door to the idea of the need for cooperation and collaboration between different parties in achieving the 'win–win' result; that no one, including business (and consumers, residents, citizens) need make large sacrifices in the process; and that industry-level and firm-level compliance and innovation is sufficient to meet the goals of 'sustainable development' (see Harvey 1996).

In the end, we are left with an interrelated set of propositions that raise as many questions about regulation as they answer, for both theory development and empirical evaluation.

- An overall increase in State regulatory power in areas such as environmental law and financial market law has been accompanied by the increasing privatisation of regulation;
- Standards setting and preferred environmental management systems reflect the interests of those who have the power to shape political agendas and/or who have the resources to implement desired regulatory regimes;
- State regulatory agencies and bodies are systematically denied the resources necessary to fully enforce environmental protection and are thus placed in a position of reliance and trust upon private sector organisations and 'good will';
- Appeal to self-regulation, smart regulation and tripartite regulatory schemes, while addressing some of the worst environmental excesses, pose little threat but rather serve to bolster overall corporate hegemony;
- Emphasis on cooperation as the lynchpin to 'good practice' in environmental regulation is a backdoor way to de-legitimate mass social action and to reinforce corporatist methods of decision-making.

Whether or not one sees regulation in terms of criminal or civil remedies, there is the larger issue that much of the present regulation debate is taking place within a culture based around the 'regulation' of inherently anti-ecological activities. That is, current regulatory apparatus, informed by the ideology of 'sustainable development', is largely directed at bringing ecological sustainability to the present mode of producing and consuming – one based upon the logic of growth, expanded consumption of resources and the commodification of more and more aspects of nature.

Conclusion: where to from here?

It is true that environmental regulation is a complex area that requires acknowledgement of many different players, strategies, approaches and techniques. These complexities should not belie the fundamentally political nature of the exercise however. For at its heart, environmental regulation is about decision-making that is favourable or unfavourable to economic, social and ecological considerations. Furthermore, the mechanics of regulation ought to be interpreted in the light of both immediate contingencies (such as firm-level characteristics and capacities), as well as broad historical political economic conjunctures (such as world system-level trends).

Research in this area has constantly to juggle issues surrounding what can be done in the here and now to prevent the worst excesses of environmental degradation, and what really ought to be done to prevent harm and sustain ecological systems more generally. In other words, while critique of specific methods and arrangements is crucial to understanding the limitations of existing systems of regulation, regulation as such remains a vital part of any reform agenda. But this, too, is a highly politicised matter.

Some argue, for example, that world's best practice in relation to environmental regulation should be based upon a cooperative rather than confrontational role for non-government organisations. In this scenario, mass mobilisation and public demonstrations are not necessarily the best way to achieve best practice (see Braithwaite and Drahos 2000: 286). Others, however, argue that one of the threats to the vitality and effectiveness of NGOs is the threat of cooptation and dilution of basic objectives in the light of negotiated deals with corporate protagonists (Walker 2001). The tension between different approaches to activism has major implications for the success or otherwise of smart regulation and enforced self-regulation models.

A key issue for regulators is how enforcement ought to work vis-à-vis its coercive elements. As observed above (and in Chapter 7), without the use and threat of the 'big stick' there is little to compel offenders to observe the rules of the regulatory game. Economic and other incentives can only go so far – when it comes to the profit margin, what works economically is what will be adopted institutionally. If a global company, for example, is bound by rules in one country but not in another, its behaviour will likewise be different in each setting.

> In Nigeria there is no government environmental regulatory intervention, therefore it is cheaper for Shell and other oil companies operating in Nigeria to pay 11 cents per every 1000 cf of gas flared per year, than to turn off the gas, save the environment and lives of the people in the community. Nigeria alone accounts for more than 28% of the total gas flared in the world. These gas emissions contribute to global warming. In contrast, Shell in Alberta is working to decrease gas emissions, coincidentally complying with the demands of the Alberta government (Hughes 2004: 45).

Resources are frequently not mobile, even though those companies that exploit them are. Those who control the resource therefore can exercise a modicum of pressure on those who wish to exploit it. But to be effective they will have to be prepared for corporate resistance of varying kinds.

The disjunction between regulation theory and what happens in regulatory practice ought to be subject to ongoing critical analysis. The overlap between contemporary theoretical currents and neo-liberal economic agendas also deserves further scrutiny. Regardless of origin or motivating rationale, recent trends in both regulatory theory and practice seem to entrench forms of regulation that work against the ideals of environmental and ecological justice. Yet, as the threats associated with global warming make clear, there is urgent need for extensive, rigorous and global regulatory systems, systems with teeth.

Chapter 9

Environmental crime prevention

The best way to respond to crime is to prevent it before it occurs. Especially for environmental harm, foresight and prudence is needed in order to modify present activities in the light of future potential harms. For environmental crime prevention, the precautionary principle is crucial. So, too, is learning from the approaches and techniques of conventional criminology that may be usefully employed to prevent environmental crime.

Introduction

The intention of this chapter is to examine the relationship between environmental harm and crime prevention. It asks the question, how do we go about improving community safety in relation to environmental issues? The chapter provides an exploration of this by considering how we might envisage crime prevention strategies and approaches that could be designed to deal with varying sorts of environmental harm.

The first part of the chapter discusses the nature and dynamics of environmental crime, and how these will necessarily impinge upon environmental law enforcement and prevention strategies. This is partly a matter of technique: for example, how do we deal with harms that we cannot see or smell, as with some forms of toxic pollution? It is also a matter of conceptualisation and value-judgement: where does the precautionary principle fit within criminological analysis? Who or what is the victim? It also relates to scope, given the globalised nature of certain types of environmental harm: how should we deal with transnational environmental harms, such as those associated with fishing and the logging of forests?

The second part discusses what we might learn from conventional crime prevention about how to prevent environmental harm. What ideas might we glean from the literature on situational prevention (e.g. satellite technology), community crime prevention (e.g. coastal watch groups) and crime prevention through environmental design (e.g. channelling of people via predetermined routes through wilderness)? What skills, capacities and organisational relationships are needed if we are adequately, and successfully, to prevent environmental harm? The more carefully we consider issues of environmental harm, and the aims and objectives of crime prevention, the more controversial we find the subject matter. Indeed, the chapter raises issues that fundamentally challenge the means and ends of criminology itself. Accordingly, it concludes with a brief review of key tensions likely to arise in criminological encounters with environmental issues.

Environmental crime prevention

Environmental crime prevention encompasses a range of substantive considerations. It must deal with acts and omissions that are already criminalised and prohibited, such as illegal fishing or illegal dumping of toxic waste. It must also come to grips with events that have yet to be designated officially as 'harmful' but that show evidence of exhibiting potentially negative consequences. Environmental crime prevention likewise has to negotiate different kinds of harms, as these affect humans, local and global environments, and nonhuman animals.

The first question that has to be addressed in any discussion of crime prevention and environmental issues, therefore, is what, precisely, are the crimes that we are talking about? How environmental harm is conceptualised is highly contested within the green criminology literature (see Chapters 1 and 4). One reason for this ambiguity over definition is that environmental harm can be conceptualised as involving acts and omissions that are both 'legal' and 'illegal'. For instance, from an ecological perspective, some activities, such as clearfelling of old-growth forests, are legal but deemed to be highly destructive. The criteria for 'harm' and 'crime', therefore, depend very much upon the values, knowledge and deliberations of those investigating the nature of the human activity.

For present purposes the notion of crime prevention refers only to those measures that apply before a crime or event has happened, and does not include coercive measures usually associated with traditional law enforcement approaches (see Sutton *et al.* 2008). Crime prevention is thus pre-emptive rather than reactionary or after the fact; and it incorporates modes of intervention that are not reliant upon hands-on coercion by authority figures.

The aims and objectives of environmental crime prevention are inseparable from ecophilosophy. That is, what it is we are trying to prevent is inherently linked to how we view human interests, the needs and requirements of specific biospheres, and the rights of nonhuman animals. Again, as alluded to in Chapter 1, this often means a weighing up of harms, interests and rights in specific contexts and circumstances.

Environmental crime prevention also necessarily encapsulates particular visions of 'the good society', as do any types of crime prevention initiative. In other words, crime prevention of any kind always has ramifications for the kind of world within which we live, and the balance we make between liberty and social control (Sutton *et al.* 2008). For instance, a strong ecological stance could well justify the prohibition of people from going into any wilderness area whatsoever, on the basis of preventing human interference in such areas. Whether or not alternatives are possible or should be made available is exactly what the political deliberations over crime prevention would have to grapple with. The answer very much depends upon the specific vision – the specific relationship between 'nature', society and animals – which is seen as ideal at any particular point in time.

If humans are allowed into specific wilderness areas, then the next question is, under what conditions? To prevent possible environment harms perpetrated by the presence of humans in these areas, rules and regulations are needed (e.g. on burying human waste, on taking litter out of the areas with you as you go). Creative architecture and strategic planning can also ameliorate the impact of humans. For instance, boardwalks and well-marked pathways can channel human traffic in certain directions and through certain areas. Provision of toilets and look-outs might have a 'honey pot' effect in drawing tourists and bush walkers into particular settings and thus away from more pristine wilderness locations. Once general decisions about the nature–human interface are made, provisions to prevent or minimise damage can be introduced.

Theoretically, good environmental crime prevention ought to be as inclusive of human, environment and animal interests as possible.

The basic principles of crime prevention need to be guided by considerations of ecological balance and from a human perspective, ecological citizenship. That is, human laws and human rights have to be tempered by the acknowledgement that human interests are intimately bound up with the well-being of the planet as a whole. Human intervention, of any kind, needs to be considered in the light of this. The notion of ecological citizenship centres on human obligations to all living things, and obliges us to carefully assess the impacts of human activity across the human and nonhuman domains.

In order to achieve this, however, we need to be clear as to what 'crime prevention' is actually intended to do. For example, balancing diverse human and nonhuman interests still means assigning some type of 'value' to the potential harm. Consider oil for instance. Is environmental crime prevention best served by ensuring that oil tankers are shipshape and tightly regulated in their transportation of oil? This would ensure a modicum of *harm minimisation*. Or, should we eliminate the threat of oil spill by banning oil tankers outright? This would entail *harm eradication*. Clearly the type and extent of environmental crime prevention will be dictated by notions of human self-interest, as well as potential threats to environments, animals and livelihoods.

One of the mandates of green criminology is to foster greater attention, analysis and action in regards to environmental harm. From the point of view of environmental crime prevention, the tasks are both instrumental and symbolic. We want to put into place strategies that protect certain peoples, places and creatures. At the same time, we want to signal to the community as a whole that this particular project is significant and that it expresses our collective values about 'what counts'. For instance, the establishment of 'green zones' in the Great Barrier Reef Marine Park is important, not only because it secludes certain areas from human interaction, but it sends a strong message that ecological well-being does count in human calculations of marine interests. The choice of words is important, as is publicity surrounding these protected areas.

As with contemporary policing, one of the key lessons from conventional crime prevention is that it ought to be based largely on a problem-solving, rather than a policy-prescribed, model of intervention. Particular problems demand particular kinds of responses. There has been little written of a specific nature about environmental crime prevention as such. However, there has been criminological work that has suggested various avenues that can serve to improve overall environmental well-being in relation to corporate activities. As described in Box 9.1, there are differing combinations of positive measures that can be used to persuade and provide incentives for companies to be good environmental citizens.

Box 9.1   Strategies for the improvement of environmental performance

Provision of information about environmental risks, responsibilities and opportunities:

- Inform people of injurious consequences of a course of action;
- Alert recipient to beneficial course of action that is in their self-interest;
- Basic information on legal requirements and why they exist;
- Communication of the logic of a programme or regime;
- Information for market about environmental risks and processes;
- Messages of 'corporate social responsibility' from fellow executives.

Self-regulatory systems for environmental compliance:

- Development and promulgation of company policy;
- Development of industry codes of practice;
- Self-certification: responsibility of attesting that one is in compliance, with the responsibility for voluntary disclosure in the event of a violation;
- Benchmarking against international practice: ISO 14000;
- Idea of a community of shared fate: mistake of one affects the others.

Commercial influences and products which are environmentally preferable:

- 'Environmentally benign' products that appeal to consumer preferences;
- 'End-of-pipe' pollution abatement technology: innovation for new markets;
- Process modification approaches, which achieve greater efficiencies in production by conserving raw materials and energy and by minimising waste;

- Buyer/supplier influences: 'cradle to grave' environmentalism;
- Institutional investors: good environmental management equals good management in general;
- Environmental services: monitoring, auditing, risk management, product testing.

Incentives for exemplary environmental performance:

- Financial incentives: grants, subsidies, price preferences for environmentally friendly products, effluent incentive payments, bounty payments for good grasslands management;
- Non-monetary incentives that are 'facilitative': compliance gives rise to procedural shortcuts or waivers, reduction in fees for early compliance, accelerated review of applications;
- Non-monetary incentives that are 'symbolic': award of a medal or trophy, prestigious environmental award programmes for industry, idea of reputational capital, public enunciation of virtuous conduct, use of simple praise in compliance activity.

Hybrid solutions combining two or more of the above.

Source: Grabosky and Gant 2000.

There are, of course, limitations to how far these measures, on their own, will go in terms of protecting and conserving environments. This is especially so in the light of systemic imperatives to expand production and consumption (see Chapter 6). Nevertheless, such ideas do provide a relatively benign approach to implementing environmental crime prevention measures, although they relate more to issues of regulation than crime prevention as such (see Chapter 8).

Not only does current thinking about crime prevention have to develop its own kind of specificity when applied to environmental issues, it also has to be abreast of other kinds of developments as well. That is, contemporary crime prevention has to incorporate a wide range of new techniques, technologies and expertise as applied to varying types of environmental issues. To take just a few examples:

DNA testing

Illegal fishing and illegal logging can be tracked through the employment of DNA testing at the point of origin and at the point of final sale. Work done on abalone DNA, for example, demonstrates that particular species within particular geographical locations can be identified as having specific (and thus unique) types of DNA (Roffey *et al.* 2004). The use of phylogenetic DNA profiling as a tool for the investigation of poaching also offers a potential deterrent in that regular testing allows for the linking of abalone species and/or subspecies to a particular country of origin. This increases the chances of detection and thus may have relevance to crime prevention as such. The use of DNA testing to track the illegal possession and theft of animals and plants can thus serve to deter would-be offenders, if applied consistently, pro-actively and across national boundaries.

Satellite surveillance

Illegal land clearance, including cutting down of protected trees, can be monitored through satellite technology. Compliance with, or transgression of, land clearance restrictions, for example, can be subjected to satellite remote sensing in ways that are analogous to the use of closed circuit television (CCTV) in monitoring public places in cities. Interestingly, the criminalisation of land clearance, which primarily affects private landholders, was due in part to images of extensive rates of land clearance provided through satellite remote sensing studies. Use of such technologies also embed certain notions of 'value' and particular relations between nature and human beings, issues that warrant greater attention in any further development of this kind of technological application (Bartel 2005).

Environmental forensics

The contamination of land, water and air can be prevented by pro-active testing of specific sites, movement routes and currents, by the establishment and collection of benchmark data, and by regular monitoring. To do this requires utilisation of methods that might include chemical analysis, study of documentary records, use of aerial photographs, and application of trend techniques that track concentrations of chemical substances over space and/or time (Murphy and Morrison 2007). Bearing in mind that some contaminations, such as nuclear radiation, are not easily visible to human detection, both alternative methods of science and communal reflexivity over potential risks will be needed (Macnaghten and Urry 1998).

Taxonomy and rare species protection

The identification of rare species, and knowledge of how trade and poaching in rare species occurs, requires both scientific and sociological expertise. Taxonomy describes the science and practice of classification and categorisation of species, both plant and animal. DNA testing can be used to 'verify' a species that is deemed to be rare. The very rarity of an exotic animal or plant means that forensic techniques can be used for prosecution if the plant or animal is protected by endangered species and/or export legislation. Plant and animal collectors either wish to add to private collections or have a commercial interest in monopolising certain species. Here a simple crime prevention measure has been to limit the type of information published in scientific journals about new species. The publication of location details has frequently been used by poachers to find rare or new species, who have subsequently collected or traded the newly discovered species, often without consideration of their environments or their future preservation (Guterman 2006). New ways of reporting scientific finds and data, such that specific geographical locations are not provided, can diminish this possibility.

A problem-solving approach to crime prevention demands a certain level of specificity. That is, general pronouncements about the nature of harm need to be accompanied by particular site or harm analysis. To illustrate how this might occur, we can consider issues surrounding harm and fishing.

Harm associated with fishing

It is important to begin this discussion by pointing out that fishing – both legal and illegal – is associated with a wide range of potentially harmful activity. Legally provided fishing, such as aquaculture and the 'scientific' harvesting of whales, can engender great harm. The distinction between legal and illegal may in fact not be the best way to conceptualise harm or responses to harm.

Consider, for example, the diverse answers to the question, 'what harm is there in fishing'? One approach has been to emphasise irresponsible fishing that is contributing to the world's most valuable fish stocks being overfished. This practice is generally referred to as illegal, unreported and unregulated (IUU) fishing, and is the subject of much legal, scientific and regulatory attention (Riddle 2006; Lugten 2005). However, when considering the many different types of fishing, beyond that related to IUU fishing on the high seas, it becomes apparent that harm can stem from and be associated with many different kinds of practice.

Fishing for profit can be distinguished from fishing for subsistence, and each of these can be distinguished from fishing for pleasure. Yet each kind of fishing entails different kinds of threat, risk and potential harm. Assessing the harms associated with fishing alerts us to the fact that environmental crime prevention has to involve lateral thinking if varying types of harms are to be prevented, reduced, minimised, eradicated or, indeed, addressed to begin with.

Case study 9.1   Aquaculture as mass production fishing

Sea-cage aquaculture, as found for example in the case of open sea salmon farming, can have negative environmental impacts. According to marine conservationists, for instance, 'it adds more pressure to the marine environment. So many wild fish are killed to make feed for the farmed fish, which at an international level is putting massive pressure on small fish stocks like pilchards, sardines and anchovies' (Craig Bohm of the Australian Marine Conservation Society, quoted in Choy 2007: 7). Intensive aquaculture methods used to produce Atlantic salmon are also of concern because untreated waste from cages is pumped straight into the marine environment. Farmed fish can also involve techniques that produce toxins, as in cases where malachite green is used in Vietnamese fish farms to treat potential fungus growth. However, this substance itself is a known carcinogen suspected of causing cancer (Cresswell 2007).

Case study 9.2   Recreational fishing as hazardous to health

The consumption of sport-caught fish from contaminated sites in the United States has been identified as an important route for human exposure to halogenated hydrocarbons thought to be risk factors for breast cancer (McGovern 2004). Pollutants such as dioxin accumulate in fish flesh and thus the fish can be harmful if regularly consumed by humans (New South Wales Food Authority 2006). Contamination of fish can affect both recreational fishers and commercial fishers. The threats to human health are increased insofar as the originating contaminants are not cleaned up and fish stocks not allowed to clean out the toxins over a period of fish generations.

> **Case study 9.3   Harm to fish stocks through human intervention**
>
> Studies are now showing that the behaviour of fish actually changes when 'adults' are taken away via over-fishing. The young fish do not return to their usual breeding sites and they exhibit different habits compared to their older counterparts (Australian Broadcasting Corporation 2007). On the other hand, intensive fish farming involving over-population of fish-farming ponds leads to a rise in bacterial infections that affects the rate of growth of the fish and may cause death (Gearin 2005). Recent studies are also indicating that exposure to sewerage leads fish to change their gender to female, due to chemicals (i.e. female hormones associated with the female contraceptive pill) in river water (in the case of the UK) and sewerage outfalls into the ocean (in the case of the US) (Pyper 2005; Cone 2005).

Scientists and professional fishers are increasingly aware of the potential dangers and hazards associated with certain kinds of production practices, such as seabed dredging in the case of scallops. According to Malcolm Haddon, an expert in resource assessment:

> We optimise catch rates, target only the best beds and minimise the impact of dredging on the seabed and other marine life. As a result, scallop fishing now provides a steady income to the fishers who manage it; the harvest is stable and of high quality, which suits customers; and the environment recovers. It's a win all round (quoted in Cribbs 2007: 47).

Many fishers are learning from past mistakes. Existing and potential harms require consciousness of the issues and a desire to engage in sustainable practices, as well as continuing commitment to change.

Conventional crime prevention approaches can in fact provide insights into how these kinds of harm might well be prevented or minimised. A proper scoping of the issues and analysis of the specific problems would therefore be accompanied by the development of particular interventions across diverse crime prevention areas (see Sutton *et al.* 2008).

In terms of *social crime prevention* methods, for example, children in schools could be exposed to programmes that reshape their concepts of 'the environment', 'fish' and 'fishing'. This could include discussions of 'catch and release' as an imperative for recreational fishing, through to doing assignments on the effects of climate change on fish species. Young people who already or who appear to be most likely to degrade environments or abuse animals could be subjected to intensive programmes aimed at changing attitudes and behaviour.

In terms of *environmental prevention* methods, boating enthusiasts and fishers generally could be advised of how best to minimise their impact on fisheries, through measures such as knowledge of marine park boundaries through to use of suitable receptacles for waste products while at sea. Regular patrols of coastlines, and use of satellites, could facilitate surveillance and monitoring of fishing 'hot spots' and areas where environmental transgressions occur on a frequent basis. The point is that, whether legal or illegal, various activities can be responded to in a manner that positively reduces their harmful consequences. On the other hand, there are occasions when official reaction is driven solely on the basis of the legal/illegal distinction.

Illegal fishing and harmful activities

Even if we are to restrict crime prevention to just those types of fishing that are deemed to be illegal, there is still considerable scoping work to do. This is because there are major variations in the specific nature of this kind of illegality. Figure 9.1 provides a brief outline of different kinds of fishing, and the activities related to each that can be described as illegal, criminal and harmful.

Different scales, motivations and techniques underpin each of these types of illegal fishing. Environmental crime prevention thus has to address the specific nature of the phenomenon in question if it is to be appropriate to the circumstances. Different kinds of illegality in fact require quite different kinds of responses, since they stem from quite different origins.

Conventional crime prevention emphasises the importance of undertaking scoping analysis before developing an intervention plan (Sutton *et al.* 2008). For example, Eck's (2003) model of crime prevention provides a useful starting point for investigation of the social processes and social relationships associated with illegal fishing. This model can be used to guide assessment of the key relationships and agencies involved in shaping targets, places and offending as this occurs in a marine environment. This is represented in Figure 9.2.

While the general contours of illegal fishing can be mapped out in this way, the structural or underpinning reasons for different types of illegal fishing still require close analysis. The case of indigenous or traditional fishing provides some indication of the complexities of the issues.

Type of fishing	Potential type of harmful activity
Commercial	• Criminal: illegal, unreported, excess to quota, false declarations; • Damage to seabed and marine environment, and to other creatures such as birds; • Destruction of by-catch and marine pollution; • Overexploitation of vulnerable species.
Recreational	• Regulatory: unlicensed, excess to quota; • Over-fishing; • Sport kills such as giant marlin; • Litter and pollution.
Indigenous	• Illegal: fishing in (traditional) but foreign waters, fishing without permit; • Over-fishing; • Non-selective fishing.
Aquaculture	• Regulatory: unlicensed, unregulated; • Conditions of penning and disease; • Fish feed and contamination; • Use of chemicals in fish farming.
Scientific	• Regulatory: excess to quota; • Depletion of vulnerable species such as whales.
Illegal	• Criminal: illegal, unreported; • Over fishing; • Super exploitation of particular species for selective food markets (e.g. shark fin).
Specialist	• Criminal: illegal, unreported; • Super exploitation of particular species for purposes of medicine or private collections such as seahorses and aquarium fish.

Figure 9.1 Fishing and related harmful activities

Place	Manager
Coastal waters	Fisheries, customs, quarantine, port authorities
High seas	Navy, fisheries
Marine parks	Park authorities, port authorities
Offender	**Handler**
Large-scale illegal operators	Buyers, market consumers
Small-scale traditional fishers	Communities, governments
Victim/target	**Guardian**
Fish	Commercial and recreational fishers
Indigenous people	Communities, governments

Figure 9.2 A model of environmental crime prevention: factors relevant to illegal fishing

Traditional fishing

The first question to ask when it comes to consideration of traditional fishing, legal or illegal, is what we actually mean by the word 'traditional'. This can in fact refer to quite different aspects of traditional fishing, such as:

- *Who specifically* (indigenous Australian, indigenous Indonesian, Papua New Guinea, Torres Strait Islander);
- *How specifically* (methods, techniques and technologies);
- *Where specifically* (traditional fisheries for particular coastal groups).

Conflicts can arise when modern technologies are utilised for what used to be simply subsistence fishing. The use of motor boats, nets and fishing rods, and sonar equipment allows for overexploitation to occur. The unrestrained exploitation of resources may be due to employment of new technologies, perceptions of resources being boundless and where management is believed to be beyond human control (Caughley *et al.* 1996). Moreover, overexploitation may be generated in the new methods of production themselves. For example, on the one hand, the mobility, range, and efficiency of 'traditional' fishing are all enhanced through modern methods and technologies. On the other hand, these technologies generate the need for cash to supplement subsistence e.g. buying the boat and petrol for the boat.

The net effect is pressure to fish beyond immediate consumption needs.

Conflicts can also occur in regards to both differing notions of 'sustainability' and encroachment by other people into traditional fishing areas.

> The concept of sustainability may be viewed slightly differently by non-Aboriginal people than by Aboriginal peoples and Torres Strait Islanders. To many non-Aboriginal people, the concept broadly implies the maintenance of maximum economic *productivity* of lands and seas. For Aboriginal peoples and Torres Strait Islanders, it often means the continuance of *use* of wildlife resources for subsistence. This small but important difference can lead to confusion over the 'sustainability' or otherwise of wildlife use. There is also an important distinction to be drawn between concerns over declines in the local abundance of a species, which may reduce its short-term availability as a resource for harvest, and declines in abundance which are sufficiently widespread and diverse to be a cause of concern for species' survival. Local declines in abundance associated with harvesting will not threaten a species with extinction unless the rate of offtake is unsustainable in the longer term (Caughley *et al.* 1996: 8, emphasis in original).

Differing perceptions of 'sustainability' also translate into different purposes and different scales of operation. In an international context, Hauck (2007: 272) points out that traditional fishers are usually associated with small-scale fisheries:

> Although each context will be different, small-scale fisheries can be broadly characterised as employing labour intensive harvesting to exploit fishery resources by operating from shore or from small fishing vessels. Furthermore, it is recognised that fishers within this sector live in fishing communities with relatively fragile livelihood conditions (Manning 2001).

Large-scale commercial fisheries, and large-scale illegal fishing operations, put these traditional fishers in a perilous position. Not only are these export-oriented, but the scale of fishing itself tends to put pressure on fishing stocks. Overfishing in some waters has immediate and dire consequences for local traditional fishers since

247

fish is part of the staple diet of these people. Moreover, overfishing in one place generates movement of both large-scale fisheries and traditional fishers to other locations, thus impinging upon traditional rights and traditional owners in these areas. In this way, conflict may occur not only between trawler operators and traditional fishers, but amongst traditional fishers themselves as they are forced further from their own traditional fishing waters in order to sustain a liveable catch. In this context, the problem is not simply one of non-compliance on the part of small-scale fishers (e.g. Indonesian fishers in Australian defined waters), but of food security and the reliance on increasingly declining fish stocks for their survival. Hence, from a crime prevention perspective, a 'big stick' approach will simply not work since it does not address the diversity of issues that may be influencing non-compliant behaviour (see Hauck 2007).

The complexities of traditional fishing are also manifest in the fact that a continuum exists between commercial and traditional fishing, and some people may practice community fishing and the fish caught may be either used for subsistence purposes or sold. That is, traditional fishing today often has an interface with the cash economy: fish to eat, fish to sell to subsist (Altman *et al.* 1996; Caughley *et al.* 1996). One issue, as mentioned above, is whether the activities of commercial (and indeed recreational) fishers adversely affect the subsistence resources of traditional communities. Another issue is to what extent these communities must themselves rely upon commercialised fishing in order to gain sufficient subsistence resources. The former requires 'external' controls of some kind to dissuade overfishing and illegal fishing. These might include monitoring and surveillance, as well as moral persuasion, to desist from harmful behaviour. The latter might well be responded to by employment of incentive measures. An example of what this might look like is provided in a Canadian initiative:

> In Canada, for example, the Income Security Programme (ISP) established for Cree hunters in north Quebec provides guaranteed income to allow the Cree to hunt. With the ISP, production is linked to people's need and there is no incentive to overexploit wildlife resources. Indeed there is a voluntary decrease in hunting in overused areas, and other wildlife conservation practices such as monitoring the numbers of certain game are recognised as hunting-related work under the ISP (Altman *et al.* 1996: 89).

Another type of incentive is to involve indigenous people directly in the co-management of the resource. In this approach indigenous fishing rights consist not just of a claim to a share of the harvest, but also a stake in the conservation and management of the resources. In other words, the right to fish can be regulated, but indigenous people ought to be part of that regulation.

What this discussion of traditional fishing illustrates is the complexities of the issues, and the need for thorough analysis before developing crime prevention options. Different types of human behaviour require different responses. While incentives might be crucial to forestalling illegal fishing by Indonesian traditional fishers in Australian waters, trade-related regulation would be more appropriate as a means to deal with large-scale illegal fishing (see Lack 2007). In other instances, a variety of situational measures can be applied that have a distinct marine application (see Smith and Anderson 2004).

In some cases, the emphasis will be on establishing protected areas, such as Australia's Great Barrier Reef Marine Park. Meanwhile, in a slightly different vein, New Zealand recently established Benthic (seabed habitat) Protected Areas (Anderton 2007). Fisheries Minister Jim Anderton said that 'these areas are being set aside to protect our seabed environment. They are not fisheries management tools and are not designed to protect the entire marine ecosystem. The government will continue to manage fisheries by setting catch limits and other rules'. Off-bottom trawl fishing is permitted with strict controls: two Ministry-approved observers on board, the vessel is satellite monitored, and an electronic net monitoring system is used to establish exactly where the fishing net is in relation to the bottom at all times. To ensure that there is little risk of any gear ever touching the bottom, a buffer zone of 100 metres has been set. Fishing within 100 metres of the bottom is a criminal offence. Furthermore, fishing within 50 metres is deemed to be touching the seabed and is a serious criminal offence, attracting a fine of NZ$100,000 and seizure of the vessel.

Brought together we can envisage a wide range of environmental crime prevention techniques, approaches and strategies that can be drawn upon in relation to illegal fishing. These are collated in Figure 9.3.

However, while suggestive of possible interventions such a list only makes sense and 'works' when put into specific fishing contexts. Studies of particular types of illegal fishing, such as abalone, lobster

Social (developmental and communal-oriented)

Incentive schemes
- Alternative sources of revenue for traditional fishers;
- Rights tied to management responsibilities.

Moral persuasion
- 'Catch and release' media advertising;
- Education in schools about species decline;
- Consumer education and fish identification.

Trade-related measures
- Schemes that require documentation to accompany product in order to authenticate its legitimacy (link to DNA testing as well);
- Schemes that rely on vessels lists that identify authorised vessels ('white lists') and/or vessels considered to have been fishing in breach of Regional Fisheries Management Organisations (RFMO) ('black lists') as a basis for imposing restrictions on the access of these latter vessels to ports and port services;
- Trade bans on particular states/entities (IUU vessels) considered to have failed to cooperate in the implementation of the RFMO's conservation and management measures.

Community mobilisation
- Coastal watch schemes and monitoring programmes;
- Indigenous coastal patrols;
- Confidential phone-in hotlines.

Situational (immediate situations and technologies-oriented)

Increasing the effort
- Fencing off key areas;
- ID badges for users;
- Partial park closure; no anchor markers;
- Vessel and employee registration.

Increasing the risks
- Harbour and jetty vessel checks;
- CCTV, satellite photos, Vessel Monitoring Scheme;

- Boat and aircraft patrolling;
- Reporting by public users.

Reducing the rewards
- Preventing access to park, relocating species;
- Licensing of vessels, fish tagging;
- Interfering with markets/distribution channels;
- Issuing permits and licensing.

Inducing guilt or shame
- Strengthening moral condemnation of over-fishing;
- Facilitating compliance by setting up community hotlines;
- Use of warning signs in ports;
- Information pamphlets about the state of fishing stocks.

Figure 9.3 Approaches and techniques of environmental crime prevention: dealing with illegal fishing
Sources: Lack 2007; Smith and Anderson 2004; Clarke 1997; White and Perrone 2005.

and toothfish, show great variation in motives, techniques, local cultures and scale of operation (Tailby and Gant 2002; McMullan and Perrier 2002; Lugten 2005; Anderson and McCusker 2005). As argued throughout this chapter, the specificity of the harm ought to drive the particular type of intervention that is adopted in any given situation. This, in turn, requires close analysis of the multiple facets of each type of harmful activity.

Issues for environmental crime prevention

It is early days in the development of environmental crime prevention as a distinct area of expertise and engagement. This section therefore briefly highlights a few of the issues that must be addressed by those trying to grapple with environmental issues.

Defining the problem

The question of how to define the problem is an intractable and necessary part of the development of environmental crime prevention. Many areas of harm to humans, environs and nonhuman animals are presently not criminalised. This includes such destructive, degrading and dehumanising practices as clearfelling of old-growth forests, reliance upon battery hen forms of egg and poultry production, and use of depleted uranium in weapons. From an analytical point of view, conceptualisation of harm ought not to rely upon the legal–illegal distinction per se, especially since some of the world's most environmentally disastrous practices are in fact still legal. Environmental crime prevention may well entail the exposure of negative, degrading and hazardous practices as a prelude to the banning and close control of such practices. New concepts of harm, as informed by ecological sciences and environmental values, will inevitably be developed as part of this process.

Prevention and precaution

The uncertainties surrounding future impacts and consequences means that debate will occur over when preventative measures need to be introduced as a precautionary measure. The politics of ecological sustainability will collide with the interests of economic growth, since greater adherence to the precautionary principle will almost always lead to curtailment of existing profit-making enterprises. Environmental crime prevention has to have a forward-looking component if human, biosphere and nonhuman interests are to be protected into the future. This means interventions now to guarantee environmental well-being later. Differences in opinion over future consequences means that those who take action now (such as protesting against a large polluting pulp mill) for the sake of up-and-coming generations may well be criminalised in the present. But the history of law reform is built precisely upon such tensions.

Tailoring the responses

While the specificity of the harm demands specificity in response, there are some forms of environmental harm that cannot be contained easily due to the enormous scope of the problem. For example, the transnational movement and illegal dumping of toxic waste will require international cooperation amongst nation-states and social movement activists. Coordination of environmental crime prevention will require free exchange of information and constant surveillance, as well as creative thinking vis-à-vis grappling with issues such as scarcity of water, diminished food sources and expanded need for adequate waste treatment facilities. Climate change and how to deal with it will ultimately require global action. It will also involve the criminalisation of what today is considered acceptable practice. For example, the imposition of severe water restrictions, and harsher penalties in regards to wasteful water use, is just one harbinger of things to come.

Problems of displacement

As with conventional crime prevention, displacement may well occur where good environmental crime prevention measures are introduced. For example, a tightening up of regulation in respect to the shipment of toxic waste in Europe or the US may well force companies to relocate their factories to places such as Mexico and Africa where vulnerable governments have less rigid controls on production and waste treatment. The Not In My Back Yard (NIMBY) syndrome will produce unintended consequences that perpetuate environmental harm. Therefore, a global perspective is essential when it comes to environmental crime prevention. So too, when subsistence fishing, farming and hunting withers due to overexploitation and climate change, then great shifts in human populations and in resource use will take place. The environmental refugee poses a whole new set of questions for criminology.

Questions of agency

What the issue of traditional fisheries highlights is that people in different circumstances have different kinds of choices. The small-scale subsistence fisher has much less power and exercise of agency, than does the large-scale trawler operator. Disparities in power and resources ought not to translate into seeing the more vulnerable and disadvantaged as easy targets for crime prevention (analogous to dealing with 'street crime') while the criminal actions of corporate polluters and large-scale organisations receive less concerted attention. Moreover, the plight of the dispossessed and disadvantaged means that often any environmental destruction brought about by their actions (cutting down of forests, overfishing) is best remedied by social justice initiatives rather than criminal justice interventions, whether these take the form of crime prevention or law enforcement.

Community crime prevention

Environmental crime prevention, as with all good crime prevention approaches, ought to incorporate the activities of ordinary people as part and parcel of the overall strategy. The involvement of diverse communities in this form of crime prevention likewise raises some interesting issues. For example, some types of engagement may be based upon Neighbourhood Watch models of citizen surveillance and monitoring – as in the case of coastal watch projects intended to alert authorities to changes in environmental conditions or the presence of illegal fishers. The place and status of community members, as volunteers or as paid auxiliary workers, can however be contentious. In Australia's Northern Territory local indigenous people would be ideal coastal watch participants given their familiarity with the lands and seas of the north. Yet, it is questionable whether indigenous people have been accorded sufficient respect and credibility from law enforcement officials from agencies such as Customs, much less mainstream police services. In other types of community participation, local residents in urban areas may well play an important and vigilant role in exposing toxic waste spills, release of pollutants into the air, water and land, and illegal harvesting of flora and fauna. How local authorities respond to such groups is crucial to the present and future contours of community crime prevention initiatives that target environmental harm.

Politics of knowing

Environmental crime prevention ought to be based upon a problem-solving approach, but it is not always easy to discern what is accurate or true when it comes to specific environmental harms. There is a need, therefore, for multidisciplinary approaches to the study of environmental harm, involving cooperation between different 'experts', including those with traditional and experiential knowledge associated with culture and livelihood (such as indigenous peoples and farmers), as well as sensitivity to ideas and research generated in intellectual domains such as law, zoology, biology, philosophy, sociology and chemistry. On the other hand, we have to be aware that there are major industries of 'denial' of environmental harm, including both corporations and governments, and this places even greater pressure on criminologists to provide affirmative data and interpretations that will bolster specific environmental crime prevention initiatives.

Much criminal and environmentally destructive behaviour is highly contingent upon particular factors and specific social circumstances. The problem of toxic waste disposal, for example, cannot be divorced from how and why toxic waste is produced in the first place, and the consequences of the commodification of waste that has occurred in the last 50 years (see Chapter 5). Accordingly, to deal with the harms associated with toxic waste disposal, a specific crime prevention plan is needed, one that fits the nature and dynamics of this specific type of environmental harm. The same goes for other forms of harm, whether this is in regards to illegal fishing or the illegal traffic in flora and fauna (see Smith and Anderson 2004; Halstead 1992).

Conclusion: where to from here?

One of the concerns of this chapter has been to provide a general overview of key elements that together form a central part of environmental crime prevention. Some of these include:

- A vision of the good society;
- Adoption of a problem-solving approach;
- Combination of community crime prevention and situational prevention measures;
- Appreciation of the symbolic as well as instrumental applications of crime prevention;
- Use of wide range of approaches, techniques and measures;
- Tailoring responses to specific harms and specific types of crime.

If preventing harm is the aim, then environmental crime prevention will inevitably have to negotiate the legal–illegal divide, and the distinction between sustainable and unsustainable activity. Likewise, reference to the precautionary principle needs to be more fully articulated in and with crime prevention principles, practices and policies. As illustrated in this chapter there are a number of issues pertaining to knowledge and predictions of harm that will need constant attention.

Innovative forensic and associated techniques need to be directly incorporated into environmental crime prevention practice. This necessarily entails forging links across disciplinary areas – from toxicology to historical investigation to place-based site analysis – and interagency cooperation will be a must in dealing with many different types of environmental harm. The field is wide open for new forms of preventive work and specialist collaborations.

Chapter 10

Global environmental issues and socio-legal intervention

Globalisation is a complex phenomenon with many different facets. The most powerful global institution is the transnational corporation. The context within which these organisations operate is fashioned through international convention and law, and global flows of information, people and finance, all of which have a major role in shaping what they do. Dealing with environmental harm will inevitably reflect deep social divisions and embody profound class conflicts. Social change thus will involve challenges to the basic institutions of late capitalism.

Introduction

Responding to environmental harm means responding to the actions of those institutions that generate so much of the destruction, pollution, degradation and extinction. Criminalising particular acts and omissions is one step toward prohibiting the worst and most obvious kinds of harm. Criminalising persistent repeat offenders, especially when they are transnational corporations, is however another thing altogether. It certainly poses a number of challenges for those wanting to uphold the principles and practices of environmental, ecological and species justice.

This chapter discusses the strategic issues associated with environmental reform and institutional change. It provides examples of corporate resilience and assertion of hegemonic power in the face of popular unease with the state of the world's environment. It also explores various ways in which community action can be directed at changing the rules and dynamics of global political economy.

There is no one path or measure or tactic that provides the answer to how we ought to deal with environmental problems and problems of unequal social power. As this book has demonstrated, responding to environmental harm requires action in and by the conventional apparatuses of the State (involving police, courts and regulators), as well as organisations and individuals working outside of the mainstream institutions (involving activists, new social movements and communities). The complexities of social change are myriad; so, too, the types of actions needed to channel reform, urgently, in desired directions will be many and varied.

Global institutions and the neo-liberal agenda

The overall direction of environmental trends can be understood as reflecting the strategic location and activities of transnational capital, as supported by hegemonic nation-states on a world scale. Capitalist globalisation, bolstered via neo-liberal State policy, means that there is great scope to increase environmentally destructive activity (see Chapters 5 and 6). This is supported by the institutions of global governance in the contemporary era, institutions such as the World Bank, the International Monetary Fund and the World Trade Organisation. Such institutions are key players in an increasingly globalised capitalist system and at least some of their policies and practices have been described outright as being 'criminal', as in the case of the World Bank's financing of a dam in Thailand (see Friedrichs and Friedrichs 2002).

The global agenda is 'free trade', under monopoly conditions, and to the advantage of the most powerful companies and countries (see Beder 2006). Privatisation of 'natural resources' such as water is part of this phenomenon.

Box 10.1 Global institutions and transnational water companies

The enormous expansion of water transnational companies in recent years could not have been possible without the World Bank and other international financial institutions such as the International Monetary

---

Fund, the Inter-American Development Fund, the Asian Development Fund and the European Bank for Reconstruction. (Marsden 2003: 2). The conceptualisation and management of drinking water as an economic resource has thus been fostered by key international organisations such as the World Bank, the International Monetary Fund, and the World Trade Organisation. Such thinking has been actively promoted by organisations such as the World Water Council (a platform for major water firms), the Global Water Partnership (initiated by senior World Bank staff), and Business Partners for Development (an industry / World Bank promoter of privatisation).

Neo-liberal 'free trade' provisions are precisely intended to allow the commodification of an ever-growing range of goods and services (many of which are essential to human well-being) and to facilitate the entry of private sector interests into previously State-owned and State-regulated spheres. The World Bank in particular has been the most significant promoter of such neo-liberal discourses. For example, it has been a principal financer of privatisation, lending about US$20 billion to water supply projects over the past decade and a half (Marsden 2003: 1). It has also increasingly made its loans conditional on the requirement that national governments privatise their waterworks. For example, a study of 276 World Bank water supply loans from 1990 to 2002 showed that 30 per cent required privatisation ... the majority in the last five years (Ravindran 2003: 1). Recent major water privatisations across the globe have taken place in cities such as Bogota, Colombia; Manila, Philippines; Jakarta, Indonesia; Buenos Aires, Argentina; Grenoble, France; and Adelaide, Australia (Whelan and White 2005).

In addition to their political connections, each of the three leading transnational water companies has enormous financial resources. Each is among the top 100 corporations in the world according to *Fortune 500*, and it has been estimated that as of 2003 the global water industry was a US$400 billion a year business, making it one third larger than the global pharmaceuticals. In specific terms it is notable that Viola Universal, the parent of 'Vivendi Environnement', reported earning over US$5 billion in water-related revenue in 1990, and that by 2002 this had increased to over US$12 billion (Marsden 2003: 2). RWE, which moved into the world market with its acquisition of Britain's Thames Water, increased its water revenue a whopping 9,786 per cent – from US$25 million in 1990 to US$2.5 billion in fiscal year 2002 (Marsden 2003:2).

> Water privatisation and full cost recovery policies have been imposed as conditions for IMF loans in many countries, particularly in Africa. The result is that water is now less accessible and less affordable, and, in some cases, people are resorting to unsafe water sources. In Ghana, to take one example, it was reported that 'the results of forcing the poor to pay "market rate tariffs" for water means that most people can no longer afford water at all. Only 36 per cent of the rural population have access to safe water and just 11 per cent have adequate sanitation within the existing system'. (South African Municipal Workers Union 2001: 22).

From the point of view of environmental stewardship, privatisation has been accompanied by corporate efforts to 'own' the problem (as well as the industries). This ownership includes both ideological manoeuvring (see the discussion of greenwashing below) and tinkering with existing regulatory systems and production methods (see Chapter 8). Levy (1997), for example, observes several interrelated ideas being promulgated through discussions of Environmental Management Systems (EMS) and other systems of self-regulation. One is the message that the environmental side-effects of capitalist political economy can be managed, enabling economic growth to continue indefinitely. The emphasis is on scientific and managerial means of mitigating environmental effects without questioning the goal of increasing production and consumption.

Related to this idea is the notion that we should leave it to corporate managers to deal with environmental problems. Adoption of EMS procedures and adherence to ISO 14000 standards implies that corporate managers are eager to address environmental problems in support of the social good. There is support of the view that corporations possess the superior technical, financial and organisational resources needed to solve environmental problems, rather than governments or other sections of the community.

There is also the fact that different businesses may have divergent orientations to the environment depending upon their market focus (e.g. public relations firms, newly emerging environmental protection industries, forestry companies). Environmental crises are not always 'bad' for business. They also open new doors of opportunity.

From the point of view of the restructuring of class relationships on a global scale, reforms in environmental management and regulation can also be seen to be intrinsically linked to the efforts of transnational corporations to further their hegemonic control over the planet's natural resources (see Goldman 1998b; Pearce and Tombs 1998). International competition among capitalist sectors for access to healthy resources is intensifying due to the overall shrinking of the natural resource base. The dominance of Western capital in this competition is sustained in part because 'environmental regulation' itself is being utilised as an entry card to new international markets. Markets can be protected through universalising environmental regulation in ways that advantage the high technology companies of the advanced industrialised countries (Goldman 1998b). The largest companies are most likely to be capable of being environmentally 'virtuous' as well as having the most input into redesigning the rules of international standardisation vis-à-vis environmental management (see also Haines 2000).

Further to this, it has been argued that the cleaning up of old, dirty industries and the rewriting of property laws, particularly in the Third World and Russia, in accordance with new international standards of environmental management and trade liberalisation, is a precursor to capitalist penetration and exploitation of nature (Goldman 1998a). To see environmental regulation in this light is to acknowledge the economic rather than ecological rationale behind the actions of global regulatory bodies such as the World Trade Organisation, the International Monetary Fund and World Bank (see Figure 10.1). The un-democratic character of these institutions stems in part from the fact that 'regulation', in this instance, is about facilitation of the exploitation of nature and humans, not about human interests and needs. As Goldman (1998b: 60) points out: 'without commoners and the State assiduously working, protecting, managing and reproducing the world's watersheds, forests, coastal waters, mountainsides and healthy communities, the *use-value* of privatised nature would dramatically diminish, yet another dimension to a changing global division of labour'. Ultimately, the appeal of 'smart regulation' and its corporate expressions in various forms of environmental management systems and voluntary codes of conduct, lies in its adherence to the 'ecological modernisation' ideological framework, which sees economic interests and environmental interests as compatible (Harvey 1996). But, in practice, the emphasis remains that of efficiency and effectiveness, and the outcome ensures corporate sector 'ownership' of environmental responses.

For instance, the set of international standards for environmental management developed by the International Organisation for Standardisation (ISO) has been put into place for particular

Global regulation strategies	Firm and industry regulation
Standards setting	*System management*
ISO 14000 environmental standards	EMS
Global ecological commons	Professionals and experts
WTO, IMF, World Bank	Self-management models

Global environmental movements
Forms and forums for participants
Consultations and conferences
Corporatist (or tripartite) bodies
Protests and activism

Figure 10.1   Global environmental regulatory developments

ideological and political purposes. Specifically, the ISO 14000 was conceived in the early 1990s as a pro-active, industry response to a host of potentially inconsistent environmental standards and to the perception that government and existing industry standards were too bureaucratic and burdensome. Its development, Wall and Beardwood (2001) argue, is consistent with the pressure for conformity and standardisation that accompanies the domination of global interests in the modern era, that is, a new infrastructure of agencies and institutions that reflect the privatisation of regulatory processes and deregulation of capital.

International agreements such as ISO 14000 constitute a parallel process of standard-making that offers opportunities for the State to divulge itself of its regulatory functions. As such it serves several purposes (Wall and Beardwood 2001):

- It fits in with the general ideological thrust of privatising public goods and services; it deflects concerns about the effects of government down-sizing and restructuring by viewing the private sector as capable of managing its own affairs;

- Privatising the regulatory process is one way for governments to defray costs in an era of fiscal constraint;

- It removes regulation and standards-setting from the democratic process and beyond the reach of citizens and social movements. Decisions are both private and international and beyond the realm of the nation-state.

The ISO's official purpose is to encourage and assist the international exchange and transfer of goods and services thereby enhancing technological, economic and scientific activity throughout the world. The objective is first and foremost framed in terms of trade, not ecological considerations.

Particular companies will benefit in different ways from the impetus to be (at least seen to be) more environmentally friendly. Logging companies can claim to be 'green' by meeting ISO standards with regard to EMS implementation. Trees are still chopped down, but the production methods can gain the ISO seal of approval. For other companies, there are genuine job and investment opportunities in areas such as ecotourism, development of new energy sources such as solar power, organic agriculture and non-timber forest products.

While climate change and environmental innovation offer outlets for investment and new profit-making enterprises, some industries are inherently 'dirty', and are not able to be 'responsible' vis-à-vis the environment. It is notable that, for example, 'just 122 corporations account for 80 per cent of all carbon dioxide emissions. And just five private global oil corporations – Exxon Mobil, BP Amoco, Shell, Chevron and Texaco – produce oil that contributes some ten per cent of the world's carbon emissions' (Bruno *et al.* 1999: 1). Some indication of the role of these corporations in poisoning the atmosphere is provided in Table 10.1, which shows that the companies are responsible for more greenhouse gases than most countries.

The response of such corporate polluters has been to adopt what has been dubbed recourse to the 'five Ds' (see Bruno *et al.* 1999). These are largely self-explanatory. They are a conscious response to public concerns about environmental problems. But in this case they retain an emphasis on business-as-usual, even in the context of rising concern about overall planetary health.

1. *Deny* (e.g. the Global Climate Coalition was formed to spread the notion that global warming is a dangerous myth);
2. *Delay* (e.g. we don't know enough, so for the sake of prosperity, delay);
3. *Divide* (e.g. jobs versus environment);
4. *Dump* (e.g. export of products, such as pesticides, to developing countries even after its use has been banned in USA);
5. *Dupe* (e.g. posing as friends of the environment, greenwashing).

The last of the 'Ds' mentioned here is certainly not the preserve of the most dirty and most obvious of corporate vandals. The phenomenon

Table 10.1 Nations vs corporations: continent, country and corporate CO_2 emissions

Company, country or continent	Million metric tons of CO_2 emitted annually
South America	747.3
Africa	745.6
BP AMOCO	622.6 (including ARCO)
EXXON MOBIL	601.4
United Kingdom	543.3
SHELL	493.7
Central America	477.0
Canada	470.8
Ukraine	430.6
Italy	410.0
France	362.0
Mexico	327.6
Brazil	287.5
Australia	286.0
Saudi Arabia	227.1
CHEVRON	187.6
Netherlands	178.8
Turkey	160.5
Thailand	155.5
TEXACO	145.7
Argentina	128.3

Source: Bruno *et al.* 1999: 7.

of 'greenwashing' has been incorporated into most companies' operational practices in one way or another. Greenwashing refers to putting a particular corporate 'spin' on environmental issues and problems. Much of it has to do with image-making, and hence it is heavily tied up with public relations and the manipulation of ideas through the mass media (see Athanasiou 1996; Beder 1997).

Techniques of greenwashing include such measures as publishing annual reports on recycled paper or online, establishing and participating in business environment institutes and awards, and sponsoring World Environment Day. It can involve manipulation of statistics:

> 3M claims in its promotional materials that 3P (Pollution Prevention Pays) prevented 72 million pounds of pollutants

from being released every year between 1975 and 1989. It does not say that because of dramatic increases in production its total output of pollutants actually increased during that period (Athanasiou 1996: 236).

What you see is not always what you get. This extends in other directions as well.

For instance, an insidious aspect of greenwashing is the creation and use of 'front organisations'. Innocuous or misleading titles are intended to hide a multitude of industry interests and links.

The oil, coal and auto industries have the Global Climate Coalition, organised and well funded to resist all moves to restrict carbon emissions. The US Council for Energy Awareness tells us that nuclear energy is essential to reduce dependency on imported oil. The American Council on Science and Health, a food industry cabal that includes Seagrams, General Motors, and Union Carbide, works to 'prove' that pesticide residues pose only a negligible risk to human health. The National Wetlands Coalition labors on behalf of mining, utility, and real estate interests to oppose wetlands protection. Beseiged chemical companies circle their wagons behind the banner of 'Responsible Care' (Athanasiou 1996: 238–239).

Investigation of front groups such as these often reveals direct funding by industry and strong personal ties between the 'community group' and the industry in question. Public relations firms have also been implicated in their establishment, as well as in creating situations which discredit 'real' community groups. Front groups are successful to the extent that they are not challenged and dismissed by journalists, government and the public; too often, however, the constructed veneer of such groups as community groups is taken at face value and they are given more credence than they deserve (Burton 1997; see also Beder 1997).

While greenwashing in its many and varied forms does exist, its success is less than definite. In other words, while undoubtedly there is a corporate ideological offensive, it is a struggle that is ongoing. To put it bluntly, people are not stupid. They have access to multiple sources of information. They are also hit with the material realities of environmental degradation in their daily lives (such as toxic waste, oil spills and bad drinking water). There is a material basis for continuing concern, and protests, about environmental destruction, regardless of how cunning the corporate sector may appear to be.

Working with and against the corporations

It is easy to demonise the transnational corporation, given the track record of such entities as producers of environmental harm and as purveyors of untruth. Yet, particularly in the light of changing world opinion about environmental issues, is there not scope to change the structure and practices of transnational corporations? This is one of the dilemmas of those who are faced with the choice of working with or against corporations.

The complexities of the strategic issues are reflected in recent debates over corporate social responsibility. Corporations know the value of putting their best foot forward. For many, responding to fears about the environment has prompted campaigns that promise a new way of working, and new operational values.

Corporate responsibility or corporate citizenship has been defined as 'the integration of business operations and values whereby the interests of all stakeholders, including customers, employees, investors, and the environment are reflected in the organisation's policies and actions' (Smith quoted in Zutshi and Adams 2004: 23). The primary means used by companies to demonstrate their corporate social responsibility are corporate social/environment reports – with some 45 per cent of the world's largest companies now producing environmental and social reports (Zutshi and Adams 2004: 23). Indications of corporate social responsibility are meant to be evidenced by, for example, the adoption of triple bottom line (TBL) reporting that features an economic dimension (e.g. creating value), an environmental dimension (e.g. impact and ecological environment), and a social dimension (e.g. workplace diversity). As well, things such as ISO 14000 certification are meant to serve to indicate commitment to environmental well-being.

There are arguments for and against the notion of corporate social responsibility. Some of the more salient ones include the following.

Arguments for corporate social responsibility

According to Gilmour (2002), from the point of view of the corporate sector, there are increasing public pressures to engage in sustainability programmes through implementing voluntary guidelines. These pressures include:

- The widespread availability of information via the Internet (e.g. consumers);
- The action of NGOs (e.g. activists);
- The concerns to prevent litigation (e.g. shareholders);
- The threat of mandatory laws and regulations.

From the point of view of the Non-government Organisation sector, there are opportunities to work with companies to improve things (Gilmour 2002: 12). Examples of this include:

- Expanding the base of support for research and conservation work;
- Accessing the skills and expertise that the business sector can bring to NGO activities;
- Maximising the educational opportunities presented by field projects and through that process to seek to engender changes in value systems within companies;
- Engaging companies in the business of triple bottom line accountability and sustainability.

Working with corporations in this way requires a basically non-confrontational relationship.

Arguments against corporate social responsibility

On the other hand, critics have issues with corporate social responsibility (see Rix 2002). For example, there is a tendency for transnational corporations to locate operations in areas with fewer regulations (e.g. less stringent waste disposal regulations in developing countries). Even within developed countries, a lack of resources (such as skills, expertise and staff) inhibits companies from implementing environmental initiatives.

It has been pointed out that appeals to corporate responsibility are necessary as a result of the victory of neo-liberalism and the demise of oppositional political movements (Rix 2002: 18). That is, voluntary initiatives emerge from an environment characterised by a voluntary absence of government. In this context, where there is little or no pressure from the top or from below, one can only appeal to the 'good nature' of the corporate sector.

As discussed by Rix (2002), the problems with corporate social responsibility as an idea and a practice are related to questions about:

- Who develops the voluntary guidelines that are constitutive of responsible corporations;

- What happens to corporate social responsibility when the bottom line is threatened;

- The ISO and similar organisations are private multinational organisations: their status, legitimacy and effectiveness depend on the commitment of national governments;

- Governments have shifted the decisions away from government (i.e. taxes used for social and public purposes) and toward companies (i.e. through massive corporate tax relief), thus making the issue of corporate philanthropy a matter of setting one's own 'tax' rates and determining social expenditure;

- What the actual track record of corporate bodies is regardless of what they say about their own corporate social responsibility (e.g. Enron).

Closer examination of corporate and governmental reform, such as that suggested along the lines of corporate social responsibility, indicate further problems. For a start, the impetus for the growth in corporate environmental consciousness has been led by insurance multinationals, for whom a decade of rising disaster payouts have provided persuasive evidence of the reality of global warming (Athanasiou 1996). In other instances, change has been brought about by the work of activists and regulatory pressure, for which the real credit for corporate reform must be attributed.

The scale of 'real' corporate environmentalism also needs to be questioned, as do the assumptions that underpin it. For example, propaganda surrounding 'triple bottom line' accounting and installation of EMS into company operations convey the sense that an ecological transition can be made within an unregulated global economy. Meanwhile, we still do not really know how 'green' our products and our production processes actually area, particularly in terms of gross levels of production, consumption and waste.

Solutions rest with private actions and global organisations flush with money to transform and regulate; global agencies mobilise a whole range of financial, intellectual and political resources to transform expeditiously the world's commons as a project of modernity. Yet these agencies are driven by discursive practices of privatisation, production intensification, integration and capitalisation. Each process, alone, runs the risk of degrading local commons, institutions and ecosystems; in combination they have proved to be disastrous (Goldman 1998b: 43).

Conservation and recycling at the individual firm level can thus mask overall effects. In many cases, as well, the problem is simply dumped into the Third World and thus disappears from the affluent countries.

It is notable, as well, that study of the international governance of the environment and the management of environmental change has been less than optimistic about the results to date. For all the talk about corporate compliance to international standards, and the development of new international protocols and conventions designed to deal with various facets of environmental degradation, the problem has gotten worse rather than better. The fact is that 'most international environmental agreements go nowhere near encoding the kinds of behaviours and targets that are required to mitigate let alone halt or reverse the negative impacts of environmental change' (Elliot 2002: 70). The governments of affluent countries have colluded with transnational companies to ensure that this has been the case.

There may well be benefits for NGOs to work with corporations. Such benefits have to be weighed up in the light of the capacity to be critical while in a collaborative relationship. Moreover, the danger of cooptation always looms large when financial incentives and funding opportunities depend upon NGO behaviour and public pronouncements. Intervention to deal with environmental harm, however, cannot rely on communities and corporations 'working it out together'. This has been demonstrated time and again throughout this book and elsewhere. At some stage, then, it is entirely appropriate and absolutely necessary to make the shift from consultation and regulation to confrontation and social action.

Contesting the global commons

Political struggle and the contest over corporate and ruling class power are central to any discussion of environmental issues. Issues of gender, ethnicity and race are important to these discussions as well, and are integral to understanding the relationship between capitalism and nature (see Pepper 1993; O'Connor 1994; Chunn et al. 2002). Social structures and cultural practices are fundamentally dependent upon what is produced, how it is produced, and how the products are exchanged. Such observations necessarily raise issues concerning private and common property, public and private ownership, how value is determined (e.g. use-value or exchange-value), distributive principles with regard to community needs and risks, the nature of democratic decision-making, access to information, and the institutionalisation of public accountability.

Issues relating to the nature of the State as a site for, and reflection of, class struggle likewise warrant further explicit consideration. There is thus a need to move from concern about the state of (environmental) crime, to concern about crimes of the State, which whether by omission or facilitation is allowing the harms to occur. Recent years have seen a massive shake-up in the role of State apparatus and in the penetration of capitalist modes of operation across all aspects of social life. This has involved substantial shifts in ownership (from public to private), in institutional orientation (from social objectives to economic efficiencies), and in patterns of social control (from rights-based to market-based forms of regulation). This has been a global pattern of change.

Thus, in determining the course of action in regards to environmental harm, we need to identify and explain the transformations in regulation along a number of dimensions (see for example, Goldman 1998a, 1998b; O'Brien et al. 2000). As reflected in this chapter and in earlier discussions, some of these include:

• The specific role of international capitalist institutions (such as the World Trade Organisation, International Monetary Fund, World Bank) in attempts to privatise nature, including via regulatory regimes designed to protect 'the world commons' for capitalist exploitation;

• The recasting of State regulation from one of control and surveillance, to that of information provider and risk management adviser;

• The transfer of regulatory functions from State authorities to private companies, as part of a wider privatisation agenda;

• The shift toward self-regulation in areas dealing with environmental harm and consumer protection, which rely upon the producers themselves to shape and define 'needs' and 'quality' criteria;

• The movement toward deregulation as such, in which faith is put into 'market forces' as the source of regulation, and where the 'command and control' powers of the State are radically diminished.

Factor into this mix phenomena such as corruption and appeals to the 'national interest' and what we have is a recipe for the perpetuation of injustice. If the opportunities are there to get away with environmental destruction, then the opportunities will be taken. Without adequate regulation and sanctions that make a difference, environmental harm is assured.

Case study 10.1   Indonesian timber baron goes free

Prosecution and regulation of environmental harm is hampered by bad laws, poor enforcement and timid sanctions. Corruption and the vested interests of national élites in perpetuating some forms of environment destruction are part of the equation, too. In early November 2007, for example, it was reported that Adelin Lis, an Indonesian businessman, had illegal logging charges against him dropped. It was alleged that companies connected to Lis had allegedly logged timber worth more than US$30 billion outside concession areas in Sumatra between 1998 and 2005. At the trial, a letter was presented from the Forestry Minister, Malam Kaban, who claimed that the companies' logging activities were not a crime but 'a mere administrative violation' (Forbes 2007). Sustained analysis of corporate loggers in the Asian-Pacific region has demonstrated the ways in which firms continue to cause irreparable harm to tropical forests. It also shows how it is not the local people who benefit from such destruction, but corporations, national governments and well-connected politicians and bureaucrats (Dauvergne 2001). The nature of profits is to profit from nature, regardless of long-term cost.

A social action approach to these kinds of incidents and trends implies the necessity of breaking with the logic of the present system and indeed of breaking the law. Lane (1998) points out that if the law were to shift from being anthropocentric (human-centred) toward ecocentric (nature-centred), then nature would be seen to have value in its own right and rights: 'not only would this criminalise previously acceptable behaviour, but also liberate behaviour that is currently seen as criminal' (Lane 1998: 245). Thus, for example, the clearfelling of old-growth forests (presently legal) would be criminalised because of its ecological damage, and the logging protestor would be free from prosecution in that they are protecting what ought to be protected by law. The transformation required for this to happen, however, demands forms of social action that will most probably cut across the legal–illegal divide. Given the powerful interests that support much environmentally harmful activity, social change will inevitably involve conflict.

Stifling dissent

A crucial aspect of environmental criminology is that it values highly the importance of deliberation and democratic participation. It is for this reason that writers also pay attention to practices that stifle dissent and prevent needed dialogue. For green criminology, the concern here is twofold: first, to investigate how the forces of the State (and capital) are mobilised against those who wish to preserve, protect and nurture; and secondly, to seriously contemplate how citizen participation can best contribute to enhanced problem solving on environmental questions (Steele 2001; Rippe and Schaber 1999). Participatory and deliberative democracy are mechanisms for potential positive change. But they, too, require critical scrutiny as well as active promotion (Martin 2004).

The contested nature of environmental issues is manifest in a number of ways, including in the efforts by the powerful to stifle environmental dissent (see Figure 10.2). Methods range from use of law suits to shut out the voices of individuals, groups and communities (see for examples, Walters 2003) through to the denial of funding to legal agencies that could provide support to those wishing to engage in environmental struggles against powerful interests (Kuehn 2000).

Use of SLAPPs
Use of strategic lawsuits against public participation (SLAPPs) as in the case of defamation and other types of law suits.

Use of FOI
Use of Freedom of Information laws against activists, as a means to undermine their work situations and professional credibility.

Use of libel
Use of libel laws to dispute what is said, and thus gagging criticism and dissent.

Use of political correctness
Use of broad ideological challenges, that serve to belittle the main message by painting activities and critics as 'holier than thou', unrealistic or on the loony Left.

Use of change in electoral rules
Use of electoral reform in ways that marginalise small political parties, and make it difficult for alternative candidates to get into government.

Propaganda campaigns
Use of images of certain elements within protest communities, such as the 'ferals' in anti-logging demonstrations, in order to misrepresent the nature of resistance and undermine the legitimacy of the claims being made.

Selective interventions by State authorities
Resource allocation and political priorities going into the policing of environmental protests rather than, and to the detriment of, law enforcement resources put into dealing with environmental crime.

Denying access to legal representation
Explicit and implicit funding restrictions put on free legal services and community legal centres that attempt to intervene on environmental matters.

Figure 10.2 Stifling dissent

The criminalisation of environmental dissent, whether it is through strategic lawsuits against public participation (SLAPPs) or through particular types of policing of environmental protests and activism, is a topic warranting close scrutiny. This is especially so if we acknowledge the centrality of public participation in decision-making processes involving environmental issues.

For example, the point of SLAPPs suits is not to 'win' in the conventional legal sense but to intimidate those who might be critical of existing or proposed developments. Beder observes that 'the cost to a developer is part of the cost of doing business, but a court case could well bankrupt an individual or environmental group. In this way the legal system best serves those who have large financial resources at their disposal, particularly corporations' (Beder 1997: 65). Claims of defamation, and for damages to company reputation and potential profits, associated with campaigns against certain developments on environmental or social grounds have started to feature more prominently in the corporate arsenal. Public discussion and attempts to more strictly regulate corporate activity becomes even more difficult than normally might be the case in such an intimidating atmosphere.

Another example of how community voices are stifled relates to State-funded legal assistance. For example, in the fall of 1996, a group of Louisiana residents approached the Tulane Environmental Law Clinic seeking legal assistance to challenge the proposed siting of a large chemical plant in their community (Kuehn 2000). To the clinic, it appeared, at first, as just another request, albeit a large one, for the type of free legal services the clinic had provided to Louisiana residents for the previous seven years. However, when the clinic slowed the plant's regulatory approval, the governor of Louisiana, certain business groups, prominent members of Louisiana's bar, and the Louisiana Supreme Court viewed the clinic's advocacy as intolerable and as an abuse of the free legal services provided by the State's law clinics. In Australia, similar kinds of responses and criticisms have been produced in regards to the Aboriginal Legal Service in relation to land rights claims, and to the Environmental Defenders Office in relation to protection of environment from industries and developers.

Strategic sites for socio-legal action

By its very nature, the development of environmental criminology as a field of sustained research and scholarship will incorporate many different perspectives and strategic emphases. For some, the point of academic concern and practical application will be to reform aspects of the present system. Critical analysis, in this context, will consist of thinking of ways to improve existing methods of environmental regulation and perhaps to seek better ways to define and legally entrench the notion of environmental crime. It might also involve working with corporations in the hope of encouraging better practices and more benign ways of dealing with the natural environment.

For others, the issues raised above are inextricably linked to the project of social transformation. From this perspective, analysis ought to focus on the strategic location and activities of transnational capital, as supported by hegemonic nation-states, and it ought to deal with systemic hierarchical inequalities. Such analysis opens the door to identifying the strategic sites for resistance, contestation and struggle on the part of those fighting for environmental justice, ecological justice and animal rights.

There are major political divisions within the broad spectrum of green criminological work (and indeed within green political movements), and these have major implications for whether action will be taken in collaboration with capitalist institutions and State authorities, or whether it will be directed towards radically challenging these institutions and authorities (see for examples, Mertig *et al.* 2002; Buttel 2003). Whatever strategies are examined and drawn upon, there are a series of questions that can serve as a guide to action (see Figure 10.3). The necessity of adopting a wide constellation of methods and intervention tactics is implicit within the imperative to see, judge and act.

The doing of critical environmental criminology is about putting things into context, about challenging the status quo, and about making the world a better place. It is essentially about three important tasks: *see, judge* and *act*. Regardless of the specific environmental harm, analysis needs to take into account several key concerns.

- Implementing 'see, judge, act' in relation to the environment means being cognisant of how environmental issues are socially constructed – *how expertise is mobilised and perceptions influenced by a variety of different actors;*
- It means identifying the social forces and actors involved in portraying, causing or responding to an environmental issue – *the institutions, people and social structures that are associated with a particular trend, event or problem;*
- It means examining how perceptions are influenced through various techniques that affirm or neutralise an issue, how ideas are contested politically and via legal and other means, and how emotions are intertwined in and through public discourses – *the modes of communication and affectation that shape the construction of social problems;*
- It means investigating how social power is organised in support of particular social interests, in ways that lead to unequal distributions of actual risks and perceived risks – *the ways in which social inequalities are manifest in environmental matters;*
- It means understanding the need for continuous deliberation about the nature of environmental harm and developing systems and activities that address these harms – *the necessity for ongoing evaluation and assessment and the use of multiple approaches in regulating and dealing with environmental harm.*

Figure 10.3 Crimes against nature: see, judge, act
Source: adapted from White 2004.

It is important to publicly expose the track record of environmental vandals as part of a public accountability process. This can be done in relation to specific environmentally-related practices, as in the case of companies supplying poor or contaminated water. It can also be achieved by highlighting the overall negative practices and reputation of a company. The targets of risk assessment and management in the case of 'environmental harm' have tended to be activities and events. Greater focus needs to be placed on the companies and individuals who perpetrate the harm.

The concentration of economic power at a global level, as manifest in the large transnational corporations, will obviously have an impact in the determination of what is deemed to be harmful or criminal, and what will not. It also means that, particularly in the case of environmental issues, the international character of capital and the transborder nature of the harm make prosecution and regulation extremely difficult. This is the case even where national legal mechanisms have been put into place to minimise environmental harm and to protect specific environments.

It is vital, therefore, that any decisions regarding environmental regulation be open to public scrutiny. The importance of independent audits of specific projects, of specific businesses and of specific government agencies, cannot be underestimated. Adoption of 'whistleblower' legislation designed to protect those who reveal 'confidential' and 'sensitive' information in the public interest is also important. These can act as both a sanction for non-compliance and an incentive to be more environmentally responsible (see Edmonds 1995). Work is needed to critically evaluate the actions of companies engaged in environmentally sensitive activities (e.g. Ok Tedi in PNG), government departments which engage in production-related activities (public utilities), and government departments which have the legal brief to monitor compliance and enforce laws (such as endangered species, fisheries, parks and wildlife).

Study of and engagement with NGOs on issues related to environmental harm is essential. Mainstream as well as radical theories of regulation stress the importance of third party participation and community involvement as part of the regulatory and prosecution processes. How members of communities respond to general and specific environmental issues will vary, and include organised and spontaneous forms of action.

Case study 10.2   Non-government actions

Green NGOs have a crucial role to play in monitoring illegal activity, challenging corporate agendas and fostering radical social change. As part of this, there will be differences in organisational structure and strategic approach. Some organisations will engage in militant and spectacular actions (e.g. Greenpeace and Sea Shepherd anti-whaling campaigns). Others will focus on specific issues and work closely with governments and international regulatory bodies to enact change. For example, the Antarctic and South Ocean Coalition (ASOC) is an NGO established in 1976 to coordinate the activities of over 250 conservation groups on matters such as Patagonian toothfish management. In so doing, it works closely with governments in confronting issues associated with illegal, unreported and unregulated fishing (Fallon and Kriwoken 2004). Other groups, such as the Animal Liberation Front (ALF) use a variety of tactics that raise awareness about systematic animal cruelty. Breaking the law (such as illegal entry into animal laboratories or battery hen farms) is considered legitimate if it means that public consciousness is heightened and immediate harms to animals diminished through such actions.

Case study 10.3   Environmental riots

The response to environmental harm takes a variety of organised and unorganised forms. The 'riot' represents a spontaneous reaction to specific issues and the perceived lack of democratic voice on environmental matters. For example, in the Dominican Republic in July 2007, local residents gathered to prevent city crews in Santa Domingo from cutting down enormous shade trees planted centuries beforehand. Angry residents lashed themselves to the threatened trees and engaged in acts of civil disobedience in frustration at not being consulted and at having their needs and wishes ignored (Stolz 2007). In the same month, thousands of Chinese residents rioted in Xinchang over three nights, demanding that the government address water pollution stemming from the local pharmaceutical plant. It was reported that in 2006, some 74,000 demonstrations took place in China, reflecting widespread anger over the failure of the political system to respond to legitimate grievances, many of which related to environmental issues (French 2007). When the people are not engaged in decision-making, the streets become an important venue for democratic participation.

A critical issue for public interest groups, whether these are global NGOs or local residents, is their capture by the corporate sector through the selling of an idea (e.g. the need to support the Green Olympics) or through corporate financial largess to those groups that reflect 'green' but relatively uncontroversial mandates (e.g. wildlife protection). As mentioned above, one also has to be aware of corporate 'grassroots' organisations, corporate-sponsored 'independent' scientific experts, and the general cooptation of environmentalists within the discursive framework of private property, free trade and individual rights.

Developing effective action around environmental harm will require thinking and acting about the environment in ways that best support this objective. Some areas that are important to consider include:

Ecophilosophy and regulation: an anthropocentric or ecocentric perspective will provide very different answers to the questions of the definition and regulation of environmental harm. Therefore, there is an ongoing need to clarify and extrapolate from the basic philosophical premises of the regulatory project – sustainable development versus ecological sustainability. This can be bolstered by the development of alternative baseline criteria for deciding what is 'good' and what is 'bad' in relation to ecophilosophy.

Democracy vs administrative mechanisms: readily available information and collective decision-making is needed rather than too heavy a reliance upon technical expertise or being subjected to government fiat. Amongst other things, this relates to the importance of 'right to know' legislation that provides access to information concerning the activities of both private companies and State agencies. Also, there is a need for the legal affirmation of the right of people to participate in public debate and public action without the threat of malicious and gratuitous law suits being used against them.

Public accountability: any decisions regarding environmental assessment and management should be open to public scrutiny. The use of independent audits, adoption of 'whistleblower' legislation and an Environmental Ombudsman may be useful here. Challenges are needed to notions of 'commercial confidentiality' that serve as cover for business-as-usual practices, and that disguise varying forms of corruption and hidden subsidies.

277

Expertise and knowledge claims: there is a need to develop specific types of expertise in areas such as investigation, detection, evidence gathering, enforcement, public advocacy and policy development, especially for environmental regulators. More work is certainly needed in regards to the determination of the status of 'experts' vis-à-vis particular vested interests. We also have to be aware of the politics of scientific rationality in relation to value and moral positions that are outside of 'scientific discourses' as such (e.g. indigenous people). On the other hand, scientists need to be protected from attempts to suppress their work, either directly or through attacks on their character.

Role of third parties: direct participation and giving of evidence by 'third parties' in court cases is essential to environmental protection. This raises issues about how best to enhance citizen suits in pursuit of social and ecological justice. The legal status of non-affected parties is important to this, as are constructions of the rights of the environment.

Eco-rights: dealing with environmental harm will lead to a reconceptualisation of rights to include expanded notions of environmental and community rights, particularly around the concepts of 'common good' and 'common property'. A questioning of the legal and social basis of 'private property' and the rights attendant to this concept is central to this task. The notion of eco-rights has to be linked to the democratisation of decision-making, the interests and actions of collectivities, and the importance granted to the concept of deliberation as an ongoing social process.

Internationalisation of action: the global nature of production and trade relations, and the enormous power of transnational capital, demand the use of international law and supra-national regulatory action, as well as international struggles on the part of NGOs. A corporate register could be utilised in order to track the environmental record of transnational companies. Financial and regulatory institutions such as the International Monetary Fund, World Bank and World Trade Organisation need to be brought to public account and subjected to democratic mechanisms of control.

The list could go on. The point of this exercise is that developing suitable responses to environmental harm will require bold and lateral thinking, as well as new forms of administrative, legal, criminal justice and direct action. Multiple strategies and many different types of alliance are required to deal with the hydra of transnational corporate capitalism. The law will be both enemy and friend in this process. And who or what gets criminalised will depend upon the contingencies of harm and the politics of the moment.

Conclusion: where to from here?

As a broad trend we have to be cognisant of how the disappearance of criminality and coercion in regard to environmental regulation, in favour of persuasion, self-regulation and cooperative strategies, shifts the locus of the problem from one of environmental and social harm to one of enhanced 'environmentally friendly' production. Such enhancements collectively degrade the global ecological commons. They also allow the main perpetrators of the harm, the transnational corporations, even more leeway to operate with little fear of sanction or the likelihood of prosecution.

Responding to environmental harm ultimately requires the testing of existing social and political limits and boundaries. The dominant structural arrangements of late capitalism are the key stumbling block to a future that is just, fair and clean. To change the future means changing the institutions of the present.

Finally, I wish to conclude with a few words about where to from here, beyond this book. My intention herein has been to stimulate thinking and research about environmental harm, and to indicate future lines of criminological inquiry. A wide range of issues and approaches have been canvassed as part of this process. From climate change to harmful fishing, ecophilosophy to assessment of risk, biopiracy to genetically modified organisms, the chapters have tried to present insights into the nature of many different types of environmental harm.

Arising from the many discussions is a series of significant political and methodological challenges for critical environmental criminology. Briefly, these include:

Need to address core issues of sustainability and survival:
Rather than being restricted by the limitations of the legal–illegal divide, we need to assert the prior importance of and urgency associated with ecological sustainability. This means assessing 'harm' in many different contexts and guises, regardless of legal status and existing institutional legitimations.

Need for a global perspective and analysis:
The international nature of issues, trends, comparisons, and networks is vital and ought to complement work done at the local, regional and country levels. Expanding the scope and vision of our work to include worldwide institutions, social processes and conduits of power and resistance, is essential.

Need to source a wide range of information and data:
What we can learn from has to include alternative sources which go well beyond conventional academic and 'official' bureaucratically provided material. It can include information provided through media stories, NGOs, the Internet, company records, medical information, traditions and legends, literature, and scientific studies of varying kinds.

Need to address issues of power and the powerful:
In gaining basic information and acting upon it, there is always the possibility of threats by capital via law suits, and threats by the State via security and surveillance measures. This raises issues about the publication of findings and critique, and how to bypass the dense protective layers that prevent 'knowing' and publicising corporate and State wrongdoing. There is also the need to find the requisite democratic space for acting upon what it is that we find out.

Need to grapple with doing critical criminology and yet participating in mainstream agencies and criminological work:
An important part of our work has to include critiques and exposures of environmental harm as state crime and as corporate crime. Yet, it is simultaneously important to assist State agencies with crime prevention, law enforcement and regulatory activities. Issues here include that of exclusion from the mainstream (for being critical) as well as incorporation into the mainstream through participation (and thus losing the critical edge).

It is my hope that this book will foster greater dialogue about how criminology might be pursued in relation to environmental harm. Many questions have been asked, many more have been left unanswered. Difficulties of definition, awkward processes of deliberation and the complexities of addressing many different types of environmental harm should be seen as part of the challenge that comes with the territory, however, not as precluding action on these matters in the here and now. For criminology, this means learning much more about the 'natural' world around us, the interrelationships between 'nature' and society, and further developing those concepts, principles and values that will best ensure planetary well-being. Our lives – and the lives of future generations and ecosystems – depend on it.

References

Akella, A. and Cannon, J. (2004) *Strengthening the Weakest Links: Strategies for Improving the Enforcement of Environmental Laws Globally.* Washington, DC: Center for Conservation and Government.

Altman, J., Bek, H. and Roach, L. (1996) 'Use of Wildlife by Indigenous Australians: Economic and Policy Perspectives', in M. Bomford and J. Caughley (eds) *Sustainable Use of Wildlife by Aboriginal Peoples and Torres Strait Islanders.* Canberra: Bureau of Resource Sciences, Australian Government Publishing Service.

Amsterdam News (2006) *More Toxic Fallout from British Oil Dumping.* [Online]. Available at: http://www.amsterdamnews.org/News/article/article.asp?NewsID=11381&sID=12 [accessed on 22 February 2008].

Anderson, K. and McCusker, R. (2005) 'Crime in the Australian Fishing Industry: Key Issues', *Trends and Issues in Crime and Criminal Justice, No. 297.* Canberra: Australian Institute of Criminology.

Anderton, J. (2007) *Groundbreaking Initiative to Protect Underwater Habitats,* press release, New Zealand Government, 4 April.

Archer, J. (1998) *Sydney on Tap.* Sydney: Pure Water Press.

Archer, J. (2001) *Australia's Drinking Water: The Coming Crisis.* Sydney: Pure Water Press.

Ascione, F. (2001) *Animal Abuse and Youth Violence,* Juvenile Justice Bulletin, Washington, DC: Office of Juvenile Justice and Delinquency Prevention, US Department of Justice.

Associated Press (2007) *EU May Make Harming Environment a Crime* [Online]. Available at: http://www.ap.org/ [accessed on 13 February 2007].

Associated Press (2008) *Total Guilty in France's Worst Oil Spill* [Online]. Available at: http://www.ap.org/ [accessed on 21 January 2008].

Athanasiou, T. (1996) *Divided Planet: The Ecology of Rich and Poor.* Boston: Little, Brown & Co.

Australian Broadcasting Corporation (2007) *Fish Schools – Teaching the Little Tackers How to Survive* [Online]. Available at: http://www.abc.net.au/catalyst/stories/s1895106.htm [accessed on 22 February 2008].

Australian Crime Commission (2004) *Annual Report 2002–2003*. Canberra: Australian Crime Commission.

The Australian (2007) *Oil Spill from Tanker Kills 30,000 Sea Birds* [Online]. Available at: http://www.theaustralian.news.com.au/story/0,25197,22754087-30417,00.html [accessed on 22 February 2008].

Ayres, I. and Braithwaite, J. (1992) *Responsive Regulation: Transcending the Deregulation Debate*. New York: Oxford University Press.

Bakan, J. (2004) *The Corporation: The Pathological Pursuit of Profit and Power*. London: Constable.

Bambrick, H. (2004) *Trading in Food Safety? The Impact of Trade Agreements on Quarantine in Australia*. Discussion Paper No. 73. Canberra: The Australia Institute.

Barlow, M. and Clarke, T. (2003) *Blue Gold: The Fight to Stop the Corporate Theft of the World's Water*. New York: The New York Press.

Bartel, R. (2005) 'When the Heavenly Gaze Criminalises: Satellite Surveillance, Land Clearance Regulation and the Human–Nature Relationship', *Current Issues in Criminal Justice*, 16(3): 322–339.

Basel Action Network/Silicon Valley Toxics Coalition (2002) *Exporting Harm: The High-Tech Trashing of Asia*. Seattle and San Jose: BAN/SVTC.

Beck, U. (1992) *Risk Society: Towards a New Modernity*. London: Sage.

Beck, U. (1996) 'World Risk Society as Cosmopolitan Society? Ecological Questions in a Framework of Manufactured Uncertainties', *Theory, Culture, Society*, 13(4): 1–32.

Beder, S. (1997) *Global Spin: The Corporate Assault on Environmentalism*. Melbourne: Scribe Publications.

Beder, S. (2006) *Suiting Themselves: How Corporations Drive the Global Agenda*. London: Earthscan.

Beirne, P. (2004) 'From Animal Abuse to Interhuman Violence? A Critical Review of the Progression Thesis', *Society and Animals*, 12(1): 39–65.

Beirne, P. (2007) 'Animal Rights, Animal Abuse and Green Criminology', in P. Beirne and N. South (eds) *Issues in Green Criminology*. Devon: Willan Publishing.

Beirne, P. and South, N. (eds) (2007) *Issues in Green Criminology*. Devon: Willan Publishing.

Benton, T. (1998) 'Rights and Justice on a Shared Planet: More Rights or New Relations?', *Theoretical Criminology*, 2(2): 149–175.

Bertell, R. (1999) 'Gulf War Veterans and Depleted Uranium', *Hague Peace Conference* [Online]. Available at: http://www.ccnr.org/du_hague.html [accessed on 22 February 2008].

Biosecurity Australia (2008) *International Standards and Obligations* [Online]. Available at: http://www.daff.gov.au/ba/about/plant/international-standards [accessed on 10 February 2008].

Black, R. (2006) *The Global Path of Pollution*, BBC News [Online]. Available at: http://news.bbc.co.uk/1/hi/sci/tech/5323258.stm [accessed on 22 February 2008].

Blacksmith Institute (2007) [Online]. http://www.blacksmithinstitute.org/ [accessed on 22 February 2008].

Blindell, J. (2006) *21st Century Policing – The Role of Police in the Detection, Investigation and Prosecution of Environmental Crime*, ACPR Issues No. 2. Adelaide: Australasian Centre for Policing Research.

Block, A. (2002) 'Environmental Crime and Pollution: Wasteful Reflections', *Social Justice*, 29(1–2): 61–81.

Bocock, R. (1993) *Consumption*. London: Routledge.

Boerner, C. and Lambert, T. (1995) 'Environmental Injustice', *Public Interest*, 118: 61–83.

Bond, P. and Bakker, K. (2001) 'Canada: Blue Planet Targets Commodification of World's Water', *Green Left Weekly*, 456, 18 July.

Boyd, D. (2003) *Unnatural Law: Rethinking Canadian Environmental Law and Policy*. Vancouver: UBC Press.

Boykoff, J and Sand, K (2003) 'Blue Gold: The Fight to Stop the Corporate Theft of the World's Water', *Capitalism, Nature and Socialism*, 14(1): 148–151.

Braithwaite, J. (1993) 'Responsive Business Regulatory Institutions', in C. Coady and C. Sampford (eds) *Business Ethics and the Law*. Sydney: Federation Press.

Braithwaite, J. and Drahos, P. (2000) *Global Business Regulation*. Cambridge: Cambridge University Press.

Brantingham, P. and Brantingham, P. (1981) *Environmental Criminology*. Beverly Hills, CA: Sage.

Bridgland, F. (2006) *Europe's New Dumping Ground: Fred Bridgland Reports on How the West's Toxic Waste is Poisoning Africa* [Online]. Available at: http://www.ban.org/ban_news/2006/061001_dumping_ground.html [accessed on 22 February 2008].

Brook, D. (2000) 'Environmental Genocide: Native Americans and Toxic Waste', *American Journal of Economics and Sociology*, 57(1): 105–113.

Brookspan, S., Gravel, A. and Corley, J. (2007) 'Site History: The First Tool of the Environmental Forensics Team', in B. Murphy and R. Morrison (eds) *Introduction to Environmental Forensics* (2nd edition). London: Elsevier Academic Press.

Bruno, K., Karliner, J. and Brotsky, C. (1999) *Greenhouse Gangsters vs Climate Justice*. San Francisco: Transnational Resource and Action Centre.

Brunton, N. (1999) 'Environmental Regulation: The Challenge Ahead', *Alternative Law Journal*, 24(3): 137–143.

Buchanan, J., Callus, R. and Briggs, C. (1999) 'What Impact Has the Howard Government Had on Wages and Hours of Work?', *Journal of Australian Political Economy*, 43: 1–21.

Bullard, R. (1994) *Unequal Protection: Environmental Justice and Communities of Color*. San Francisco: Sierra Club Books.

Burns, R. and Lynch, M. (2004) *Environmental Crime: A Sourcebook*. New York: LFB Scholarly.

Burton, B. (1997) 'Invisible PR: Dirty Tricks for Media Consumption', *Australian Journalism Review*, 19(1): 133–143.

Buttel, F. (2003) 'Environmental Sociology and the Explanation of Environmental Reform', *Organization and Environment*, 16(3): 306–344.

Caldicott, H. (2006) *Nuclear Power Is Not The Answer*. New York: The New Press.

Carrabine, E., Iganski, P., Lee, M., Plummer, K. and South, N. (2004) *Criminology: A Sociological Introduction*. London: Routledge.

Carson, R. (1962) *Silent Spring*. Boston: Houghton and Mifflin.

Casey, S. (2007) *Plastic Ocean: The Great Pacific Garbage Patch* [Online]. Available at: http://www.cdnn.info/news/article/a071104.html [accessed on 22 February 2008].

Caughley, J., Bomford, M. and McNee, A. (1996) 'Use of Wildlife by Indigenous Australians: Issues and Concepts', in M. Bomford and J. Caughley (eds) *Sustainable Use of Wildlife by Aboriginal Peoples and Torres Strait Islanders*. Canberra: Bureau of Resource Sciences, Australian Government Publishing Service.

Chi, N. (2006) *Poor Countries Bear Brunt of Toxic Burden* [Online]. Available at: http://vietnamnews.vnagency.com.vn/showarticle. php?num=01OUT151206 [accessed on 22 February 2008].

Choy, H. (2007) 'A Bone of Contention – Say No To Scallops and Tassie Salmon: Guide', *Mercury*.

Christensen, R. (2002) 'Canada's Drinking Problem: Walkerton, Water Contamination and Public Policy', in S. Boyd, D. Chunn and R. Menzies (eds) *Toxic Criminology: Environment, Law and the State in Canada*. Halifax: Fernwood Publishing.

Christoff, P. (2000) 'Environmental Citizenship', in W. Hudson and J. Kane (eds) *Rethinking Australian Citizenship*. Melbourne: Cambridge University Press.

Chunn, D., Boyd, S. and Menzies, R. (2002) '"We all live in Bhopal": Criminology Discovers Environmental Crime', in S. Boyd, D. Chunn and R. Menzies (eds) *Toxic Criminology: Environment, Law and the State in Canada*. Halifax: Fernwood Publishing.

Clarke, R. (ed.) (1997) *Situational Crime Prevention: Successful Case Studies*. New York: Harrow and Heston.

Cohen, S. (1993) 'Human Rights and Crimes of the State: The Culture of Denial', *Australian and New Zealand Journal of Criminology*, 26(2): 97–115.

Cohen, S. (2001) *States of Denial: Knowing About Atrocities and Suffering*. Cambridge: Polity Press.

Cone, M. (2005) 'Sewage Altering Fish, Study Reports', *Los Angeles Times*, 14 November.

Cooper, M. (2002) 'Bush and the Environment: Are the President's Policies Helping or Hurting?', *The CQ Researcher*, 12(7): 865–896.

COSMOS Magazine (2006) *Ivory Coast Toxic Waste May Have Entered Food Chain* [Online]. Available at: http://www.cosmosmagazine.com/node/650 [accessed on 22 February 2008].

Cresswell, A. (2007) 'Fertile Ground', *The Weekend Australian*, 5–6 May.

Cribbs, J. (2007) 'Fishing for a Perfect Catch', *The Australian*, p. 47.

Croall, H. (2007) 'Food Crime', in P. Beirne and N. South (eds) *Issues in Green Criminology*. Devon: Willan Publishing.

Crook, S. and Pakulski, J. (1995) 'Shades of Green: Public Opinion on Environmental Issues in Australia', *Australian Journal of Political Science*, 30: 39–55.

Crowley, K. (1998) '"Glocalisation" and Ecological Modernity: Challenges for Local Environmental Governance in Australia', *Local Environment*, 3(1): 91–97.

Cullinan, C. (2003) *Wild Law: A Manifesto for Earth Justice*. London: Green Books in association with The Gaia Foundation.

Curson, P. and Clark, L. (2004) 'Pathological Environments', in R. White (ed.) *Controversies in Environmental Sociology*. Melbourne: Cambridge University Press.

Dadds, M., Turner, C. and McAloon, J. (2002) 'Developmental Links between Cruelty to Animals and Human Violence', *Australian and New Zealand Journal of Criminology*, 35(3): 363–382.

Dauvergne, P. (2001) *Loggers and Degradation in the Asia-Pacific: Corporations and Environmental Management*. Cambridge: Cambridge University Press.

Davison, A. (2001) *Technology and the Contested Meanings of Sustainability*. Albany NY: State University of New York Press.

Davison, A. (2004) 'Sustainable Technology: Beyond Fix and Fixation', in R. White (ed.) *Controversies in Environmental Sociology*. Melbourne: Cambridge University Press.

Deacon, B. (1983) *Social Policy and Socialism: The Struggle for Socialist Relations of Welfare*. London: Pluto Press.

Deleage, J-P. (1994) 'Eco-Marxist Critique of Political Economy', in M. O'Connor (ed.) *Is Capitalism Sustainable? Political Economy and the Politics of Ecology*. New York: Guilford Press.

del Frate, A. and Norberry, J. (eds) (1993) *Environmental Crime: Sanctioning Strategies and Sustainable Development*. Rome: UNICRI / Sydney: Australian Institute of Criminology.

Deutsche Welle (2006) *European Hazardous Waste to Africa and Back* [Online]. Available at: http://www.dw-world.de/ [accessed 20 October 2006].

Deville, A. and Harding, R. (1997) *Applying the Precautionary Principle*. Sydney: Federation Press.

Eck, J. (2003) 'Police Problems: The Complexity of Problem Theory, Research and Evaluation', in J. Knutsson (ed.) *Problem-oriented Policing*. Monsey, NY: Criminal Justice Press.

Edie News Centre (2007) *Pollution Monitoring and Control – Review of the Year 2006* [Online]. Available at: http://www.edie.net/index.asp [accessed on 22 February 2008].

Edmonds, S. (1995) 'The Environmental Audit as a "Sanction" or Incentive under the Victorian Environment Protection Act 1970', in N. Gunningham, D. Sinclair and S. McKillop (eds) *Environmental Crime*. Canberra: Australian Institute of Criminology.

Elkington, J. and Hailes, J. (1991) 'Green Consumerism', in A. Dobson (ed.) *The Green Reader*. London: Andre Deutsch.

Elliot, L. (2002) 'Global Environmental Governance', in R. Wilkinson and S. Hughes (eds) *Global Governance: Critical Perspectives*. London: Routledge.

Elliot, L. (ed.) (2007) *Transnational Environmental Crime in the Asia-Pacific: A Workshop Report*. Canberra: Department of International Relations, Australian National University.

Environment Australia (2007) *Compliance and Enforcement Policy* [Online]. Available at: http://www.environment.gov.au/epbc/publications/compliance.html [accessed on 22 February 2008].

Environment News (2006) *World Governments Asked to Pay for Ivory Coast Cleanup* [Online]. Available at: http://www.ens-newswire.com/ens/nov2006/2006-11-24-02.asp [accessed on 22 February 2008].

Ericson, R., Baranek, P. and Chan, J. (1991) *Representing Order: Crime, Law and Justice in the News Media*. Milton Keynes: Open University Press.

Fallon, L. and Kriwoken, L. (2004) 'International Influence of an Australian Nongovernment Organization in the Protection of Patagonian Toothfish', *Ocean Development and International Law*, 35(1): 221–266.

Faure, M. and Heine, G. (2000) *Criminal Enforcement of Environmental Law in the European Union*. Copenhagen: Danish Environmental Protection Agency.

Field, C. (1999) 'The New Face of Consumer Protection', *Alternative Law Journal*, 24(3): 157–159.

Field, R. (1998) 'Risk and Justice: Capitalist Production and the Environment', in D. Faber (ed.) *The Struggle for Ecological Democracy: Environmental Justice Movements in the US*. New York: Guilford Press.

Fine, B. (1984) *Democracy and the Rule of Law: Liberal Ideals and Marxist Critiques*. London: Pluto.

Forbes, M. (2007) 'Outrage as Timber Baron Walks Free', *Sydney Morning Herald*, 7 November, p. 11.

Fortney, D. (2003) 'Thinking Outside the "Black Box": Tailored Enforcement in Environmental Criminal Law', *Texas Law Review*, 81(6): 1609–1630.

Foster, J. (2007) 'The Ecology of Destruction', *Monthly Review*, 58(9): 1–14.

Franklin, A. (1999) *Animals and Modern Cultures: A Sociology of Human–Animal Relations in Modernity*. London: Sage.

Freiberg, A. (1997) 'Commercial Confidentiality, Criminal Justice and the Public Interest', *Current Issues in Criminal Justice*, 9(2): 125–152.

French, H. (2007) 'Riots in a Village in China as Pollution Protest Heats Up', *The New York Times*, 19 July, p. 3.

Friedrichs, D. and Friedrichs, J. (2002) 'The World Bank and Crimes of Globalization: A Case Study', *Social Justice*, 29(1–2): 13–36.

Gearin, M. (2005) *Greater Reliance on Overseas Fish* [Online]. Available at: http://www.abc.net.au/7.30/content/2005/s1526227.htm [accessed 22 February 2008].

Gibson, R. (2006) 'Sustainability Assessment: Basic Components of a Practical Approach', *Impact Assessment and Project Appraisal*, 24(3): 170–182.

Gilmour, J. (2002) 'Can Partnerships be an Agent for Change in Corporations?', *Alternative Law Journal*, 27(1): 11–12.

Glasbeek, H. (2003) *The Invisible Friend: Investors are Irresponsible. Corporations are Amoral* [Online]. Available at: http://www.newint.org/issue358/friend.htm [accessed on 22 February 2008].

Glasbeek, H. (2004) *Wealth by Stealth: Corporate Crime, Corporate Law and the Perversion of Democracy*. Toronto: Between the Lines.

Goldman, M. (1998a) 'Introduction: The Political Resurgence of the Commons', in M. Goldman (ed.) *Privatizing Nature: Political Struggles for the Global Commons*. London: Pluto Press in association with Transnational Institute.

Goldman, M. (1998b) 'Inventing the Commons: Theories and Practices of the Commons' Professional', in M. Goldman (ed.) *Privatizing Nature: Political Struggles for the Global Commons*. London: Pluto Press in association with Transnational Institute.

Gorz, A. (1989) *Critique of Economic Reason*. London: Verso.

Gosine, A. (2005) 'Dying Planet, Deadly People: "Race"–Sex Anxieties and Alternative Globalizations', *Social Justice*, 32(4): 69–86.

Grabosky, P. (1994) 'Green Markets: Environmental Regulation by the Private Sector', *Law and Policy*, 16(4): 419–448.

Grabosky, P. (1995) 'Regulation by Reward: On the Use of Incentives as Regulatory Instruments', *Law and Policy*, 17(3): 256–279.

Grabosky, P. and Gant, F. (2000) *Improving Environmental Performance, Preventing Environmental Crime*. Research and Public Policy Series No. 27. Canberra: Australian Institute of Criminology.

Green, P. and Ward, T. (2000) 'State Crime, Human Rights and the Limits of Criminology', *Social Justice*, 27(1): 101–15.

Green, P. and Ward, T. (2004) *State Crime: Governments, Violence and Corruption*. London: Pluto Press.

Gunningham, N. and Grabosky, P. (1998) *Smart Regulation: Designing Environmental Policy*. Oxford: Clarendon Press.

Gunningham, N., Norberry, J. and McKillop, S. (eds) (1995) *Environmental Crime, Conference Proceedings*. Canberra: Australian Institute of Criminology.

Gunningham, N., Sinclair, D. and Grabosky, P. (1998) 'Instruments for Environmental Protection', in N. Gunningham and P. Grabosky (eds) *Smart Regulation: Designing Environmental Policy*. Oxford: Clarendon Press.

Guterman, L. (2006) 'Poachers Prey on Research Publications', *The Australian*, 30 August, p. 27.

Hager, N. and Burton, B. (1999) *Secrets and Lies: The Anatomy of an Anti-environmental PR Campaign*. New Zealand: Craig Potton Publishing.

Haines, F. (1997) *Corporate Regulation: Beyond 'Punish or Persuade'*. Oxford: Clarendon Press.

Haines, F. (2000) 'Towards Understanding Globalisation and Control of Corporate Harm: a Preliminary Criminological Analysis', *Current Issues in Criminal Justice*, 12(2): 166–180.

Halsey, M. (1997a) 'Environmental Crime: Towards an Eco-human Rights Approach', *Current Issues in Criminal Justice*, 8(3): 217–242.

Halsey, M. (1997b) 'The Wood for the Paper: Old-growth Forest, Hemp and Environmental Harm', *Australian and New Zealand Journal of Criminology*, 30(2): 121–148.

Halsey, M. (2004) 'Against "Green" Criminology', *British Journal of Criminology*, 44(4): 833–853.

Halsey, M. and White, R. (1998) 'Crime, Ecophilosophy and Environmental Harm', *Theoretical Criminology*, 2(3): 345–371.

Halstead, B. (1992) *Traffic in Flora and Fauna*. Trends and Issues in Crime and Criminal Justice, No. 41. Canberra: Australian Institute of Criminology.

Hannigan, J. (1995) *Environmental Sociology: A Social Constructionist Perspective*. London: Routledge.

Hannigan, J. (2006) *Environmental Sociology* (2nd edition). London: Routledge.

Harding, R. and Fisher, E. (1999) 'Introducing the Precautionary Principle', in R. Harding and E. Fisher (eds) *Perspectives on the Precautionary Principle*. Sydney: Federation Press.

Hartman, C. and Squires, G. (eds) (2006) *There is No Such Thing as a Natural Disaster: Race, Class and Hurricane Katrina*. New York: Routledge.

Harvey, D. (1996) *Justice, Nature and the Geography of Difference*. Oxford: Blackwell.

Harvey, N. (1998) *Environmental Impact Assessment: Procedures, Practice and Prospects in Australia*. Melbourne: Oxford University Press.

Hauck, M. (2007) 'Non-compliance in Small-scale Fisheries: A Threat to Security?', in P. Beirne and N. South (eds) *Issues in Green Criminology*. Devon: Willan Publishing.

Hayward, T. (2006) 'Ecological Citizenship: Justice, Rights and the Virtue of Resourcefulness', *Environmental Politics*, 15(3): 435–446.

Heine, G., Prabhu, M. and del Frate, A. (eds) (1997) *Environmental Protection: Potentials and Limits of Criminal Justice*. Rome: UNICRI.

Herbig, F. and Joubert, S. (2006) 'Criminological Semantics: Conservation Criminology – Vision or Vagary?', *Acta Criminologica*, 19(3): 88–103.

Hessing, M. (2002) 'Economic Globalization and Canadian Environmental Restructuring: The Mill(ennium)-end Sale', in S. Boyd, D. Chunn and R. Menzies (eds) *Toxic Criminology: Environment, Law and the State in Canada*. Halifax: Fernwood Publishing.

Higgins, V. and Natalier, K. (2004) 'Governing Environmental Harms in a Risk Society', in R. White (ed.) *Controversies in Environmental Sociology*. Melbourne: Cambridge University Press.

Hindmarsh, R. (1996) 'Bio-policy Translation in the Public Terrain', in G. Lawrence, K. Lyons and S. Momtaz (eds) *Social Change in Rural Australia*. Rockhamptom: Rural Social and Economic Research Centre, Central Queensland University.

Hogg, R. and Brown, D. (1998) *Rethinking Law and Order*. Sydney: Pluto Press.

Hollander, R. (2006) 'Light-handed Regulation: The Case of the Tasmanian Forest Practices System', *Australasian Journal of Environmental Management*, 13(1): 17–27.

Hughes, S.D. (2004) 'The Current Status of Environmental Performance Reporting', *National Environmental Law Review*, 4: 41–58.

Iafrica.com (2007) *West Should Pay for 'Ruining' Africa* [Online]. Available at: http://www.iafrica.com/news/sa/752001.htm [accessed on 22 February 2008].

Ibrahim D. M. (2006) 'The Anti-cruelty Statute: A Study in Animal Welfare', *Journal of Animal Law and Ethics*, 1(1): 175–203.

Interpol (2007) *Environmental Crime* [Online] Available at: http://www.interpol.int/Public/EnvironmentalCrime/Default.asp [accessed on 22 February 2008].

Irvine, S. (1991) 'Against Green Consumerism', in A. Dobson (ed.) *The Green Reader*. London: Andre Deutsch.

Irwin, A. (2001) *Sociology and the Environment: A Critical Introduction to Society, Nature and Knowledge*. Cambridge: Polity Press in association with Blackwell.

Israel Police and the Israeli Ministry of Environmental Protection (various dates) [Online]. Available at: http://www.police.gov.il and http://www.sviva.gov.il [accessed on 22 February 2008].

Jackson, H. (2003) 'Prosecutions under the Environmental Protection Act 1970', *National Environmental Law Review*, 2(1): 22–30.

Jackson, N. (2004) 'When the Population Clock Stops Ticking', in R. White (ed.) *Controversies in Environmental Sociology*. Melbourne: Cambridge University Press.

Jalee, P. (1977) *How Capitalism Works*. New York: Monthly Review Press.

Julian, R. (2004) 'Inequality, Social Differences and Environmental Resources', in R. White (ed.) *Controversies in Environmental Sociology*. Melbourne: Cambridge University Press.

Kirkland, L-H. and Thompson, D. (1999) 'Challenges in Designing, Implementing and Operating an Environmental Management System', *Business Strategy and the Environment*, 8: 128–143.

Kuehn, R. (2000) 'Denying Access to Legal Representation: The Attack on the Tulane Environmental Law Clinic', *Journal of Law and Policy*, 4(1): 33–147.

Kuehn, R. (2004) 'Suppression of Environmental Science', *American Journal of Law and Medicine*, 30(2): 333–369.

Lack, M. (2007) *Catching On? Trade–related Measures as a Fisheries Management Tool*. Cambridge: TRAFFIC International.

Lambrecht, B. (2006) *Exported E-waste Pollutes Africa* [Online]. Available at: http://www.dibella.biz/news/209938989.htm [accessed on 22 February 2008].

Lane, P. (1998) 'Ecofeminism Meets Criminology', *Theoretical Criminology*, 2(2): 235–248.

Langton, M. (1998) *Burning Questions: Emerging Environmental Issues for Indigenous Peoples in Northern Australia*. Darwin: Centre for Indigenous Natural and Cultural Resource Management.

Larsen, N. and Smandych, R. (eds) (2008) *Global Criminology and Criminal Justice: Current Issues and Perspectives*. Peterborough, Ontario: Broadview Press.

Leiss, W. and Hrudey, S. (2005) 'On Proof and Probability: Introduction to "Law and Risk"', in Law Commission of Canada (ed.) *Law and Risk*. Vancouver: UBC Press.

Leonard, G. (2004) Personal communication in his capacity as Chief Investigations Officer, Fisheries Monitoring and Quota Audit Unit, Tasmania, 9 November.

Levy, D. (1997) 'Environmental Management as Political Sustainability', *Organization and Environment*, 10(2): 126–147.

Lewis, P. (2004) *Apple Growers Square up for Biosecurity Stoush*, television programme 'Landline', ABC TV, 13 June.

Little, C. (2004) Personal communication in his capacity as Tasmania Police member of Operation Oakum, 9 November.

Living On Earth – UK (2007) *Toxic Delivery* [Online]. Available at: http://www.livingonearth.org/shows/shows.htm?programID=07-P13-00008 [accessed on 22 February 2008].

Lockie, S. (2004) 'Social Nature: The Environmental Challenge to Mainstream Social Theory', in R. White (ed.) *Controversies in Environmental Sociology*. Melbourne: Cambridge University Press.

Lorenz, A. (2005) *Choking on Chemicals in China* [Online]. Available at: http://www.spiegel.de/international/spiegel/0,1518,387392,00.html [accessed on 22 February 2008].

Lovelock, J. (2006) *The Revenge of Gaia*. London: Penguin.

Low, N. and Gleeson, B. (1998) *Justice, Society and Nature: An Exploration of Political Ecology*. London: Routledge.

Lugten, G. (2005) 'Big Fish to Fry – International Law and Deterrence of the Toothfish Pirates', *Current Issues in Criminal Justice*, 16(3): 307–321.

Lynch, M. (1990) 'The Greening of Criminology: A Perspective on the 1990s', *The Critical Criminologist*, 2(3): 1–4 and 11–12.

Lynch, M. and Stretesky, P. (2003) 'The Meaning of Green: Contrasting Criminological Perspectives', *Theoretical Criminology*, 7(2): 217–238.

Lynch, M. and Stretesky, P. (2006) 'Toxic Crimes: Examining Corporate Victimization of the General Public Employing Medical and Epidemiological Evidence', in N. South and P. Beirne (eds) *Green Criminology*. Aldershot: Ashgate.

Lynch, M., Stretesky, P. and McGurrin, D. (2002) 'Toxic Crimes and Environmental Justice: Examining the Hidden Dangers of Hazardous Waste', in G. Potter (ed.) *Controversies in White-collar Crime*. Cincinnati: Anderson Publishing.

Macnaghten, P. and Urry, J. (1998) *Contested Natures*. London: Sage.

Macpherson, C. (1962) *The Political Theory of Possessive Individualism: Hobbes to Locke*. Oxford: Oxford University Press.

Maguire, S. and Ellis, J. (2005) 'Redistributing the Burden of Scientific Uncertainty: Implications of the Precautionary Principle for State and Nonstate Actors', *Global Governance*, 11(4): 505–526.

Mahony, H. (2007) *EU Court Delivers Blow on Environment Sanctions* [Online]. Available at: http://euobserver.com/ [accessed on 22 February 2008].

Malthus, T. (1798/1973) *An Essay on the Principles of Population*. London: Dent.

Mandel, E. (1975) *Late Capitalism*. London: Verso Books.

Manning, P. (2001) 'Small-scale Fisheries Management in Sub-Saharan Africa', background document for the *FAO Expert Consultation on Small-scale Fisheries Management in Sub-Saharan Africa*, December 2001, Accra, Ghana,

Marigza, L. (2007) *Earth Day Interfaith Project Collects Discarded Drugs* [Online]. Available at: http://www.umc.org [accessed on 22 February 2008].

Marsden, B. (2003) *Cholera and the Age of the Water Barons* [Online]. Available at: http://www.publicintegrity.org/water/report.aspx?aid=44 [accessed on 22 February 2008].

Marsden, S. (1998) 'Importance of Context in Measuring the Effectiveness of Strategic Environmental Assessment', *Impact Assessment and Project Appraisal*, 16(4): 255–266.

Martin, E. (2004) 'Sustainable Development, Postmodern Capitalism and Environmental Policy and Management in Costa Rica', *Contemporary Justice Review*, 7(2): 153–169.

Martin, R. (2005) 'Trends in Environmental Prosecution', *National Environmental Law Review*, 4(1): 38–46.

Marx, K. (1973) *Grundrisse*. New York: Vintage Books.

Marx, K. (1975) 'Economic and Political Manuscripts (1844)', *Marx: Early Writings*. Harmondsworth: Penguin.

Mass, B. (1976) *Population Target: The Political Economy of Population Control in Latin America*. Toronto: Latin American Working Group.

Massey, R. (2001) 'United States: Arsenic from Your Tap', *Green Left Weekly*, 449, 23 May.

Maxwell, G. (2007) 'Quest for Sustainability, After a Stop at Canadian Tire', *PIQUE Newsmagazine*, 26 July, p. 98.

McCulloch, J. (2005) 'Loggerheads over Old-growth Forests: Growing Civil Society Against State Crime and the Timber Wedge', *Current Issues in Criminal Justice*, 16(3): 351–367.

McGovern, V. (2004) 'Sport-caught Fish and Breast Cancer', *Environmental Health Perspectives*, 112(2): p. A112.

McMullan, J. and Perrier, D. (2002) 'Lobster Poaching and the Ironies of Law Enforcement', *Law and Society Review*, 36(4): 679–720.

Medical Association for Prevention of War, Australia (2003) *Policy Statement: Uranium Munitions – 'Tolerable' Radiological Weapons?* [Online]. Available at: http://www.mapw.org.au/mapw-policy/03-11uranium.html [accessed on 22 February 2008].

Meiksins, P. (1986) 'Beyond the Boundary Question', *New Left Review*, No. 157: 101–120.

Merchant, C. (2005) *Radical Ecology: The Search for a Liveable World* (2nd edition). New York: Routledge.

Mercury (2006) *Green Talks Focus on Hazardous Waste*, 29 November.

Mercury (2007) *Pulling Wings off an Angel*, 1 October, p. 14.

Mertig, A., Dunlap, R. and Morrison, D. (2002) 'The Environmental Movement in the United States', in R. Dunlap and W. Michelson (eds) *Handbook of Environmental Sociology*. Westport, Connecticut: Greenwood Press.

Mgbeoji, I. (2006) *Global Biopiracy: Patents, Plants and Indigenous Knowledge*. Vancouver: UBC Press.

Moore, R. (1990) 'Environmental Inequities', *Crossroads*, No. 1.

Munro, L. (2004) 'Animals, "Nature" and Human Interests', in R. White (ed.) *Controversies in Environmental Sociology*. Melbourne: Cambridge University Press.

Munro, M. (2007) 'Biofuels Come Up Short as Way to Reduce Carbon Load, Study Finds', *The Vancouver Sun*, 17 August, p. A3.

Murphy, B. and Morrison, R. (2007) *Introduction to Environmental Forensics*. Amsterdam: Elsevier.

Murray, G. (2006) *Capitalist Networks and Social Power in Australia and New Zealand*. Aldershot: Ashgate.

National Toxics Network Inc. (no date) *The Precautionary Principle Gets Real* [Online]. Available at http://www.oztoxics.org/ [accessed 25 February 2008].

New South Wales Bureau of Crime Statistics (2003) *Number of Charges by Offence Type, NSW Local Court 1998 to 2002* [Online]. Available at: http://www.bocsar.nsw.gov.au/ [accessed 25 February 2008].

New South Wales Food Authority (2006) *Dioxins in Seafood in Port Jackson and its Tributaries: Report of the Expert Panel.* Sydney: NSW Food Authority.

News.scotsman.com (2008) *Burning Issue: Biofuel Targets and Subsidies: Is it Time for a Moratorium?* [Online]. Available at: http://news.scotsman.com/climatechange/Burning-issue-Biofuel-targets-and.3692044.jp [accessed 25 February 2008].

Nichols, D. (ed.) (1999) *Environment, Capitalism and Socialism.* Sydney: Resistance Books.

O'Brien, R., Goetz, A., Scholte, J. and Williams, M. (2000) *Contesting Global Governance: Multilateral Economic Institutions and Global Social Movements.* Cambridge: Cambridge University Press.

O'Connor, J. (1994) 'Is Sustainable Capitalism Possible?', in M. O'Connor (ed.) *Is Capitalism Sustainable?: Political Economy and the Politics of Ecology.* New York: The Guilford Press.

O'Riordan, T. and Cameron, J. (1994) 'The History and Contemporary Significance of the Precautionary Principle', in T. O'Riordan and J. Cameron (eds) *Interpreting the Precautionary Principle.* London: Earthscan.

Onimode, B. (1985) *An Introduction to Marxist Political Economy.* London: Zed Books.

Page, T. (1991) 'Sustainability and the Problem of Valuation', in R. Costanza (ed.) *Ecological Economics: The Science and Management of Sustainability.* New York: Columbia University Press.

Pakulski, J., Tranter, B. and Crook, S. (1998) 'The Dynamics of Environmental Issues in Australia: Concerns, Clusters and Carriers', *Australian Journal of Political Science*, 33(2): 235–252.

Pauw, J (2003) *Metered to Death: How a Water Experiment Caused Riots and a Cholera Epidemic* [Online]. Available at: http://www.publicintegrity.org/water/report.aspx?aid=49 [accessed on 25 February 2008].

Pearce, F. and Tombs, S. (1998) *Toxic Capitalism: Corporate Crime and the Chemical Industry.* Aldershot: Dartmouth Publishing Company.

Pearce, N. (2007) *The Reality of Environmental Regulation: An Analysis of the Environmental Regulatory Structure of Forestry Tasmania*, Masters Thesis in Criminology and Corrections, School of Sociology and Social Work, University of Tasmania.

Peel, J. (2005) *The Precautionary Principle in Practice: Environmental Decision-making and Scientific Uncertainty.* Sydney: The Federation Press.

Pellow, D. (2004) 'The Politics of Illegal Dumping: An Environmental Justice Framework', *Qualitative Sociology*, 27(4): 511–525.

Pepper, D. (1993) *Eco-socialism: From Deep Ecology to Social Justice.* New York: Routledge.

Perry, M. (2006) *Toxic Waste Ends Sydney Harbour Commercial Fishing* [Online]. Available at: http://www.planetark.com/dailynewsstory.cfm/newsid/35014/newsDate/10-Feb-2006/story.htm [accessed on 25 February 2008].

Pezzullo, P. and Sandler, R. (2007) 'Introduction: Revisiting the Environmental Justice Challenge to Environmentalism', in R. Sandler and P. Pezzullo (eds) *Environmental Justice and Environmentalism: The Social Justice Challenge to the Environmental Movement*. Cambridge, MA: The MIT Press.

Pinderhughes, R. (1996) 'The Impact of Race on Environmental Quality: An Empirical and Theoretical Discussion', *Sociological Perspectives*, 39(2): 231–248.

Plumwood, V. (2005) 'Gender, Eco-feminism and the Environment', in R. White (ed.) *Controversies in Environmental Sociology*. Melbourne: Cambridge University Press.

Pollan, M. (2007) 'Unhappy Meals', *The New York Times Magazine*, 28 January.

Powell, S. (2007) 'How we're Destroying our Habitat', *The Australian*, 14 November, p. 28–29.

Priest, M. (1997–98) 'The Privatization of Regulation: Five Models of Self-regulation', *Ottawa Law Review*, 29(2): 233–302.

Public Citizen Organisation (2004) *Why Oppose the Privatisation of Water* [Online]. Available at: http://www.citizen.org/cmep/Water/general/whyoppose/index.cfm [accessed on 25 February 2008].

Pyper, W. (2005) 'On the Trail of Sexual Chemistry', *ECOS*, 123: 26–28.

Ravindran, P (2003) 'Water Privatisation: Reaching Epidemic Proportions', *Business Line*, 25: 1–2.

Redbolivia.com (2006) *Ivory Coast Toxic Waste Cleanup Nears End* [Online]. Available at: http://www.redbolivia.com/ [accessed on 1 November 2006].

Reliable Plant (2007) *New Study Favors Tree Over Corn as Biofuel Source* [Online]. Available at: http://www.reliableplant.com/article.asp?articleid=10046 [accessed 25 February 2008].

Reuters (2007) *Corrected – EU Cracks Down on Shipment of Toxic Waste* [Online]. Available at: http://www.alertnet.org/thenews/newsdesk/L12823000.htm [accessed on 26 February 2008].

Reuters (2008) *Committee Calls for Biofuel Moratorium* [Online]. Available at: http://uk.reuters.com/article/topNews/idUKL1885287820080121?sp=true [accessed on 26 February 2008].

Rhodes, E. (2003) *Environmental Justice in America*. Bloomington, IN: Indiana University Press.

Riddle, K. (2006) 'Illegal, Unreported and Unregulated Fishing: Is International Cooperation Contagious?', *Ocean Development and International Law*, 37: 265–297.

Rippe, K. and Schaber, P. (1999) 'Democracy and Environmental Decision-making', *Environmental Values*, 8(1): 75–88.

Rix, S. (2002) 'Globalisation and Corporate Responsibility', *Alternative Law Journal*, 27(1): 16–22.

Robinson, B. (1995) 'The Nature of Environmental Crime', in N. Gunningham, J. Norberry and S. McKillop (eds) *Environmental Crime*. Canberra: Australian Institute of Criminology.

Robinson, B. (2003) *Review of the Enforcement and Prosecution Guidelines of the Department of Environmental Protection of Western Australia*. Perth: Communication Edge.

Robinson, D. (2000) *Environmental Racism: Old Wine in a New Bottle* [Online]. Available at: http://www.oikoumene.org/en/home.html [accessed on 26 February 2008].

Robyn, L. (2002) 'Indigenous Knowledge and Technology', *American Indian Quarterly*, 26(2): 198–220.

Roffey, P., Provan, P., Duffy, M., Wang, A., Blanchard, C. and Angel, L. (2004) 'Pyhlogenetic DNA Profiling – A Tool for the Investigation of Poaching', *Crime in Australia: International Connections*, Melbourne, 29–30 November. Canberra: Australian Institute of Criminology.

Rosoff, S., Pontell, H. and Tillman, R. (1998) *Profit Without Honor: White-collar Crime and the Looting of America*. Upper Saddle River, NJ: Prentice Hall.

Rowe, R. (2007) 'Wanted: More Bio-detectives', *The Australian*, 17 January, p. 26.

Rush, S. (2002) 'Aboriginal Resistance to the Abuse of Their National Resources: The Struggles for Trees and Water', in S. Boyd, D. Chunn and R. Menzies (eds) *Toxic Criminology: Environment, Law and the State in Canada*. Halifax: Fernwood Publishing.

Saha, R. and Mohai, P. (2005) 'Historical Context and Hazardous Waste Facility Siting: Understanding Temporal Patterns in Michigan', *Social Problems*, 52(4): 618–648.

Sandler, R. and Pezzullo, P. (2007) (eds) *Environmental Justice and Environmentalism: The Social Justice Challenge to the Environmental Movement*. Cambridge, MA: MIT Press.

Schmidt, C. (2004) 'Environmental Crimes: Profiting at the Earth's Expense', *Environmental Health Perspectives*, 112(2): A96–A103.

Schneider, R. and Kitchen, T. (2002) *Planning for Crime Prevention: A TransAtlantic Perspective*. London: Routledge.

Schwendinger, H. and Schwendinger, J. (1975) 'Defenders of Order or Guardians of Human Rights?', in I. Taylor, P. Walton and J. Young (eds) *Critical Criminology*. London: Routledge & Kegan Paul.

Scott, D. (2005a) 'When Precaution Points Two Ways: Confronting "West Nile Fever"', *Canadian Journal of Law and Society*, 20(2): 27–65.

Scott, D. (2005b) 'Shifting the Burden of Proof: The Precautionary Principle and Its Potential for the "Democratization" of Risk', in Law Commission of Canada (eds) *Law and Risk*. Vancouver: UBC Press.

Seis, M. (1993) 'Ecological Blunders in US Clean Air Legislation', *The Journal of Human Justice*, 5(1): 58–81.

Silva, C. and Jenkins-Smith, H. (2007) 'The Precautionary Principle in Context: US and EU Scientists' Prescriptions for Policy in the Face of Uncertainty', *Social Science Quarterly*, 88(3): 640–664.

Simon, D. (2000) 'Corporate Environmental Crimes and Social Inequality: New Directions for Environmental Justice Research', *American Behavioral Scientist*, 43(4): 633–645.

Situ, Y. and Emmons, D. (2000) *Environmental Crime: The Criminal Justice System's Role in Protecting the Environment*. Thousand Oaks, CA: Sage.

Smith, M. (1998) *Ecologism: Towards Ecological Citizenship*. Minneapolis, MN: University of Minnesota Press.

Smith, R. and Anderson, K. (2004) *Understanding Non-compliance in the Marine Environment*. Trends and Issues in Crime and Criminal Justice, No. 275. Canberra: Australian Institute of Criminology.

Smith, S. (1997) 'Customer Charters: The Next Dimension in Consumer Protection?', *Alternative Law Journal*, 22(3): 138–140.

Snider, L. (2000) 'The Sociology of Corporate Crime: An Obituary (Or: Whose Knowledge Claims Have Legs?)'. *Theoretical Criminology*, 4(2): 169–206.

Snider, L. (2002) 'Zero Tolerance Reversed: Constituting the Non-culpable Subject in Walkerton', *Annual Meetings, Canadian Law and Society Association*, Vancouver, 31 May 2002. Vancouver: Canadian Law and Society Association.

South African Municipal Workers Union (2001) 'Union "Mourns" on World Water Day', SAMWU statement on World Water Day, reprinted in *Green Left Weekly*, 442, 28 March.

South, N. (1998) 'A Green Field for Criminology? A Proposal for a Perspective', *Theoretical Criminology*, 2(2): 211–233.

South, N. (2007) 'The "Corporate Colonisation of Nature": Bio-prospecting, Bio-piracy and the Development of Green Criminology', in P. Beirne and N. South (eds) *Issues in Green Criminology*. Devon: Willan Publishing.

South, N. and Beirne, P. (2006) *Green Criminology*. Aldershot: Ashgate.

Steele, J. (2001) 'Participation and Deliberation in Environmental Law: Exploring a Problem-solving Approach', *Oxford Journal of Legal Studies*, 21(3): 415–442.

Stern, N. (2007) *The Economics of Climate Change: The Stern Review*. Cambridge: Cambridge University Press.

Stinus-Remonde, M. (2006) 'Mission Impossible: Address our Serious Waste Problems First', *The Manila Times*, 31 October.

Stolz, K. (2007) *Environmental Riots* [Online]. Available at: http://gristmill. grist.org/print/2007/7/24/94820/1911?show_comments=no [accessed on 25 February 2008].

Stretesky, P. (2006) 'Corporate Self-policing and the Environment', *Criminology*, 44(3): 671–708.

Stretesky, P. and Hogan, M. (1998) 'Environmental Justice: An Analysis of Superfund Sites in Florida', *Social Problems*, 45(2): 268–287.

Stretesky, P. and Lynch, M. (1999) 'Corporate Environmental Violence and Racism', *Crime, Law and Social Change*, 30: 163–184.

Sutherland, E. (1949) *White Collar Crime*. New York: Dryden Press.

Sutton, A., Cherney, A. and White, R. (2008) *Crime Prevention, Perspectives and Practices*. Melbourne: Cambridge University Press.

Swingewood, A. (1975) *Marx and Modern Social Theory*. London: Macmillan Press.

Sydee, J. and Beder, S. (2006) 'The Right Way to Go? Earth Sanctuaries and Market-based Conservation', *Capitalism, Nature, Socialism*, 17(1): 83–98.

Szentes, T. (1988) *The Transformation of the World Economy: New Directions and New Interests*. London: Zed Books.

Tailby, R. and Gant, F. (2002) *The Illegal Market in Australian Abalone*, Trends and Issues in Crime and Criminal Justice No. 225. Canberra: Australian Institute of Criminology.

Tappan, P. (1947) 'Who is the Criminal', *American Sociological Review*, 12: 96–102.

Tasmania Police (2004) *Annual Report 2002–2003*. Hobart: Department of Police and Public Safety.

The Scotsman (2008) *Oil Giant Must Pay Millions for Slick* [Online]. Available at: http://thescotsman.scotsman.com/world/Oil-giant-must-pay-millions.3681415.jp [accessed 25 February 2008].

Thornton, J. and Tromans, S. (1999) 'Human Rights and Environmental Wrongs: Incorporating the European Convention on Human Rights: Some Thoughts on the Consequences for UK Environmental Law', *Journal of Environmental Law*, 11(1): 35–57.

Thottam, J. (2007) 'Made in China: The Growing Dangers of the China Trade', *Time Magazine*, 9 July, p. 24–27.

Time Magazine (1999) 'Attention All Shoppers', *Time Magazine*, 22 August.

Tombs, S. and Whyte, D. (2004) *Unmasking the Crimes of the Powerful: Scrutinizing States and Corporations*. New York: Peter Lang Publishers.

Tomkins, K. (2005) 'Police, Law Enforcement and the Environment', *Current Issues in Criminal Justice*, 16(3): 294–306.

Topalov, A. (1999) 'Environmental Reporting by Australian Corporations', *Griffith Law Review*, 8(2): 411–438.

Tranter, B. (2004) 'The Environment Movement: Where to from Here?', in R. White (ed.) *Controversies in Environmental Sociology*. Melbourne: Cambridge University Press.

United Nations Environment Programme (2003) *Desk Study on the Environment in Iraq*. Geneva: UNEP.

United Nations Environment Programme (2006) *Call for Global Action on E-waste*. New York: UNEP.

United Nations Environment Programme (2007) *Global Environment Outlook*. New York: UNEP.

United States Food and Drug Administration (2007) *Counterterrorism* [Online]. Available at: www.fda.gov/oc/opacom/hottopics/bioterrorism.html [accessed on 25 February 2008].

van der Velden, J. (1998) *Productive Labour in Contemporary Economy: Capitalised Services and State Privatisations*, unpublished paper, Canberra.

van der Velden, J. and White, R. (1996) 'Class Criminality and the Politics of Law and Order', in R. Kuhn and T. O'Lincoln (eds) *Class and Class Conflict in Australia*. Melbourne: Longman.

Verry, J., Heffernan, F. and Fisher, R. (2005) 'Restorative Justice Approaches in the Context of Environmental Prosecution', *Safety, Crime and Justice: From Data to Policy Conference*, Canberra, 6–7 June. Canberra: Australian Institute of Criminology.

Victoria, Environmental Protection Authority (2003) *Annual Report 2002–2003: Compliance Report*. Melbourne: Victorian Government Printer.

VOA News.com (2006) *International Conference Seeks to Reduce Hazardous Waste* [Online]. Available at: http://www.voanews.com [accessed on 25 February 2008].

Walker, C. (2001) 'Time to Choose Sides: The Green Movement and Corporate Power in the Twenty–First Century', *Arena Magazine*, 54: 22–24.

Wall, E. and Beardwood, B. (2001) 'Standardizing Globally, Responding Locally: The New Infrastructure, ISO 14000 and Canadian Agriculture', *Studies in Political Economy*, 64: 33–58.

Walters, B. (2003) *Slapping On the Writs: Defamation, Developers and Community Activism*. Sydney: University of New South Wales Press.

Walters, R. (2004) 'Criminology and Genetically Modified Food', *British Journal of Criminology*, 44(1): 151–167.

Walters, R. (2005) 'Crime, Bio-agriculture and the Exploitation of Hunger', *British Journal of Criminology*, 46(1): 26–45.

Weidner, M. and Watzman, N. (2002) *Paybacks – Policy, Patrons and Personnel: How the Bush Administration is Giving Away Our Environment to Corporate Contributions*. Washington, DC: Earthjustice and Public Campaign.

Weinstein, T. (2005) 'Prosecuting Attacks that Destroy the Environment: Environmental Crimes or Humanitarian Atrocities?', *Georgetown International Environmental Law Review*, 17(4): 697–722.

Weisskopf, M. (2007) 'Something's Fishy in Mississippi', *Time Magazine*, 9 July.

The West Australian (2007) 'Mafia Fear in Illegal Tuna Fish Racket', *The West Australian*, 30 June, p. 49.

Wexler, L. (2006) 'Limiting the Precautionary Principle: Weapons Regulation in the Face of Scientific Uncertainty', *University of California Davis Law Review*, 39: 459–527.

Whelan, J. (2005) 'Neo-liberal Water Policy and Socio-environmental Harm', *Current Issues in Criminal Justice*, 16(3): 286–293.

Whelan, J. and White, R. (2005) 'Does Privatising Water Makes Us Sick?', *Health Sociology Review*, 14(2): 135–145.

White, R. (1994) 'Green Politics and the Question of Population', *Journal of Australian Studies*, 40: 27–43.

White, R. (1998) 'Environmental Criminology and Sydney Water', *Current Issues in Criminal Justice*, 10(2): 214–219.

White, R. (1999) 'Criminality, Risk and Environmental Harm', *Griffith Law Review*, 8(2): 235–257.

White, R. (2002) 'Environmental Harm and the Political Economy of Consumption', *Social Justice*, 29(1–2): 82–102.

White, R. (2003) 'Environmental Issues and the Criminological Imagination', *Theoretical Criminology*, 7(4): 483–506.

White, R. (2004) 'Introduction: Sociology, Society and the Environment', in R. White (ed.) *Controversies in Environmental Sociology*. Melbourne: Cambridge University Press.

White, R. (2005a) 'Environmental Crime in Global Context: Exploring the Theoretical and Empirical Complexities', *Current Issues in Criminal Justice*, 16(3): 271–285.

White, R. (2005b) 'Stifling Environmental Dissent: On SLAPPS and Gunns', *Alternative Law Journal*, 30(6): 268–273.

White, R. (2007a) 'Green Criminology and the Pursuit of Social and Ecological Justice', in P. Beirne and N. South (eds) *Issues in Green Criminology*. Devon: Willan Publishing.

White, R. (2007b) 'Fishing for the Future: Exploring the Ambiguities of Environmental Harm', *Criminology Public Lecture*, James Cook University, Townsville, 22 May, Old Magistrate's Court.

White, R. (2007c) *Dealing with Environmental Harm: Green Criminology and Environmental Law Enforcement*, Briefing Paper No. 5, Tasmanian Institute for Law Enforcement Studies. Hobart: University of Tasmania.

White, R. (2008a) 'A Green Criminological Perspective', in E. McLaughlin and T. Newburn (eds) *The Sage Handbook of Criminological Theory*. London: Sage.

White, R. (2008b) 'Depleted Uranium, State Crime and the Politics of Knowing', *Theoretical Criminology*, 12(1): 31–54.

White, R. (2008c) 'Toxic Cities: Globalising the Problem of Waste', *Social Justice*, 35(3).

White, R. and Habibis, D. (2005) *Crime and Society*. Melbourne: Oxford University Press.

White, R. and Perrone, S. (2005) *Crime and Social Control* (2nd edition). Melbourne: Oxford University Press.

White, R. and Watson, S. (2007) 'Animal Abuse and Green Criminology', *Animals and Society II Conference*, Hobart, 3–6 July. Hobart: University of Tasmania.

Williams, C. (1996) 'An Environmental Victimology', *Social Justice*, 23(4): 16–40.

Williams, F. (1977) *Why The Poor Pay More*. London: National Consumer Council.

Wise, S. (2001) *Rattling the Cage: Toward Legal Rights for Animals*. Cambridge, Mass: Perseus Books.

Wise, S. (2004) 'Animal Rights, One Step at a Time', in C. Sunstein and M. Nussbaum (eds) *Animal Rights: Current Debates and New Directions*. New York: Oxford University Press.

Worley, M. (2007) 'Weld Angel's Heart Still in Forest Cause', *Mercury*, 1 October, p. 7.

Wynne, B. (1996) 'May the Sheep Safely Graze? A Reflexive View of the Expert/Lay Knowledge Divide', in S. Lash, B. Szerszynski and B. Wynne (eds) *Risk, Environment and Modernity: Toward a New Ecology*. London: Sage.

Zilney, L., McGurrin, D. and Zahran, S. (2006) 'Environmental Justice and the Role of Criminology: An Analytical Review of 33 Years of Environmental Justice Research', *Criminal Justice Review*, 31(1): 47–62.

Zutshi, A. and Adams, C. (2004) 'Voluntary Guidelines: Are They Enough to Sustain the Environment?', *Alternative Law Journal*, 29(1): 23–26.

Index